TACKLING DISABILITY DISCRIMINATION AND DISABILITY HATE CRIME

of related interest

Supporting Disabled People with their Sexual Lives
A Clear Guide for Health and Social Care Professionals
Tuppy Owens with Claire de Than
ISBN 978 1 84905 396 9
eISBN 978 0 85700 762 9

**Sexuality and Relationships in the Lives of
People with Intellectual Disabilities**
Standing in My Shoes
*Edited by Rohhss Chapman, Louise Townson
and Sue Ledger with Daniel Docherty*
ISBN 978 1 84905 250 4
eISBN 978 0 85700 530 4

**Preventing the Emotional Abuse and
Neglect of People with Intellectual Disability**
Stopping Insult and Injury
Sally Robinson
Foreword by Hilary Brown
ISBN 978 1 84905 230 6
eISBN 978 0 85700 472 7

Safeguarding Adults and the Law
2nd edition
Michael Mandelstam
ISBN 978 1 84905 300 6
eISBN 978 0 85700 626 4

Learning Difficulties and Sexual Vulnerability
A Social Approach
Andrea Hollomotz
ISBN 978 1 84905 167 5
eISBN 978 0 85700 381 2

Autism, Discrimination and the Law
A Quick Guide for Parents, Educators and Employers
James Graham
ISBN 978 1 84310 627 2
eISBN 978 1 84642 768 8

TACKLING DISABILITY DISCRIMINATION AND DISABILITY HATE CRIME

A MULTIDISCIPLINARY GUIDE

EDITED BY
ROBINA SHAH
AND PAUL GIANNASI

FOREWORD BY
PROFESSOR SHEILA BARONESS HOLLINS
AND DR KERI-MICHÈLE LODGE

Jessica Kingsley *Publishers*
London and Philadelphia

Contains public sector information licensed under
the Open Government License v3.0.

First published in 2015
by Jessica Kingsley Publishers
73 Collier Street
London N1 9BE, UK
and
400 Market Street, Suite 400
Philadelphia, PA 19106, USA

www.jkp.com

Library of Congress Cataloging in Publication Data
Tackling disability discrimination and disability hate crime
: a multidisciplinary guide / edited by Robina
Shah and Paul Giannasi.
pages cm
ISBN 978-1-84905-528-4 (alk. paper)
1. Discrimination against people with disabilities. 2. People
with disabilities--Crimes against. I. Shah,
Robina, editor. II. Giannasi, Paul, editor.
HV6250.4.H35T33 2015
305.9'08--dc23

2014041408

British Library Cataloguing in Publication Data
A CIP catalogue record for this book is available from the British Library

ISBN 978 1 84905 528 4
eISBN 978 0 85700 941 8

Printed and bound in Great Britain

CONTENTS

FOREWORD

PROFESSOR SHEILA BARONESS HOLLINS
AND DR KERI-MICHÈLE LODGE

Across the world, people with physical disabilities, a learning disability or a mental health difficulty have been subject to hostility, stigma, exclusion and neglect for centuries. And today, people with disabilities continue to experience very real challenges in dealing with discrimination and hate crime as they go about their daily lives. Children, young people, women and those with a learning disability or mental health difficulty are particularly at risk. Yet, the concept of disability hate crime is relatively new and poorly understood. This perhaps reflects how as a society we are really only just beginning to accept the uncomfortable idea that some of our most vulnerable citizens are the target of discrimination and hate crime because they have, are thought to have or are associated with someone who has a disability.

Media reports of shocking cases such as Fiona Pilkington and Francecca Hardwick have highlighted the failings of professionals from health, social care, education and criminal justice services to adequately respond to the victimisation of disabled people, showing how this often follows a pattern of low-level persistent incidents that, if not acted upon, can result in tragic consequences. Alongside this, we have seen the scandal of the systematic criminal abuse of people with a learning disability in care settings exposed by a BBC Panorama documentary at Winterbourne View Hospital, and of deaths through neglect of people with a learning disability in NHS hospitals uncovered by Mencap's *Death by Indifference* report. These stories prompted Government responses, and the need to address disability discrimination and hate crime has become a political priority that can no longer be ignored.

Despite recent relevant policy and legislation, there remains a lack of understanding and awareness of disability hate crime and discrimination, particularly among practitioners in health, social care, and education or criminal justice systems. Furthermore, data and research evidence to help those organisations tasked with planning, delivering and providing such services to better address these issues is scarce. Collecting data on disability hate crime is particularly difficult, not least because victims may not report harassment or crimes for many reasons – a fear they will not be believed, significant communication barriers or dissatisfaction with agency responses when they have tried to report crimes previously. This book is therefore very timely, and we welcome *Tackling Disability Discrimination and Disability Hate Crime* as a much needed exploration of the nature of discrimination and hate crime against people with disabilities and how these can be addressed in the current policy context.

Dr Shah and Superintendent Giannasi have skilfully edited insightful contributions from distinguished authors from a variety of backgrounds – professional, academic, as well as individuals with disabilities and their family members. These accessible, jargon-free accounts are grounded in real-life personal experiences, contextualising what disability discrimination and hate crimes are, why these occur and their impact. By presenting a variety of viewpoints, the book reflects the cross-governmental approach required to tackle these matters. The different voices presented are all drawn together by a common message – that disability discrimination and hate crime have been overlooked for too long, that these experiences should not be seen as inevitable and that we can and must work together to tackle these matters.

Some of the accounts are challenging to read, and you may find yourself feeling disbelief, anger or sadness at the experiences recounted. But ultimately, the book instils within the reader a sense of determination to achieve change. The book's call for action is compelling – that the victimisation of people with disabilities can no longer be tolerated. And the book goes further: it provides clear, concise, practical, evidence-based (where possible) recommendations on the steps professionals and practitioners in health, social care, education and criminal justice settings can take to better identify and respond to disability discrimination and hate crime. Alongside this, the book considers the challenge to policymakers in ensuring an effective multi-agency approach to tackling these matters. The need for action at a broader level to change societal attitudes and prejudice against people with disabilities is also made clear.

Written for professionals, practitioners, academics, policymakers, as well as those who themselves have been affected by disability discrimination and hate crime, *Tackling Disability Discrimination and Disability Hate Crime* fills an important gap, providing a well-timed investigation of the key issues from a multi-agency perspective. We do hope you will read it and share its important lessons with your friends, family and professional colleagues.

Professor Sheila Baroness Hollins, Cross Bench Member of the House of Lords and Dr Keri-Michèle Lodge, Higher Trainee in Psychiatry of Intellectual Disability

ACKNOWLEDGEMENTS

Dr Robina Shah MBE

This book is dedicated to the special people in my life who supported me when I needed them most; my husband Tariq and our beautiful children, Zainab, Raabiyah, and Sulaymaan, without their love, selflessness and encouragement this book would not have been written. It is also dedicated to my wonderful parents for their prayers, love and guidance.

Many thanks to my colleagues at Frenkel Topping Ltd, particularly Richard Fraser for giving me the time to complete this book and his personal commitment to support carers and disabled people.

I would also like to express my sincere gratitude to all the contributors that shared my vision and gave their time so generously. Collectively we have delivered a powerful message, 'a call to action' to tackle disability hate crime and disability discrimination.

A final thank you to my co-editor Paul Giannasi for his support, expert advise, insight and invaluable contribution.

Paul Giannasi OBE

I am also grateful to the contributors to the book for their insight and to Robina for her hard work and for keeping us on track.

Most importantly I want to thank my daughter Lucy Giannasi for making me grammar gooder.

PREFACE

DR ROBINA SHAH MBE

What's in a Name?

My name is Fred!
Not retard, not spastic, not filth,
My name is Fred!
But this did not stop the kicking, the
spitting, the punching in my face,
This didn't stop the bystanders looking in disgrace,
shaking their head but still moving on!
The tears roll down my face, I feel wretched
and alone, without value or purpose.
My head hits the pavement hard, I collapse
in a bundle but nobody cares,
The group move quickly, laughing as they go,
I get up slowly in the knowledge that this
will happen again tomorrow.
I will walk around the corner and they will be waiting,
Once again ready to ask me the same question:
What is your name?
And before they pounce I will still say proudly my name is Fred!

(Dr Robina Shah)

Disability hate crime has emerged as one of the most challenging problems facing our society today. It is not 'emerging' because it is a new problem, but rather, it appears to be part of the historical reality of many disabled people. It is 'emerging' because agencies only began to measure the problem nationally in 2008. There were, of course, many violent crimes against disabled people before this date but they were regarded as individual, horrific acts rather than the widespread problem this now appears to be. Thankfully, data collection has begun to focus on the hostility suffered by many disabled people on a regular basis. The aim of this book is to identify the work needed to ensure that disabled people live and are looked after in an environment that is safe and secure, something that most people in our society take for granted.

Academia has not agreed, and probably never will agree, on a definition of what a hate crime is or even whether the concept is valuable to engender equality for all or, as some detractors would claim, whether it is a flawed policy which provides a two-tier criminal justice system 'minorities' receive an enhanced service. It is not the intention of this book to engage in this debate; rather, the focus will be on the nature of the victim's experience and what agencies and practitioners can do to reduce the harm caused.

For us, the concept is a simple one: it is where a disabled person is physically or sexually abused, harmed, bullied or even killed because of the perpetrator's hostility to their disability.

The poem on the previous page is written as a reflective piece to describe what disability hate crime may look like in our everyday world, seen and yet unnoticed. It is a stark reminder that, every day, somewhere; a person who is perceived to be 'different' is attacked, harmed or abused. For many it is such a regular occurrence that it has become a daily feature of their lives and sadly it is tolerated because there is no escape. However, the poem also illustrates the power and strength of self-awareness, dignity, respect and the determination to be heard, irrespective of the known outcome.

It is the urgency of this voice's desire to be heard and to be valued that provides the inspiration for writing this book. The collective voice of all the contributors presents a powerful example of what can be achieved when passionate and committed colleagues from different backgrounds come together to give a voice to a 'cause' worthy of the attention of all caring professionals.

In the chapters that follow, several contributors have offered useful explanations of what disability hate crime means in the context of their personal lives or their professional practice or discipline.

We live, work and occupy a space in our society which feels safe for most of us; however, how confident are we that this is also true for our most vulnerable members, the elderly, children, and people with disabilities? This confidence has been challenged through a number of damning reports (see Chapter 12) about the treatment and experience of disabled people who were receiving advice, care services or support from a range of government departments such as health, social care, education and criminal justice.

What is more alarming is the lack of awareness about disability-related hate crime, discrimination and harassment and its impact upon the lives of disabled people who become its victims. There is an absence of awareness in much of our society that this type of crime exists and even a common disbelief or denial that disabled people can be targeted in this way. It makes people uncomfortable when it is spoken about in individual conversations or in group settings. There is a common discomfort, shared by everyone, about the fact that crimes of this nature are present in our society.

We know that discrimination takes place on many levels and can sometimes involve more than one characteristic, for example, disability, race and sexuality. The Equality Act (2010) brings together a number of existing laws and sets out the personal characteristics that are protected by the law and the behaviour that is unlawful. The protected characteristics under the Act are: age, disability, gender reassignment, marriage and civil partnership, pregnancy and maternity, race, religion and belief, sex and sexual orientation.

Under the Act it is interesting to note that people are not allowed to discriminate, harass or victimise another person because they have any one of the protected characteristics. Furthermore, in the context of disability hate crime it is also interesting to note that the Act also provides protection against discrimination for someone who is perceived to have one of the protected characteristics or where they are associated with someone who has a protected characteristic; such as a carer or family member looking after a disabled person.

The Act requires public sector organisations to demonstrate how they are promoting equality and to collect data about their employees and service users to ensure they are complying with public sector equality duty. One of the key issues discussed in this book is the lack of data collection about disability hate crime by some organisations and the difficulty this creates in raising awareness about it and, more importantly, in monitoring the impact of policies and practices on disabled people affected by hate crime.

With this realisation comes the 'call for action' and the need to address this issue as a matter of urgency. This book presents a series of academic, professional and personal accounts that, combined, argue why this call must be heard. The chapters are written in an inclusive style and manner that is honest, grounded, passionate and, where possible, evidence based. Collectively they form a conversation piece to deliver a message that resonates throughout the book, which is that this crime against disabled people in all its forms must no longer be tolerated. Adults, children and young people with disabilities and their families need to feel safe in our society and protected from harm whilst in our care. This book conveys that aspiration, hope and the need for change, making an argument that no one agency is capable of solving the problem unilaterally. We all have a role to play whether we are educators or health, social care or law enforcement professionals. This book will help professionals to understand the nature of this problem and to identify how they can help reduce such hostility.

The contributors are known for their passion and commitment to this area and for their personal motivation to share their expertise and experience to 'make a difference'. Some chapters are written in the first person while others follow the traditional academic style of writing; irrespective of the format, collectively they seek to contextualise the experience of hate crime towards disabled people across a spectrum of public services.

In order to provide a coherent story, the book is divided into four key parts which address the following themes: what disability hate crime is, what it feels like to experience it, what we know about disability hate crime and what we can do to respond to the challenges raised.

Part 1: What is Disability Hate Crime?

Chapter 1 discusses the historical roots of disability hate crime, drawing on international and academic perspectives including the UK government legislative and policy context. Chapter 2 sets the tone and context for the book by presenting a personal insight into the impact and implications of the Equality and Human Rights Commission (EHRC) inquiry into the harassment of disabled people.

Chapter 3 uses a selection of case studies to discuss the diverse circumstances in which disability hate crime takes place and highlights the nature of the escalation required to identify the various stages of that abuse. The cases studies of Fiona Pilkington, Brent Martin and others are explored to demonstrate how disability hate crime became a significant policy area for government and criminal justice agencies.

Chapter 4 considers a range of issues relating to those who commit disability hate crimes and examines what is known about offenders and their offending behaviour. It discusses the factors that make disability hate offenders 'unique' including the contextual issues that set them apart and often shield them from outside scrutiny.

Part 2: Disability Hate Crime – The Impact on Victims

Chapter 5 presents two personal stories. The first provides an individual and personal account of the experience of disability hate crime and why, as a victim, Mark chose to advocate for others. This is followed by David's account of his experience growing up with one of his triplet brothers, Paul, who has cerebral palsy.

Through personal stories, Chapter 6 discusses the impact on the life experience of carers/parents looking after a person who has experienced disability hate crime. It considers issues around personal safety in the context of education, training, supported living and community inclusion. This chapter also addresses how families (and the professionals who support them across schools, colleges, health and social care) help their relatives to develop and use coping strategies to avoid hate crime and to handle it when it occurs.

Chapter 7 introduces the concept that hate crime leaves an 'absent presence', long after the crime has been committed. It highlights the need for enhanced services for victims of hate crime and recommends support services based on the individual needs of each victim and not on the assumption that 'one size fits all'.

Chapter 8 explores the concept of disability hate crime being everyone's business and the need to consider disability hate crime in the same context as safeguarding. The discussion looks at what health and social care professionals need to do and why it's important to co-design a new professional and values-based approach.

Part 3: Disability Hate Crime – Lessons from Other Disciplines

Chapter 9 discusses the learning from rape and sexual abuse cases, legislation and policy and the implications for professional practice. It also explores the practitioner response to understanding the impact of hate crime in the context of rape, violence and sexual abuse. The chapter also looks at the link between hate crime and sexual offending, both in terms of shared practices which can assist professionals and about those sexual offences that are motivated by hostility.

Chapter 10 explores the role of an educationalist through the experience of Sylvia Lancaster who faced every parent's nightmare when her daughter, Sophie, was murdered by young, hate-motivated offenders in 2007. The hostility that fuelled the attack on Sophie and her boyfriend Robert was towards their dress and lifestyle, but Sylvia believes that such hostility is homogeneous with other hate crime. This chapter discusses Sophie's attack but also demonstrates how we can educate young people to reduce all hostility including disability hate crime.

Chapter 11 discusses the response in higher education and the importance of raising awareness among the student and teaching community about reporting disability hate crime. Chapter 12 begins with an overview of the strategic and policy landscape and how partners across government and the third sector can work together to improve the circumstances of disabled people injured, harmed or abused because of their disability. Second, it is discussed how regulation can support the policy changes required in a cross-government approach by considering generic standards that all departments can sign up to in order to inform a change and reform context.

Part 4: How to Respond to Disability Hate Crime

Chapter 13 explores the role of local authorities and, in particular, social services. It discusses the challenges of working with other disciplines and considers the difficulties practitioners may face when a victim chooses to be in the company of abusive 'friends' and therefore is a risk to their own personal safety. Chapter 14 presents the primary care picture, looking at the role of the general practitioner and their response to improving support to disabled people and carers in the context of hate crime.

Chapter 15 focuses on the contributions that healthcare agencies, practitioners and professionals can make in tackling hate crime whilst working with colleagues in the criminal justice system, social care, the third sector and others. It explores the value that multi-agency working brings in helping overcome the challenges that disability hate crime presents and considers how to empower professionals and practitioners, in particular those working within health and social care, to be able to reduce the impact that hate crime has on the lives of disabled people.

Chapter 16 describes the policy of the criminal justice agencies and how their response to the challenges of disability hate crime has changed massively since 2007. Disability hate crime has been named as a priority area by the police and Crown Prosecution Service, yet many crimes never get reported to authorities and others are reported to the police but are never recorded as disability hate crime. This chapter will look at policy and performance progress since 2007 and will explore the three greatest challenges.

Chapter 17 uses a personal perspective to explain how necessary change can be achieved through influence over policy, legislation and politics. The chapter is grounded in 'realpolitik', ignoring 'ideal-world' solutions but concentrating on the one we all occupy.

Chapter 18 considers next steps and how organisations can work collaboratively to provide a coherent and robust response to the issues raised in this book. It concludes with a series of recommendations that will inform local and national strategies to improve the life circumstances of disabled people and deliver better outcomes for victims of disability hate crime.

PART 1

WHAT IS DISABILITY HATE CRIME?

CHAPTER 1

JOHNNY COME LATELY?

THE INTERNATIONAL AND DOMESTIC POLICY CONTEXT OF DISABILITY HATE CRIME

JEMMA TYSON, PAUL GIANNASI OBE AND DR NATHAN HALL[1]

In terms of understanding, awareness and legislation, disability hate crime is regarded by many as lagging behind other challenges such as racial and religious discrimination. However, with an emergent literature base and the exposure of high-profile crimes, such as those suffered by Brent Martin and Fiona Pilkington, there has emerged an increased pressure to introduce disability hate crime to the world of politics. Or, perhaps, to introduce politics to the world of disability hate crime. Either way, in doing so, this provides an essential stage to highlight the victimisation and ill-treatment that people with disabilities face, which seemingly occur on a daily basis, yet are frequently overlooked.

In this chapter we discuss the international and domestic policy context of disability hate crime and the significant differences between the two. When international comparisons are made, the UK has a far greater number of disability hate crimes committed than anywhere else in the world, at least officially. It would be naive to believe that such offences are not happening in other countries, yet questions remain about the causes of this disparity and in particular why there are such vast differences in levels of reporting and recording. The reasons behind the statistics of other countries – whether they are a result of societal ignorance or a lack of education and understanding – is a debate in itself, beyond the scope of this chapter. Rather, we consider the importance of ensuring that

---

1   Excerpts within this chapter have previously been published in Hall (2013).

disability hate crime is viewed as a political priority if it is to be responded to appropriately.

In this regard, we argue that there has been a shift in focus within the UK that has led to disabled people's organisations and more generally victims increasing pressure on the authorities, in particular the UK government, to make disability hate crime a political priority. Elsewhere in this book, Giannasi (Chapter 3) discusses the addition of 'disability' to the UK's national hate crime policy, demonstrating a political acknowledgement of the issue in response to high-profile crimes. We will suggest that whilst the UK is not perfect in its responses to disability hate crime, in many ways those responses can be viewed, comparatively at least, as examples of best practice.

This book provides an abundance of information surrounding disability hate crime and is one of a limited number of publications that does. However, without any policy recognition of this issue, from an international and domestic perspective, these efforts are likely to be fruitless and made in vain. It is this political prioritisation, provided that it is sustained, that we expect to be the catalyst for significant improvements in the ways in which disability hate crimes are responded to.

Johnny come lately? Disability hate crime on (or off) the international stage

Perhaps unsurprisingly, and reflective of our choice of title for this chapter, information concerning the extent and nature of disability hate crime around the world is hard to find. Although organisations such as Human Rights Watch[2] document human rights abuses against people with disabilities in a number of countries around the world, specific data is rare. This is starkly illustrated by the hate crime reports of the Organization for Security and Co-operation in Europe (OSCE – the world's largest regional security organisation, with members from 57 States across Europe, Central Asia and North America).

---

2   See www.hrw.org.

In 2012, only 14 of the 56 participating OSCE States (the fifty-seventh and most recent State to join, Mongolia, was not included in this report) recorded data on crimes against people with disabilities. However, at the time the report was written in November 2013, Finland, Germany and the UK were the only participating States that had provided data for 2012, recording 19, 29 and 1853 respectively (OSCE 2013). Furthermore, unlike other recognised strands of hate crime, the OSCE received no information from non-governmental organisations (NGOs) relating to crimes or incidents motivated by bias against people with disabilities. Moreover, the FBI (2013) reported just 58 disability hate crimes across the whole of the US, a country with seven times the population of the UK.

The new kid in town: the arrival of disability hate crime as a UK policy concern

So, why is it that the UK, officially at least, records far more disability hate crimes than anywhere else, and how did we get to the position where this situation now exists? In no small part, the answer lies in an event completely unrelated to disability hate crime that took place in London on the night of 22 April 1993.

Twenty years ago, black teenager Stephen Lawrence was murdered in Eltham, south-east London. For those of us involved in hate crime scholarship and those involved in criminal justice policy and practice in the UK, this was undoubtedly our watershed moment. The murder, and in particular the public inquiry that was published in 1999 with damning conclusions and sweeping recommendations for change, went far beyond just issues of policing. With the benefit of hindsight, this was the single most important event in bringing issues of hate crime to the forefront in the UK.

This was not just because of the inquiry's focus on racism, victimisation and the responses to it, and not just because of the far-reaching implications for change that it was to have across the board, but also because the Lawrence's fight with 'the system' has left a legacy that has allowed other voices to be heard where they previously would not have been. Ultimately, a deep sense of injustice relating to racism and the unwavering commitment of Doreen and Neville Lawrence in their search for truth has opened the door for the proper and formal recognition of other forms of targeted victimisation, giving us our academic and political focus on what we now call 'hate crime'.

This shift is evident in the attention now paid by scholars, researchers, law and policy makers and practitioners alike to hate crimes motivated by prejudices other than just race, often themselves highlighted by high-profile and tragic cases. Such examples include, but are not limited to, the manslaughter of Johnny Delaney in Cheshire in 2003, the murder of Sophie Lancaster in Lancashire in 2007 (which have respectively served to bring Gypsy and Irish Traveller and 'alternative lifestyle' issues to the forefront), the homophobic murder of Jody Dobrowski in London in 2005 and a number of murders and other serious offences against people with disabilities, which are discussed later in this book (see Chapter 16). In addition to the response to high-profile crimes, Mason-Bish (2010) rightly states that the role of various campaign groups has also been central to the way that policy has developed in the UK in recent years. The victim groups included in the formal definitions of hate crime represent those who have activists and campaigners working on their behalf, many of whom will have benefited either directly or indirectly from the efforts of the Lawrence family.

More recently, a key milestone in the development of disability as part of hate crime policy has been the inquiry of the Equality and Human Rights Commission (EHRC) into the harassment of disabled people. The inquiry, which reported initially in September 2011, is discussed in detail in this book (see Chapter 2) but it is worthy of mention here because of the impact it had on raising awareness of the problems faced by disabled people and the focus it brought to the governments of England, Wales and Scotland as well as the agencies and authorities who have the responsibility of protecting the community from harm.

The first steps on a long journey?

Hall (2013) has reflected upon the progress made in the UK in furthering the hate crime agenda and upon the 'paradigm shift' that he suggests has taken place since the publication of the Stephen Lawrence Inquiry. He suggests that:

> the outcomes of this 'paradigm shift' in terms of radically changing the goals of policy and practice, which in many ways is still in progress, can be seen in the range of outcomes that to me set the UK apart from its international counterparts... In comparative terms, then, in my view the UK is the 'world leader' in terms of responding to hate crimes. (Hall 2013, p.198)

Arguably, however, the key word in the quotation above is 'comparative'. Given the OSCE data above, it is clear that more disability hate crimes come to the attention of the authorities in the UK than anywhere else. Indeed the official figure in England and Wales reported above represents an almost 150 per cent increase since data was first collected in 2008. Arguably, this is a product of the increased attention that has been drawn to the issue of disability victimisation in recent years, culminating in the EHRC's inquiry published in 2012, and the inevitable resulting pressure for those in authority to respond to this emerging social problem.

Whilst this is of course a cause for some optimism, it is clear that there can be no room for complacency. Behind the 'headline' figure of 1853 recorded disability hate crimes recorded nationally in 2012/13, there is a worrying disparity across police forces. For example, Leicestershire Police (the force covering the area where Fiona Pilkington was victimised) recorded 188 disability hate crimes whilst in the same period the Metropolitan Police in London (with a population of over seven million people) recorded 85. Rather disturbingly, 11 forces across England and Wales recorded fewer than ten disability hate crimes each (ACPO 2014).

Of course one might suggest that these low figures are simply because disability hate crimes don't occur in those areas, but to suggest as much would, to our minds, demonstrate a woeful ignorance of the realities of the situation. Indeed, it is starkly apparent from the research undertaken by various disability-related organisations and others that disability-related harassment remains vastly under-reported. For example, a study by Mind (2007) found that, with reference to people with mental health problems, 71 per cent of respondents had been victimised in the community at least once in the previous two years; 41 per cent were victims of ongoing bullying; 22 per cent had been physically assaulted; 27 per cent had been sexually harassed; and 34 per cent had been victims of theft. Crucially, the reporting of these incidents was low and a finding that perhaps helps to explain the levels of under-reporting is that 64 per cent of victims reported being dissatisfied with the overall response they received from the authorities. These findings are not unique, with other studies in the field reporting similarly (see, for example, DRC 2004; Mind 2007; Mencap 2007; Quarmby 2008; EHRC 2012).

Numerically speaking, however, the extent of the problem of under-reporting is most brutally apparent from the data provided by the British Crime Survey, now known as the Crime Survey of England and Wales (Smith *et al.* 2012) which estimates that around 65,000 disability hate crimes occur annually. This huge 'dark figure' of unreported, or at least unrecorded, disability hate crime, coupled with an ever expanding research base reveals the considerable barriers that victims with disabilities face when trying to access justice. This makes it clear that despite the progress made, and notwithstanding comparative advances, the journey ahead for the UK in this regard remains a very long one indeed.

A road map for the journey? The legal and policy context of disability hate crime

Later in this book, Giannasi sets out the legal framework for the criminalisation of hate crime in England and Wales (see Chapter 16). Whilst the cornerstone of hate crime legislation is the enhanced sentencing that is available for any offence that is found to be motivated wholly or partially by a hostility to one of the five protected strands (including disability), it will be seen that there are also some potential gaps that have been identified by the EHRC and others. In addition to the criminalisation of offending behaviour, Giannasi also explores the proactive legal duties placed on all agencies by the requirements of the Equality Act (2010).

Perhaps one of the most comforting elements for affected communities is that hate crime has been stated as a priority area for successive governments in the UK, including Scotland and Northern Ireland, with the subject receiving almost universal prioritisation. Key to that commitment is the recognition of the harm caused to communities by hate crime and also the transparency of data, both in terms of recorded crime and community experiences of crime. This cross-party leadership and transparency has doubtless contributed to the situation which exposes such huge gaps in the OSCE reports and places the UK in a comparatively strong position.

The cross-party consensus is demonstrated in a number of publications. For example, under the Labour guardianship there was the Home Secretary's Action Plan in response to the Stephen Lawrence Inquiry (Home Office 1999) and *Hate Crime – The Cross-Government Action Plan* (Home Office 2009). When the Coalition Government came to power in 2010, both parties had commitments concerning hate crime in their manifestos. Their joint manifesto, *The Coalition: Our Programme for Government* (Home Office 2010) included a commitment to increase the recording of hate crimes, including a specific mention of disability hate crimes which it recognised were often not recorded.

The broad recognition of hate crime as a priority area was further demonstrated during a Westminster Hall debate in Parliament on 23 November 2011 (HC Deb 23 November 2011 105–97WH). MPs from a broad range of political and geographical backgrounds expressed their deep concern at the level of hostility towards disabled people in the community. In response to the debate Maria Miller MP, then the Minister for Disabled People, stated that:

> It is important that we recognise, both within the House and outside, the magnitude of the problem that we face. Any form of discrimination against disabled people is absolutely unacceptable. Hate crime is a particularly disgusting and disgraceful abuse of disabled people, which has no place in civilised society… Our starting point must be that disabled

people have to be absolutely clear that they are adequately protected by the law... Crimes targeted at disabled people by friends, relatives and carers are a significant challenge for the criminal justice agencies and the Government. I reassure [MPs] that the issue is seen as a priority. (HC Deb 23 November 2011 105–97WH)

In March 2012 the UK government published its action plan to tackle hate crime. Notwithstanding the content, this was symbolically important, not least because the last Conservative government (in power until 1997) showed little interest in furthering the race-hate agenda as a political and legislative concern, meaning that nearly all of the progress made in this regard happened under the Labour administration (see Hall 2013, for a discussion of this issue). Perhaps unsurprisingly, the removal of Labour from office in the 2010 general election, and replacement coalition government with a Conservative Prime Minister caused considerable concern in some quarters that hate crime might start to disappear from the political agenda. The publication of the action plan suggests that this is not the case.

There is not the space here for a full consideration of the content of the 2012 action plan, but nevertheless some overarching aspects are useful for our purposes in this chapter. The government's approach to crime in general is based upon a withdrawal from top-down micro-management towards more locally administered responses that should reflect the needs of local areas and communities. As such, the government sees its role as setting strategic direction, making information available, sharing good practice and, where necessary, passing legislation (Home Office 2012).

In the context of hate crime, the action plan (Home Office 2012) is underpinned by three core principles, the ongoing responsibility for which is shared across government departments and the agencies of the criminal justice system:

- preventing hate crime (by challenging attitudes and early intervention)
- increasing reporting and access to support (through increased victim confidence and supporting local partnerships)

- improving operational responses (through better identification and management of cases and dealing effectively with offenders).

Under the theme of preventing hate crime, the government identified 23 action points including the need to develop and improve the evidence base upon which interventions are based (see Chapter 4 for a discussion of the complexities involved here), reducing negative media stereotypes of different groups (again, see Chapter 4 for a consideration of media stereotypes in shaping offender behaviour), supporting educational and anti-bullying initiatives, supporting the work of charities and others (including sports organisations) involved in challenging hateful discourse, working with relevant others to address hate on the internet, developing resources for use by local partnerships, and supporting the work of the antisemitism and anti-Muslim cross-government working groups.

With regard to increasing reporting and access to support, 16 points for action are identified. These are broadly based on the need for the improved collection and dissemination of data, the identification of statistical gaps, the need to engage with 'at risk' communities, working with the voluntary sector to establish and share 'good practice' in reporting and preventing hate crimes, supporting the work of True Vision[3] and providing funding for selected organisations and projects in the field.

Finally, with the goal of improving operational responses, 14 action points are highlighted including the publishing of a hate crime manual to guide police organisations, the updating of training for all police roles, the development of various tools to assist professionals dealing with hate crimes, the amendment of legislation as necessary, the development of a hate crime framework covering prisons and the probation service to assist with the management of offenders, and assessing the scope for alternative disposals such as restorative justice (see Chapter 16 for a discussion of criminal justice responses to disability hate crime).

Of course, the action plan is rather short on specific detail and many of the undertakings within are ongoing at least until

---

3   See www.report-it.org.uk.

the next general election in May 2015. However, the first two core principles do at least recognise and acknowledge the need for an holistic approach to the problem, rather than simply relying on a retributive response through law and the criminal justice system, which the literature suggests can be problematic (Hall 2013; also see Chapter 16 in this book).

In considering the UK government's formal response to *Hidden in Plain Sight* (EHRC 2012) which refers to a number of the significant new policy or legislative approaches outlined above, the EHRC concluded that the UK government's response is comprehensive and robust in relation to: the government's clear commitment to tackling this issue, commitments to improving data collection on the application of Section 146 of the Criminal Justice Act (2003) and data sharing, safeguarding measures in health services, tackling anti-social behaviour in social housing and a commitment to developing reciprocal reporting arrangements in transport.

However, the EHRC (2012, p.7) also identified areas where more needs to be done and stated their intention to continue discussions with government departments on other areas including a better understanding of the motivations of perpetrators and societal causes of disability-related harassment (see Chapter 4), the collection of comprehensive data on disability-related harassment, improving decision making and accountability, empowering local leadership and other local agents of change to have access to the right information and support to hold authorities to account and make change happen, addressing cyber-bullying and the impact of terminology and language in bringing about cultural change.

The importance of political prioritisation

Meaningful approaches to tackling hate crime, such as those discussed above, can, inevitably, only take place if governments, and therefore policy makers, have an interest in furthering the hate crime agenda. The EHRC's (2012) acknowledgement of the UK government's commitment in this area is encouraging. In keeping with the theme of policy and politics, something that strikes us as particularly important is the extent to which hate crime is regarded as a political priority by governments.

Undoubtedly, the role and political inclinations of the state (and its institutions) can have serious implications for shaping an environment in which hate can potentially flourish. The extent to which a country's political stance serves either to protect or infringe human rights therefore represents an important issue for consideration. Hall (2013), Human Rights Watch (2013) and others have variously noted concerns relating to the (mis)treatment of different minority groups in a number of countries around the world. Therefore, one might reasonably assume that the numbers of recorded hate crimes in any given country (noted above) are, at least in part, an indication of the importance (or otherwise) in which it is held politically if it is recognised at all. At the very least, the various calls for improvements to state responses in a number of countries (see, for example, the OSCE report of 2013) are an indicator of considerable concern in this regard.

Of course there are different ways in which the politics of a country can shape its policy responses to these issues. This is illustrated by Bleich (2007), for example, who notes that in recent years different countries of the European Union have pursued distinctive paths in their responses to hate crimes. To illustrate this Bleich highlights (in relation to racism) the primacy of a criminal justice approach in the UK, whilst Germany has devoted resources to civil society groups with the intention of countering right-wing extremism and France has taken symbolic and educational approaches to the problem. As Bleich suggests:

> broadly speaking, states have choices to make about how much they use repressive policies aimed at preserving public order versus instructive policies aimed at promoting tolerance and liberal democratic values... Most commentators agree that much has changed during the past few years, yet most also agree that each state's commitment to eradicating [hate crime] is not as strong as it could be. Developing nationally effective policies thus depends on learning from other states about the pragmatic steps a country can take. It also depends on responding to domestic actors who articulate concerns about

specific problems and suggest possible solutions. Obeying this rule of thumb will go a long way toward limiting the impact of [hate] violence and toward promoting national cohesion. (Bleich 2007, pp.160–162)

It is true that 'commitment', the 'international learning process' and listening and responding to 'articulated concerns' are by no means guaranteed, as reflected in some of the global political stances on this issue. Thus, in comparative terms, as we have already suggested, in our view the UK is the 'world leader' in terms of responding to hate crimes. This position, as argued elsewhere (Hall 2013; Hall, Grieve and Savage 2009), is, as we have seen, largely a product of the 'legacies of Lawrence', which have been instrumental in generating or accelerating far-reaching and multi-tiered changes to the UK's political and policy responses to hate crime.

The outcomes of this 'paradigm shift', in terms of radically changing the goals of policy and practice, which in many ways is still in progress, can be seen in the range of outcomes that set the UK apart from its international counterparts. These include, but are not limited to, the broad and inclusive definitions of hate crime employed, the focus on appropriate service provision to victims and communities, the True Vision online (and other) third party reporting system, the volume of incidents reported to the police, the number of diversity strands for which data is collected and published, the scope and strength of legal recognition for diversity issues, the number of cases prosecuted, the level of financial support thus far provided by government (most noticeably through the Victim's Fund, to support the valuable work of NGOs in this area), the previous and current governments' Hate Crime Action Plan, the engagement with Independent Advisory Groups and other community representatives, the ACPO Hate Crime Policing Manuals, the hate crime 'diagnostic tool' for police and the demand from other countries for knowledge transfer.

But, whilst the comparative position of the UK should be a source of some satisfaction, concerns still exist in many quarters. In recent times, the political commitment of the UK government and the response of key agencies has attracted some criticism. In 2009, the tenth anniversary of the publication of the public inquiry into Stephen Lawrence's murder provided an opportunity to reflect on the extent of progress made in relation to the areas covered by the Inquiry's original recommendations. The general consensus of opinion was that much had been achieved, but that much still remained to be done (EHRC 2009; Hall, Grieve and Savage 2009; Rollock 2009; Stone 2009). However, as we noted above, the period since the tenth anniversary has seen a change of government and, for the first time since the inquiry was originally published, the 'hate crime' agenda is not under the guardianship of the administration that instigated it. This situation, as also suggested above, has been the source of anxiety for those who expressed concerns relating to the new government's desire and commitment to further pursue the agenda set in motion by its predecessor, not least in times of considerable financial austerity.

In what are increasingly difficult (financial) times globally, sustaining political interest and creating and maintaining an environment in which hate cannot flourish therefore seems to be crucial for the furtherance of the hate crime agenda. Notwithstanding recent domestic concerns, we would still contend that those of us in the UK are in a comparatively privileged position in this regard, although much still remains to be done here too.

However, the question of how to secure the protection of human rights of others elsewhere in the world where combating hate crime has been, and remains, somewhat less of a political priority (perhaps shaped by deep-rooted cultural differences) is both problematic and unanswered. As Perry suggests:

> hate-motivated violence can flourish only in an enabling environment…such an environment historically has been conditioned by the activity – or inactivity – of the state… State practices, policy, and rhetoric often have provided the formal framework within which hate crime – as an informal mechanism of control – emerges. (2001, p.179)

Examples in this regard are not hard to find. For example, Russia's courts have already banned gay pride events for 100 years, nine regions in Russia have outlawed the promotion of 'homosexual propaganda' and, in the time between this being written and you reading it, the ban may well have been extended into national law

(Grekov 2013). As noted by Hall (2013), elsewhere one might point to the popularity of the anti-immigration position of Greece's Golden Dawn party and recent Italian political rhetoric concerning the Roma. We might also consider France's 'voluntary repatriation' of Roma in 2010 and the controversial banning of the niqab and burqa in public spaces in 2011 to be influential in shaping an environment conducive to the development of prejudice.

Closer to home, as Hall and Tyson (in Chapter 4) note in relation to the shaping of offender attitudes, there have been apparent recent increases in levels of hostility towards people with disabilities. They note that perceived increases in the occurrence of disability hate crime are, at least in the view of many disabled people, being attributed to what is claimed by some to be irresponsible political rhetoric from the British government in relation to statements concerning the numbers of people claiming incapacity benefit who are 'faking' disabilities (Riley-Smith 2012). As Hall and Tyson note in Chapter 4, research by ComRes (2012) on behalf of the disability charity Scope found that disabled people identified the small number of people falsely claiming disability benefits and the way the actions of this minority of claimants are reported as primary causes of public hostility. Crucially, Scope concluded that it was impossible to ignore that the results came at the same time as the government continued to focus the welfare debate on a few benefit 'scroungers' as part of efforts to make the case for more radical reform to the welfare system.

The monumental challenge in furthering the disability hate crime agenda and securing positive change, it would seem, is to secure the commitment of states in terms of carefully shaping rhetoric, policy and practice, to create safe and inclusive environments where the human rights of all are both respected and protected. On the available evidence, international organisations and others seeking to improve national responses to hate crime undoubtedly have some way to go in this unenviable undertaking. Once that commitment has been achieved, however, the next challenge is to sustain it. In the UK at least, this long journey has already begun. In disability hate crime, there is indeed a new kid in town.

References

Association of Chief Police Officers (ACPO) (2014) *Recorded Hate Crime Data for 2013/14 for England, Wales and Northern Ireland.* Available at www.report-it. org.uk/hate_crime_data1, accessed on 17 October 2014.

Bleich, E. (2007) 'Hate crime policy in Western Europe: responding to racist violence in Britain, Germany and France.' *American Behavioral Scientist 51,* 25, 149–165.

Commons Hansard Debates, 23 November 2011. Available at www.publications. parliament.uk/pa/cm201011/cmhansrd/cm111123/halltext/111123h0001. htm, accessed on 9 February 2015.

ComRes (2012) *Scope Disability Survey.* Available at www.comres.co.uk/poll/712/ scope-disability-survey.htm, accessed on 17 October 2014.

Disability Rights Commission (DRC) (2004) *Hate Crime Against Disabled People in Scotland: A Survey Report.* Edinburgh: Capability Scotland.

Equality and Human Rights Commission (EHRC) (2009) *Police and Racism: What Has Been Achieved 10 Years After the Stephen Lawrence Inquiry Report?* London: EHRC. Available at www.equalityhumanrights.com/uploaded_ files/raceinbritain/policeandracism.pdf, accessed on 17 October 2014.

EHRC (2011) *Hidden in Plain Sight: Inquiry into Disability-Related Harassment.* London: EHRC. Available at www.equalityhumanrights.com/uploaded_ files/disabilityfi/ehrc_hidden_in_plain_sight_3.pdf, accessed on 17 October 2014.

EHRC (2012) *Out in the Open: Tackling Disability-Related Harassment – A Manifesto for Change.* London: EHRC. Available at www.equalityhumanrights.com/ publication/out-open-tackling-disability-related-harassment-manifesto-change, accessed on 17 October 2014.

FBI (2013) *Hate Crime Statistics 2011.* Available at www.fbi.gov/about-us/cjis/ ucr/hate-crime/2011, accessed on 17 October 2014.

Grekov, I. (2013) *Will 'Promoting Homosexuality' Become a Crime in Russia?* New York: Human Rights First.

Hall, N. (2013) *Hate Crime (Second Edition).* Oxon: Routledge.

Hall, N., Grieve, J. and Savage, S. P. (eds) (2009) *Policing and the Legacy of Lawrence.* Oxon: Routledge.

Human Rights Watch (2013) *World Report 2013.* Available at www.hrw.org/ world-report/2013, accessed on 17 October 2014.

Mason-Bish, H. (2010) 'Future challenges for hate crime policy.' In Chakraborti, N. (ed.) *Hate Crime: Concepts, Causes, Controversies.* Cullompton: Willan.

Mencap (2007) *Bullying Wrecks Lives: The Experiences of Chilren and Young People with a Learning Disability.* London: Mencap.

Mind (2007) *Another Assault.* London: Mencap.

Organisation for Security and Co-operation in Europe (OSCE) (2013) *Hate Crimes in the OSCE Region – Incidents and Responses. Annual Report for 2012.* Warsaw: OSCE.

Perry, B. (2001) *In the Name of Hate: Understanding Hate Crimes.* New York: Routledge.

Quarmby, K. (2008) *Getting Away With Murder: Disabled People's Experiences of Hate Crime in the UK.* London: Scope. Available at www.scope.org.uk/Scope/media/Images/Publication%20Directory/Getting-away-with-murder.pdf, accessed on 17 October 2014.

Riley-Smith, B. (2012) 'Disability hate crime: is 'benefit scrounger' abuse to blame?' *The Guardian*, 14 August, 2012.

Rollock, N. (2009) *The Stephen Lawrence Inquiry 10 Years On: An Analysis of the Literature.* London: The Runnymede Trust. Available at www.runnymedetrust.org/uploads/publications/pdfs/StephenLawrenceInquiryReport-2009.pdf, accessed on 17 October 2014.

Smith, K., Lader, D., Hoare, J. and Lau, I. (2012) *Hate Crime, Cyber Security and the Experience of Crime Among Children: Findings from the 2010/11 British Crime Survey.* London: Home Office.

Stone, R. (2009) *Stephen Lawrence Review – An Independent Commentary to Mark the 10th Anniversary of the Stephen Lawrence Inquiry.* Available at www.stoneashdown.org/images/stories/slr_report.pdf, accessed on 14 October 2014.

CHAPTER 2

DISABILITY HATE CRIME – A CALL FOR ACTION

MIKE SMITH

Introduction

I was a Commissioner at the Equality and Human Rights Commission[1] from December 2009 until December 2012. My background was private sector, working for one of the big four accountancy firms, PricewaterhouseCoopers, from university until 2010. As a Commissioner, I chaired the Commission's statutory Disability Committee and was also Lead Commissioner for our formal inquiry into disability-related harassment.

I had been involved in various equality initiatives for the previous ten years, but nothing had prepared me for the issues I would be exposed to during this inquiry. Some of the evidence was truly shocking in terms of what one human being can do to another. Some of it showed disconcerting complacency on the part of some public bodies. All of it built a picture, over 18 months, of a problem that was significant, complicated and clearly not well recognised or well understood.

The inquiry's final report, *Hidden in Plain Sight*, has been much acclaimed. There is a lot in it and I won't be wasting the precious words I have for this chapter just by repeating its contents. Instead I want to take you on a journey through the different stages of the inquiry. In the following pages I set out:

- how the inquiry came about

- what happened along the way

---

1   The Equality and Human Rights Commission is a non-departmental public body set up to promote the UK's equality and human rights laws. It covers all protected strands and operates in England, Scotland and Wales. It is the UK's A-rated National Human Rights Institution for the United Nations.

- the findings of the inquiry

- the impact of the inquiry

- what should happen next.

I am mindful that there are certain obligations placed upon me under Section 16 of the Equality Act (2010), as the Lead Commissioner for the inquiry, in terms of confidentiality. Where I make references within this chapter to events during the inquiry which are not already in the public domain, I will ensure the identity of the relevant individuals or organisations cannot be determined.

I was lucky enough to have a fantastic team working on the inquiry with me. Staff who are/were internal to the Commission, you know who you are and what a great job you did. I was also very grateful for the guidance of the members of my external advisory group and Disability Committee, who were a constant source of good advice, reason and sense.

Some of the rest of this book is about the responses of different agencies following the inquiry. It's great to know that progress is being made. I can honestly say that leading this inquiry is the thing that I am most proud of in my life so far.

The context of the inquiry

In 2009, the Commission conducted research into the safety and security of disabled people.[2] The research findings included:

- Disabled people are at greater risk of experiencing violence than non-disabled people.

- Disabled children and young people and disabled women, particularly those with learning disabilities, are particularly at risk.

- Ongoing low-level incidents are widespread and may go undetected but may escalate at some point. These incidents

---

2   *Promoting the Safety and Security of Disabled People* see www. equalityhumanrights.com/key-projects/good-relations/safety-and-security-for-disabled-people.

are often ignored by public agencies even though they have a significant impact on disabled people.

- Disabled people restructure their lives to minimise real and perceived risk to themselves even if they have not experienced targeted violence personally.

There had, for some time afterwards, been a discussion within the Commission around what we should do next. We had been discussing whether to use our inquiry powers under Section 16 of the Equality Act (2006).[3] Section 16 inquiries are quite lengthy and relatively resource-intensive and costly procedures for the Commission and so deciding on what topics to cover under an inquiry takes some time.

In the meantime, the case of Fiona Pilkington hit the headlines. This case is explored and referred to in many of the forthcoming chapters, probably because it was certainly something that hit the newspaper headlines and TV news in a big way and was useful in crystallising action within the Commission. We committed to conducting the inquiry and set about drafting and consulting upon the terms of reference for it (a requirement of the legislation).

So we embarked upon an 18-month inquiry. At the outset we didn't know it would take so long but we also didn't fully appreciate just how complex an issue it was going to be to investigate.

The process of the inquiry – getting going

I was determined that disabled people should be key in leading this inquiry, both at the outset and throughout. After all, the mantra of the disability rights movement is 'Nothing about us, without us'. So we held consultation events around England, Scotland and Wales with disabled people and representatives of their organisations.

The inquiry's budget was limited and in order to deliver the best impact a decision was taken to frame it within the context of equalities legislation (specifically observance of and compliance with public sector equality duty responsibilities), together with human rights law.[4]

---

3   See www.legislation.gov.uk/ukpga/2006/3/section/16.

4   See *Hidden in Plain Sight* (EHRC 2011) for the full terms of reference.

What was interesting about these initial consultations was the apparent difficulty individual people had differentiating between what was 'hate crime' and what was 'discrimination' based on the grounds of disability. Indeed this was later reinforced in the call for written evidence.

Part of the issue seemed to be that so many unpleasant things happen to so many disabled people on an often daily basis and so there was a blurring between indirect discrimination, direct discrimination, offensive or anti-social behaviour, 'hate incidents' and 'hate crimes'. While trying to agree a definition that would explain the terms of reference for the inquiry, it was difficult trying to explain that we weren't going to be addressing every evil that happens to disabled people. It was only later on in the inquiry, as we were analysing all of the information, that it became apparent that it was difficult for people to differentiate precisely because there is a continuum of activities and behaviour, which can often lead to the most serious of hate crimes.

Predominantly, the inquiry focused on the actions of public bodies which excluded the activities of organisations and individuals as employers. This met with a lot of resistance, as many people felt that disability-related harassment happened in the workplace particularly. However, this would have meant significantly widening the scope of the inquiry, which was already much wider than originally planned. Personally, I believe the team made the right call on the basis that employers had a duty to prevent harassment in the workplace and including that would also extend the terms of reference to cover employment law, which was not in the remit of the Commission. We also considered that our findings should translate across a wide range of environments.

However, there were two main things that were added to the inquiry as a result of these consultations. First of all, the language was moved from 'disability hate crime' to 'disability-related harassment'. It was clear, right from the outset, that we needed to look more widely and more deeply than just at crimes. There was also the very common point made to us that people didn't perceive what was happening to them as 'hate crime'. They didn't associate what had happened to them with being 'hated', just taken advantage of or targeted because of their disability. So we defined disability-related harassment as:

> Unwanted, exploitative or abusive conduct against disabled people which has the purpose or effect of either:
>
> - violating the dignity, safety, security or autonomy of the person experiencing it, or
>
> - creating an intimidating, hostile, degrading or offensive environment.

Ultimately, I believe this wider definition gave us a much broader understanding of the issues than we would have obtained had we limited ourselves to conventional definitions of disability hate crime and disability hate incidents.

The other significant change was extending the scope to include transport providers, whether public sector or not. It had become clear through the consultations that high levels of disability-related harassment occurred on public transport, whether due to conflict over shared space or because the actions of others were not adequately monitored and controlled.

Getting evidence – having a robust understanding

We used a number of evidence-gathering approaches. These included:

- reviewing existing research and reports
- key informant interviews with disabled people's organisations (DPOs), other targeted violence organisations, academics, public authorities and public transport operators
- a questionnaire aimed at capturing individual experiences[5]
- a pro forma for organisations and interested parties
- regional events for disabled people's organisations, public authorities and public transport operators

---

5   The questionnaire was available to individuals in various ways including through the Commission's website, via regional roundtable events and through disabled people's organisations.

- a questionnaire on Disability Equality Duty for public authorities

- focus groups, supplemented by individual interviews with disabled people, to explore disabled people's experiences of harassment and their views about the way this is currently addressed by public authorities

- formal evidence hearings in London, Manchester, Glasgow, Cardiff and north Wales, primarily aimed at national and local public authorities and public transport operators, and government departments

- roundtable events on specific themes including:
  - for friends and family of people killed as a result of disability-related harassment and for survivors of serious violence and abuse
  - the role of media regulators and intermediary bodies which represent parts of the media sector in influencing the portrayal of disabled people and disability-related harassment
  - cyber-bullying and cyber-harassment with a number of experts from the public, private and voluntary sectors.

The evidence base for the inquiry included:

- more than 90 research and policy papers

- transcripts of 85 key informant interviews; interviewees included:
  - 46 experts from the disability sector and eight from other third sector organizations
  - 17 from the public sector
  - 13 academics

- 287 disabled people's questionnaires

- 159 submissions to the call for evidence from organisations and interested parties

- 13 regional events for disabled people's organisations, public authorities and public transport operators

- 272 questionnaires from public authorities on the DED

- a report of qualitative research conducted for this inquiry, based on 12 focus groups and 16 in-depth interviews; in this report, we draw on both the evidence provided by disabled people in this research, and on the researchers' analysis of their findings (Sykes, Groom and Desai 2011)

- transcripts of 76 formal evidence hearings (including three themed roundtables) held in London, Manchester, Glasgow, Cardiff and north Wales, involving 234 witnesses and 132 organisations. Witnesses included:

  ◦ 11 local authority chief executives, one local authority leader and nine directors of adult social care

  ◦ seven chief constables, three deputy chief constables and five assistant chief constables

  ◦ the following inspectorates: Ofsted, Care Quality Commission, Her Majesty's Inspectorate of Constabulary, Audit Commission, Ofcom, Her Majesty's Crown Prosecution Service Inspectorate, Press Complaints Commission, Her Majesty's Inspectorate of Education Scotland, Her Majesty's Inspectorate of Constabulary for Scotland, Audit Scotland, Inspectorate of Prosecution Scotland, Her Majesty's Inspector of Education Scotland, Scottish Commission for Regulation of Care, Scottish Housing Regulator, Estyn, Care and Social Services Inspectorate Wales, Wales Audit Office

  ◦ six NHS chief executives and three housing chief executives

  ◦ two head teachers, one deputy head and a principal of a Further Education College

  ◦ the Victims' Commissioner, Information Commissioner and the chief executives of the National Offenders

Management Service and Her Majesty's Court Service, respectively

- ○ four Permanent Secretaries and 11 Directors of government departments (England, Scotland and Wales)
- ○ the Director of Public Prosecutions, Solicitor General (Scotland) and two judges

• written evidence from 59 organisations in advance of formal inquiry hearings sessions and from 55 organisations following hearings.

Formal evidence hearings – emerging issues

I chaired the majority of the London-based formal evidence sessions. It was a fascinating experience and one that I can honestly say I truly enjoyed. Maybe it was because it gave me the chance to play the barrister I never got to be; at my disabled boarding school I was advised by the careers guidance service that it was not a sensible career choice because 'when have you ever seen a lawyer in a wheelchair?' Luckily things have moved on a little since the mid-1980s.

There were broadly three kinds of formal evidence hearings:

1. with informed or learned individuals, who would have particular insightful contributions that we knew they could make

2. heads of national or other public bodies that had an interest in or responsibility for some of the areas

3. so-called 'incident' or 'geography' based sessions – these were usually targeting an area where there had been a significant case (not necessarily where a serious case review had been conducted) in the past, for example the Fiona Pilkington case, and would typically involve senior figures in the local authority, social services, police, health services, housing providers and so on.

In Group 1, the interviewees were generally very forthcoming and pleased that we were doing the inquiry. They gave us great insight and background to conducting Groups 2 and 3.

Group 2 were more challenging. Initially I was surprised at how cautious and careful the interviewees were when responding to questions. I attributed this to the fact that these were formal evidence sessions under an inquiry underpinned by legislation. It was only later on that I started to realise that it was just as much because they often simply didn't know the answer to the questions – they didn't have the evidence base upon which to base their answers. I was starting to wonder how they could properly fulfil their responsibilities under the Disability Equality Duty without this information. But I genuinely think it is fair to say that, approximately halfway through each evidence session, the majority of interviewees understood better that they did not in fact understand the issue or their domain of responsibility in relation to it, and realised that they had some work to do when they got back to the office. The process of change and action started simply by virtue of doing the inquiry itself; the inquiry's findings were the justification for continuing action.

In many ways, the Group 3 sessions were where much of the learning came from. By getting so many agencies together in the same room at the same time we were able to better understand what had gone wrong leading up to particular incidents and what learning had occurred subsequently. Often the cross-agency working had either not existed or had not worked effectively at the right levels.

It was through these Group 3 sessions that I started to map the complex interactions between different policy areas such as housing, social care, education, transport, anti-social behaviour management and the design of public space. In each case, something that was happening in one policy area impacted or adversely affected another. For example, if someone has inadequate social care support they may feel isolated and without friends. It's easy to fall into the wrong company if you don't have good support – 'bad friends' are usually better than social isolation.

Yet the majority of the responses to disability hate crime were being looked at within a specific sector only. We were going to have to find a way, in our final report, of showing just how inter-linked all of the different issues were, and that they would only be addressed effectively with significantly improved cross-sector working.

Many of these sessions were quite revealing. Most organisations submitted written evidence in advance of their formal evidence sessions, which then formed the basis of some of our questioning. I remember one chief executive of a national body had in their report that there were no discernible cases of disability hate crime in their area of responsibility. Later on in the same report it said that they did not monitor the constituency for disability/impairment when addressing violent or other 'crime incidents'. When I asked how the first statement could be made given the second, there was a notable unease on the other side of the table. The issue was, of course, that they hadn't found a problem because they simply weren't looking for it.

In another evidence session's previously submitted written evidence there was a narrative around a particular disabled person's experience of a significant number of crimes over a period of just a few years. The submission said they had concluded that none of these were hate crimes, as each one had been investigated and not found to have a disability-related motive. I asked the particular Chief Constable whether, given the pattern of events that had happened in other situations such as those that ultimately ended in the death of Fiona Pilkington or Stephen Hoskin, he saw a parallel. He agreed to revisit the case. In this situation, the evidence should have been in front of people's faces, yet they just didn't see it.

It was for this and other reasons that we called the report *Hidden in Plain Sight*. Parts of the disability movement had been campaigning on the issue for years; they knew perfectly well that there was a problem. If many of the public bodies had looked more effectively at the information they already had, they could have seen it themselves. In other cases, the data simply wasn't collected to enable them to see it. If anyone had been looking, the issue of disability-related harassment would be in plain sight, but it was hidden from the collective consciousness of those organisations that should be doing something about it.

Writing the report – how to make change happen?

Our key findings were:

- The inquiry confirmed that the cases of disability-related harassment which come to court and receive media attention are only the tip of the iceberg. Our evidence indicated that, for many disabled people, harassment is a commonplace experience. Many come to accept it as inevitable.

- Disabled people often do not report harassment, for a number of reasons: it may be unclear who to report it to, they may fear the consequences of reporting or they may fear that the police or other authorities will not believe them. A culture of disbelief exists around this issue.

- There is a systemic failure by public authorities to recognise the extent and impact of harassment and abuse of disabled people, take action to prevent it happening in the first place and intervene effectively when it does. These organisational failings need to be addressed as a matter of urgency and the full report makes a number of recommendations aimed at helping agencies to do so.

- Any serious attempt to prevent the harassment of disabled people will need to consider more than organisational change, although that will be an important precondition to progress. The bigger challenge is to transform the way disabled people are viewed, valued and included in society.

A central aim of the inquiry was to investigate how disability-related harassment was dealt with by public authorities, public transport operators and others. We concluded that the current system is not succeeding in preventing harassment occurring in the first place, neither is it ensuring that perpetrators face the consequences of their actions. Taken together, this amounted to systemic institutional failure to protect disabled people and their families from harassment. We found:

- Incidents are often dealt with in isolation rather than as a pattern of behaviour.

- There is a lack of consideration by agencies of disability as a possible motivating factor in bullying, anti-social behaviour and crime. As a result, the response to harassment is given low priority and appropriate hate incident policy and legislative frameworks are not applied.

- Left unmanaged, low-level behaviour has the potential to escalate into more extreme behaviour. Opportunities to bring harassment to an end are being missed.

- There is sometimes a focus on the victim's behaviour and 'vulnerability' rather than dealing with the perpetrators.

- Agencies do not tend to work effectively together to bring ongoing disability-related harassment to an end.

- There has been little investment in understanding the causes of harassment and preventing it from happening in the first place.

- There are barriers to reporting and recording harassment across all sectors.

- There are barriers to accessing justice, redress and support so most perpetrators face few consequences for their actions and many victims receive inadequate support.

- There is a lack of shared learning from the most severe cases, so the same mistakes are repeated again and again.

Due to the broad-ranging nature of the inquiry and the fact that many public bodies would need to be involved in making change happen, *Hidden in Plain Sight* was launched with initial recommendations that we would then consult on. I knew that individual public bodies would be unlikely to buy into the actions that we were proposing for them without understanding the bigger picture. To do that would have required sharing the whole report with them prior to its publication, something that we were not allowed to do under the rules governing our inquiries. So we launched with a pledge to consult on these recommendations and report one year later on the 'final recommendations' that other organisations had committed to.

In our initial recommendations, we came up with a number of specific recommendations for sectors such as the criminal justice system, social care, education, housing, transport and so on. But we also came up with the seven core recommendations that were relevant across all sectors and all organizations. I offer these for consideration by readers at the end of this chapter.

Everything that we wanted to write up in the final report had to be based on evidence. Yes, we had tens of thousands of pages of evidence in the files, and analysed, but still there were some of areas that I instinctively knew about but where we did not have concrete evidence. So we crafted our conclusions carefully and, where necessary, I included narrative in my foreword instead.

The impact of the report

9 September 2011 was launch day and is a day I will remember for a long time. In the period running up to launch our media team had been working to get coverage of the report but they were finding it hard. It seemed that the 'culture of disbelief' was fully 'live and kicking' in the journalistic fraternity and it was hard to get commitment to coverage in advance.

But, confirmed the night before, the day started with my debut appearance on BBC Radio 4's *Today* programme. I was on at 6.55am, and was interviewed by James Naughtie. Overall it went pretty well, but I was fairly staggered when I was asked a question along the lines of 'But is it really all that bad, I mean, haven't things improved for disabled people over the last few years?'.[6] Maybe it was good forensic journalism, but one commentator subsequently wrote '...#disbelief from James himself, I felt'.[7]

In fact, the coverage we got on the day was significantly better than first hoped, with coverage on Channel 4, ITV and the majority of the broadsheets and red tops. I also did further radio interviews all day for various regional stations, Radio 5 Live and

---

6   Unfortunately I no longer have the recording to give the exact transcript.
7   '#disbelief' was the hashtag used on Twitter to promote the report.

on the Vanessa Feltz show on BBC Radio London. I have to say, Vanessa was brilliant and seemed to be the person who really got what we were talking about. I was meant to be on the show for ten minutes and it got extended to around 30 minutes with phone-ins.

I have a schedule covering some nine pages detailing all of the audio-visual, online and print media coverage over the next week. But then what was the coverage? Really, very little. If anything, the online campaigns against the media for negative stereotyping of disabled people as benefits scroungers have increased in the last year and a half. This is juxtaposed with continuing coverage of continuing attacks on disabled people, but very little mention of sentence uplifts under Section 146.[8]

But Rome wasn't built in a day. There's been some great other work going on. For example:

- The Commission helped draft the amendments to the Legal Aid, Sentencing and Punishment of Offenders Bill, which successfully equalised the sentencing provisions for murder offences aggravated by disability with those of other protected characteristics.

- Both the Welsh Assembly and the Association of Chief Police Officers commissioned research into perpetrators.

- A joint inspection into disability hate crime was announced by Her Majesty's Inspectorate of Constabulary, Her Majesty's Crown Prosecution Service Inspectorate and Her Majesty's Inspectorate of Probation.

- The government asked the Law Commission to review the law on disability-related aggravated offences and the incitement offences.

- The Mental Health (Discrimination) (No. 2) Act 2013 eliminated some of the discriminatory provisions in our law which the report called to have addressed.

---

8   See www.legislation.gov.uk/ukpga/2003/44/section/146.

I've also spoken at numerous conferences on the topic in the UK, Denmark (for the European Fundamental Rights Agency)[9] and in Poland (Office for Democratic Institutions and Human Rights).[10]

Also, one year after the publication of *Hidden in Plain Sight* we published our follow-up report *Out in the Open*.[11] In that we reported on the 81 formal responses that we had received in relation to our recommendations, together with the responses from the three national governments in England, Scotland and Wales. Each response is a public statement by that organisation of what they have already done to make progress and their commitments on what they will do in the future.

Based on the responses, and the Commission's own further work, we narrowed the original list of recommendations down to 43 strategic recommendations grouped under seven sections:

1. Reporting, recording and recognition.

2. Addressing gaps in legislation and policy.

3. Ensuring adequate support and advocacy.

4. Improved practice and shared learning.

5. Redress and accessing justice.

6. Prevention, deterrence and understanding motivation.

7. Transparency, accountability and involvement.

The Commission also committed to take action going forward, in its *Strategic Plan 2012–2015*, by stating:

> The implementation of our Disability Harassment Inquiry recommendations – including their application to the other protected groups – will be tracked annually and reported in a progress review in 2015. (p.22)

---

9   See http://fra.europa.eu/en/event/2012/conference-autonomy-and-inclusion -people-disabilities.

10 See www.osce.org/hdim_2012 (I was the Introducer at the Human Dimensions Implementation Meeting on Tolerance and Non-Discrimination).

11 See www.equalityhumanrights.com/uploaded_files/disabilityfi/out_in_the_ open_dhi_manifesto.pdf.

So what next?

I remain convinced that one of the key drivers for change will be decent statistics on the incidence of hate incidents and hate crimes. Only then will there be the evidence base to appropriately apply resources not only to properly addressing hate crime when it happens, but to preventing it in the first place. But with the direction of travel from Westminster being to require police to reduce crime, there is a perverse incentive to reduce the amount of recording rather than increase it.

There has to be better end-to-end thinking throughout the criminal justice system. During the inquiry I perceived a funnelling effect, where it didn't occur to officers that something might be disability related, so they didn't look for the evidence appropriately, so the evidence wasn't there when it went the CPS, so sentence uplifts under Section 146[12] of the Criminal Justice Act (2003) were not requested and so they weren't applied by judges. There was plenty of evidence that showed that individuals at all stages of the criminal justice system did not properly understand Section 146.

Moving forward will also need genuine cross-sector responses, nationally and locally. Some of the chapters later in this book explain well the role different individuals, such as GPs, can play in the identification and prevention of disability hate crime. But again, that's only going to happen if those individuals accept and recognise that it happens in the first place.

This brings me to two more things. I spent two and a half years from the beginning of the inquiry through until the publication of *Out in the Open*, yet I can still talk to some people I know personally, and they still can't quite accept or believe that disability hate crime happens. I know that the Westminster government, in its response to *Hidden in Plain Sight*, disagreed with our original recommendation to review the language of disability hate crime. Their response was that this would not be in line with hate crime language for other protected strands. But what does this matter if this language prevents:

---

12   See www.cps.gov.uk/legal/d_to_g/disability_hate_crime.

- victims from recognising what has happened to them (and so reporting it)

- other people accepting that it has happened or could happen.

Probably as a result of the work of charities in promoting positive feelings for disabled people, people just can't identify with the notion that some people 'hate' disabled people. Instead they see 'hate' as the language of extremists such as the Westboro Baptist Church in the US. Even if the language doesn't get changed (and it's not defined in legislation anyway), organisations will at least need to develop strategies for overcoming the above barriers to recognition and reporting.

I also have concerns that the move to Police and Crime Commissioners (PCCs) may reduce the focus on disability hate crime. They are, after all, only as human as the rest of us and there may well be a tendency to focus on the issues that attract votes. Furthermore, if the population at large has a collective denial that disability hate crime exists or occurs, why would PCCs consider it a policing priority?

In late February 2013, a local councillor in Cornwall[13] was forced to apologise by the Council's standards committee after saying 'disabled children cost the council too much and should be put down'. When figures of authority and leadership say things like this is it any surprise that would-be criminals think it's OK to target disabled people specifically?

Sadly, I think it will take at least another ten years before society at large properly recognises the issue that is disability-related harassment/hate crime, and therefore society (and its institutions) responds appropriately. The last three years have seen progress, but there is so, so much further to go.

---

13   See www.bbc.co.uk/news/uk-england-cornwall-21594109.

Recommendations from *Hidden in Plain Sight*

These were the seven core recommendations of our first report:

1. There is real ownership of the issue in organisations critical to dealing with harassment. Leaders show strong personal commitment and determination to deliver change.

2. Definitive data is available which spells out the scale, severity and nature of disability harassment and enables better monitoring of the performance of those responsible for dealing with it.

3. The criminal justice system is more accessible and responsive to victims and disabled people and provides effective support to them.

4. We have a better understanding of the motivations and circumstances of perpetrators and are able to more effectively design interventions.

5. The wider community has a more positive attitude towards disabled people and better understands the nature of the problem.

6. Promising approaches to preventing and responding to harassment and support systems for those who require them have been evaluated and disseminated.

7. All frontline staff who may be required to recognise and respond to issues of disability-related harassment have received effective guidance and training.

References

Equality and Human Rights Commission (EHRC) (2009) *Promoting the Safety and Security of Disabled People*. London: EHRC. Available at www.equalityhumanrights.com/key-projects/good-relations/safety-and-security-for-disabled-people, accessed on 25 October 2014.

EHRC (2011) *Hidden in Plain Sight: Inquiry into Disability-Related Harassment*. London: EHRC. Available at www.equalityhumanrights.com/uploaded_files/disabilityfi/ehrc_hidden_in_plain_sight_3.pdf, accessed on 17 October 2014.

Sykes, W., Groom, C. and Desai, P. (2011) *Disability-Related Harassment: The Role of Public Bodies – A Qualitative Research Report*. Research Report No. 78. London: EHRC.

CHAPTER 3

THE NARRATIVE FOR CHANGE
HOW DISABILITY BECAME INCLUDED IN UK HATE CRIME POLICY

PAUL GIANNASI OBE

In Chapter 1, Tyson, Giannasi and Hall outlined that there is no clear criminological consensus about hate crime. Policy does not stem from a single incident or strategic decision but has developed over many years. However, the term 'hate crime' is well established, recognised by many states and international multi-state bodies. Whilst we have heard that the inquiry into the murder of Stephen Lawrence in 1993 was the catalyst for most policy development within the UK, the concept remains a 'fluid' policy area that responds to emerging crime trends, community concerns and, most importantly, the tragic crimes that shock the nation. The inclusion of disability within national hate crime policy in 2007 follows this same pattern. In this chapter I will explore the background to that decision.

Later in this volume (Chapter 16), I discuss how the police and criminal justice partners came to include disability as a core part of their hate crime policy but show that the decisions were taken amid a backdrop of a series of high-profile and tragic crimes where disabled people were targeted by prolonged and often escalating violence that, on occasions, had the characteristics of torture. The crimes outlined below are some of the more distressing offences, but they had characteristics in common that led many to believe that the disability of the victim was more than just a coincidental factor, rather that it was indicative of a more widespread hostility which is all too prevalent in our society.

It would be wrong to suggest that the crimes outlined below were a new phenomenon as, in reality, similar crimes have been present throughout modern history. The movement away from housing disabled people in residential institutions to community residency (often referred to as 'care in the community') in the latter part of the twentieth century undoubtedly changed the nature of victimisation of many disabled people. However, a lack of historical data makes it difficult to establish whether this policy change made disabled people more or less exposed to violence and hostility.

The abuse of disabled people in a 'care setting'

Whilst it would be naive to suggest that closed institutions completely protected individuals from abuse, community living meant that victimisation was more visible to the general population. Evidence of the abuse of disabled people within residential care settings has always been present, both within the UK and globally, whether that be the complaints of ill-treatment or poor service in the traditional 'asylum' of the early twentieth century or the ill-treatment of residents in a modern commercial care facility. The potential for widespread abuse in a care setting was exposed in 1969 when a report to Parliament from the Secretary of State for Health exposed widespread violence and abuse of patients at Ely Hospital in Cardiff.

Despite the move to help more people to reside in the community, there is still contemporary evidence of abuse, including the systematic criminal abuse uncovered by a BBC *Panorama* documentary at the Winterbourne View Hospital. The documentary aired in May 2012 uncovering evidence which led to the conviction of 11 staff and brought about a formal government response.

Historically, authorities have tended to treat violence or abuse in a care setting as ill-treatment and abuse rather than targeted hostility to the victim's disability. The exposure of the crimes at Winterbourne View came to light after disability had been embedded into the shared justice system definition of hate crime and after the enactment of Section 146 of the Criminal Justice Act (2003) which gives powers in England and Wales for courts to 'enhance' sentences where they believe a crime was motivated wholly or partially by hostility to a person's disability.

With these legal and policy changes embedded, both the police and the Crown Prosecution Service (CPS) recorded and responded to the Winterbourne View crimes as disability hate crimes. In October 2012, after the convictions, Ann Reddrop, head of the CPS's South West Complex Casework Unit, said:

> Every member of society has the right to live free from intimidation and fear, but the offending that took place at Winterbourne View undermined that right in an appalling and systematically brutal way. People who should have been able to trust their carers had that trust cruelly and repeatedly abused.
>
> The CPS treated these offences as disability hate crimes, crimes based on ignorance, prejudice and hate. We brought this aggravating factor to the attention of the court and it was reflected in the sentencing today. The CPS works closely with the police and other agencies to tackle hate crimes and will always prosecute where there is sufficient evidence and it is in the public interest to do so. Today's sentences send a clear message to those who believe there will be no consequences for their abuse of disabled people. (Crown Prosecution Service 2012)

Disability hate crime in 'the community'

In 2007, when the review of hate crime policy was being undertaken by criminal justice partners in England and Wales, there was a series of high-profile crimes where disabled people were targeted in degrading, abusive, torturous and even fatal violence. Many of the crimes targeted adult victims, often people with a learning disability, and often they had befriended the offenders who went on to abuse them. Worryingly, many of the groups who go on to commit these crimes include children or young people.

In these examples we explore some of the high-profile crimes that involved young people either as victims or perpetrators and were sharp in the background as agencies considered which strands of hate crime should be included in the shared definition in the UK.

Steven Hoskin

Steven was 38 when he was murdered in 2006 in St Austell, Cornwall. He had a learning disability and lived alone in a bedsit. He 'befriended' a group, including five individuals who would go on to abuse, torture and eventually murder him. The group included two men in their twenties and three teenagers, although only one of these was involved in the fatal incident.

Over a period of time, Steven's friendship was abused and he was subjected to prolonged humiliation and violence. He was tied up in his home, made to wear a dog's collar and lead before being dragged around his home. He had multiple injuries from cigarette burns and other violence. Steven was forced to confess to being a paedophile and was found guilty in a 'kangaroo court'. As a punishment, Steven was sentenced 'to death'. He was forced to take around 70 Paracetamol tablets before being taken to a nearby viaduct, where he was forced to climb over the railings. Shockingly, as Steven held on to the viaduct, the youngest of those present, a 16-year-old girl, stamped on his fingers causing him to fall 35 metres to his death.

Five offenders were convicted in relation to Steven's death: the 16-year-old girl and her 29-year-old boyfriend were convicted of murder, a 21-year-old man was convicted of manslaughter and two teenage boys were convicted of assault and false imprisonment. The hearing took place before disability was included in the national agreed hate crime definition and it does not appear that any of the criminal justice agencies considered it to be a disability hate crime.

At the time of the court hearing the most serious offence charged, that of murder, was not included in the enhanced sentencing provision of the Criminal Justice Act, although as we explore later in this volume this anomaly has since been put right. That said, the eldest of the offenders, who was considered by many to be the ringleader, was given a minimum 25 year tariff to his life sentence which would imply that the court recognised the circumstances when calculating the 'seriousness' of the crime.

Brent Martin

Brent was 16 years old when, because of a mental health issue, he was detained under the Mental Health Act; he also had a learning disability. Brent was eventually released to live with his family in 2007, now aged 23. At the time of his death, just three months after his release, Brent was living with his mother on a housing estate in Sunderland. He died because of what the sentencing Judge John Milford called 'sadistic conduct on an extremely vulnerable victim'.

Brent entered into the community with significant savings but lacking the friendships that most of his peers, who had been educated and grew up on the estate, had been able to develop. In his efforts to form friendships, Brent began spending time with a group of youths from the estate, including three who were younger than him, aged 16, 17 and 22. Brent considered the youths to be his friends but they would go on to abuse him financially and ultimately violently. It appears that as the violence escalated, Brent was 'dehumanised' in the eyes of the perpetrators. Before his death the youths had taken bets, offering £5 to the first of them to knock him out by punching him.

The youths went on to kick, punch and stamp on Brent. The post-mortem examination revealed at least 18 separate injuries to his head and neck. In the ultimate act of degradation, Brent's murderers stripped him of his trousers and underwear before leaving him to die in the street whilst they posed for photographs. Witnesses heard one of the perpetrators declare, 'I'm not going down for a Muppet' which perhaps demonstrated that their actions were fuelled by a view that Brent's life was less worthy because of his disability. ('Muppet' is a common derogatory slang term used to describe someone with a learning disability.)

As in the case of Steven Hoskin, the minimum tariff of the life sentence for murder could not (at that time) be enhanced under the Criminal Justice Act, but again the sentencing judge appears to reflected the circumstances of the offences when calculating the 'seriousness' of the offence. Brent's family expressed their satisfaction at the sentences which had minimum tariffs of 15, 18 and 22 years to the life sentences. However, some charities and advocates expressed their disappointment that the sentences were not transparently enhanced, as they could have been for other types of hate crime.

In an article to challenge the fairness of this position Quarmby (2008) compares the sentencing of murder convictions. She quotes Julie Newman, then chair of the UK Disabled People's Council as saying:

> The matter of sentencing for those who are convicted of disability hate crime will be of concern as long as there continues to be a difference between this and other forms of hate crime.

Fiona Pilkington and Frankie Hardwick

In October 2007 Fiona Pilkington drove with her 18-year-old daughter Francecca (Frankie) Hardwick to a lay-by near to their home which they shared with Frankie's brother Anthony, who was then 16. The bodies of the mother and daughter were later discovered in the burnt-out shell of the vehicle.

An inquest into their deaths was held in 2009; the jury found that Fiona Pilkington killed herself and Frankie 'due to the stress and anxiety regarding her daughter's future, and ongoing anti-social behaviour'. The jury said the police's response had contributed to Fiona Pilkington's decision to 'unlawfully kill her daughter and commit suicide'. They said that 'calls were not linked or prioritised' and they also highlighted the lack of action by local borough and county councils.

The inquest was told that Frankie had a learning disability and that Fiona was her carer; Anthony also suffered from dyslexia. The family had suffered torment over a period of around ten years before their deaths. Their abuse was varied in its nature and severity, taking place in many different locations and targeting all family members. Incidents ranged from rowdiness around their home through to occasions where Anthony was forced into a shed at knife-point and detained there until he was able to break free. There were other occasions where property around the family home was set on fire.

It does not appear from the evidence heard in the inquest or the subsequent investigation of the Independent Police Complaints Commission (IPCC) that the issue of the children's disability was a consideration when responding to incidents. At the time of the tragic deaths, Leicestershire Police, in common with many police forces, did not include disability as one of its strands of hate crime recording. Sadly, Fiona and Frankie died a month before ACPO's Cabinet agreed to the common definition of hate crime which included disability.

However, the inquest and the IPCC investigation found fundamental flaws in the response of the police and local authorities. There were systemic and individual failings in the agencies' responses but perhaps most damaging was the fact that the incidents tended to be responded to in isolation, with different officials responding to the circumstances they faced at that time, rather than recognising the escalating harm caused by the holistic situation faced by the family.

Fiona had sought the support of agencies repeatedly but her family gave evidence that she died with a sense of desperation, fearing that there was no other escape from the torment that she and Frankie were suffering.

It is worth taking time here to consider the situation Fiona faced – ask yourself: how could we envisage a life so tormented and frustrating that we would choose to take our own life and that of our child, in such horrific circumstances, in an attempt to escape the fear and suffering within our everyday life?

In May 2011 the IPCC launched the report of their investigation; Commissioner Amerdeep Somal said:

> I was deeply saddened to hear of the tragic deaths of Fiona Pilkington and her daughter…no one person gripped these reports and took charge to strategically manage and oversee what should have been a targeted police response.

> I struggle to see what more Fiona could have done. She did all the right things. She informed the police and other agencies involved with her family of the ongoing problems. She did as she was told and she even kept a diary and records of the incidents… [Fiona's] records portray a sense of resignation that nothing would be done and the youths would just carry on.

When agencies were considering the inclusion of disability as a strand of the national hate crime definition, the plight of Fiona and Frankie was not clearly related. Whilst the tragedy of their deaths was reported extensively in 2007, the true horrors of what they faced in and around their home did not become commonly discussed by society, the media or agencies until the time of the inquest in 2009.

Whilst the tragedy did not influence the formation of the definition, it has gone on to have a huge influence on policy and operational practices in police and other agencies. Due to the concerns highlighted by the inquest, the subsequent considerations by the EHRC and the public concerns, it has perhaps become, as charities such as Mencap and Scope called for it to be, 'The Stephen Lawrence moment for disabled people'.

Lobbying for change

In addition to the focus placed on disability hate crime by the above and other similar crimes, 2007 also saw significant momentum to the lobbying by and on behalf of disabled people. Disabled people's organisations (DPOs) had been highlighting the plight of disabled people for some considerable time; however, their voice and claims did not have the traction or influence that they would achieve once society in general had become aware of cases such as those mentioned above. Many DPOs were frustrated by their inability to bring about change in the criminal justice system and their task was made more difficult by the lack of available data on the extent of the problem they were trying to expose.

In November 2007, the mental health charity Mind produced a report called *Another Assault* to highlight the problems experienced in the community by people with mental health distress. Whilst the survey was relatively small, with 304 questionnaires completed from the 5100 that were distributed to people with mental health issues (and a further 86 from the 1100 distributed to support workers), it was able to highlight the prevalence of abuse. As mentioned in Chapter 1, 71 per cent of those who responded had been 'victimised' in the community in the previous two years and 41 per cent said that they were the victims of 'ongoing bullying'. It was noted by some criminologists that the research methodology may limit the reliability of those findings, fearing that only those with a positive 'story to tell' would be motivated to return the questionnaire.

Whilst the limitations of a relatively small survey were clear, *Another Assault* was influential amongst policy makers at the time of publication. In the absence of official data its findings highlight the nature of problems faced and it did 'chime' with the testimony of DPOs who felt that agencies needed to become aware of the nature of the problem and begin to measure crimes and encourage reporting. Paul Farmer, Chief Executive of Mind, said:

> Inequality in access to justice poses a serious threat to the dignity, rights and equal citizenship of people with mental health problems. [The research] shows that people with mental distress feel disempowered to speak out against injustices. A third of people who had been victimised in our survey told no one at all. Two-thirds of victims of crime who did report the incident were completely or somewhat dissatisfied with the overall response of the authorities, and just six per cent were completely satisfied.
>
> It is unacceptable for such an overwhelming majority of users of any service to feel disappointed by it. It is particularly unacceptable in the criminal justice system. (Mind 2007, p.3)

In addition to the DPOs and charities who would try to raise concerns about abuse suffered by disabled people, there were some journalists who were also trying to raise public consciousness of the problem. However, many journalists who became committed to the subject found it difficult to gain traction in the mainstream media. Specialist media, such as *Disability Now*, provided regular material on the subject, but in 2007 it seemed difficult for journalists to break stories into the national media. Some, like Katharine Quarmby, would have success in getting material out into the mainstream media in the following years but in 2007 such material was sparse and individual crimes, even the most horrific, were treated by the media largely in isolation, rather than in recognition of a trend of similar crimes and prevalent hostility in our communities.

As Quarmby herself (2011) notes:

The targeting of disabled people has happened while society has looked the other way. Disability hate crime was the invisible crime, the crime that people looked straight through because they could not recognise it for what it was. Now it is coming into focus and we can ignore it no longer. (p.236)

The nature of disability hate crime in the UK

The crimes mentioned above are illustrative of some of the more serious and prolonged disability hate crimes but the list is far from exhaustive. There were many others which shared similar fates and the EHRC report includes ten examples of such cases; however, there were and have been many others that could equally have been used to highlight the nature of the problem.

However, it is important to note that whilst the examples highlighted above include some of the more severe and prolonged examples of abuse, there are many spontaneous and isolated examples of abuse and violence.

It is relatively rare in other monitored strands of hate crime for victims to suffer the prolonged and escalating abuse highlighted in this chapter. The vast majority of those reported to the police are spontaneous incidents where the perpetrator's hostility is demonstrated at the time of their offending. As Iganski (2008) argued, whilst hate crimes that reach our attention will inevitably be the more serious, most hate crimes are 'one-off', 'situational' incidents where the offender demonstrates their hostility at the time of committing the offence.

I believe it is likely that the majority of disability hate crimes are also spontaneous and isolated; however, we cannot ignore the more prolonged, repeated and escalating violence highlighted in many of the attacks mentioned here and in reports such as *Hidden in Plain Sight* (EHRC 2011).

Many disabled people can give individual examples of adverse reactions from unknown members of the public, whether they are the wheelchair user facing the anger of other passengers as they try to utilise ill-equipped public transport or whether they face spontaneous bullying from groups or individuals in public space, in schools or elsewhere. In Chapter 5 Mark Brookes outlines some of those experiences that he and his friends have faced. He also goes on to talk about the adjustments he makes in his life to try and avoid the situations where harm is likely to be prevalent. For those of us who do not regularly suffer targeted abuse, these adjustments would be intolerable but they remain a constant part of the life of those who suffer or fear such abuse.

In Chapter 4 Tyson and Hall outline the dearth of evidence to accurately describe the perpetrators of disability hate crime, but we should ask ourselves a basic question – does society in general, or sections of it, hate disabled people? This question has exercised academics interested in disability hate crime and was also considered during the inquiry of the EHRC (2011) which concluded that much more evidence was needed from authorities to fully understand the nature of offending and to enable effective rehabilitation work to be embedded as part of the criminal justice response.

Quarmby (2011) examined this question; she highlighted that hostility is present throughout history and not something new. She said:

> [I don't believe] that society, in general, hates disabled people. But I think there is an underlying feeling that disabled people have not earned the equality they enjoy in name. This is why so many are attacked in our community, because some people believe they should be still shut away. They are infuriated by disabled people demanding that they too should have the freedoms that non-disabled people take for granted. (Quarmby 2011, p.236)

The prevalence of disability hate crime

Whilst the UK has arguably the most advanced hate crime data recording processes in the world (see Chapter 1), available data is relatively new. The police commenced the national hate crime data collection in 2008 and it is broadly accepted that, given the vast numbers of under-recorded crimes, any fluctuation in data is more likely to be a result of improved recognition and recording structures, rather than being direct evidence of an increase in hostility.

We do, however, have the benefit of the British Crime Survey (BCS), now more accurately called the Crime Survey of England and Wales. Following on from the decision to include disability in hate crime recording, questions about its prevalence were included in the survey. The first set of data was published in March 2012 and discussed in Chapter 1 (see p.25).

The value of the BCS data is further limited when considering the focus of this volume since it is a household survey and does not include individuals who are resident in a care setting. It would not, for example, include the victims who suffered abuse at Winterbourne view. The second key limitation to the data is that it only includes respondents over the age of 16 years.

Despite these limitations, the BCS data does expose a huge gap between the police-recorded hate crimes and actual victim experiences. As we explored earlier in Chapter 1 the data suggests that fewer than 1 in 30 actual disability hate crimes appear in the recorded crime data. This is not to say that the crimes identified by the respondents as being motivated by hostility were not recorded by the police and it is possible that many victims did not express their perceptions at the time of reporting. It does, however, highlight the challenges faced by the police and others in raising awareness of hate crime amongst victims, advocates and professionals. It also highlights the need to improve systems to recognise those crimes that are motivated by such hostility.

Given the restrictions in the BCS data, it is perhaps sensible to consider the under-recording gap to be the minimum estimate of the challenges faced, because hate crimes against children or institutional residents would be included in police-recorded data but not in the BCS data.

The Coalition Government manifesto set out its view that closing the gap between actual crimes and police-recorded data is an important priority.

Common traits of disability hate crime

As we have explored here it would be dangerous to base policy solely on those tragic crimes that gain public attention because they result in the death of an individual. This could lead us to ignore the myriad of experiences that happen in the day-to-day life of disabled people who face hostility, abuse and discrimination. To do so would be to fail in our duty to protect disabled people from abuse and to provide the equality of protection from harm that is a legal and moral duty for agencies and, at least as regards the moral duty, for society in general.

Recognising this, it is also important to note some of the common traits that have been prevalent in the more high-profile, prolonged or tragic offences. Given the relatively small number of offences discussed here and in other literature, it is difficult to effectively research and quantify common factors. There is no evidence to suggest that there was a 'common cause' that motivated the perpetrators outlined here, in a way that we have seen in, for example, 'white supremacist' or sectarian violence. For these reasons these observations should be seen as anecdotal rather than establishing any reliable model of offending; this perhaps best highlights an area ripe for empirical analysis.

Repeat offending

The BCS identifies that hate crime victims are more likely to suffer repeat victimisation where it involves 'household crime'. Whereas 'personal crime' shows little difference from crime victims in general the norm, 37 per cent of victims of household hate crime had been victimised more than once in the previous year, compared with 29 per cent of victims in general (Smith *et al.* 2012). Many of the fatal crimes identified since 2007 have been characterised by repeated and escalating offending by the same group or individuals. Some, such as Fiona Pilkington, suffered over many years but others, like Brent Martin, had a short exposure to escalating offending.

Learning disability – mental ill-health

Whilst there are undoubtedly crimes suffered by a broad range of disabled people, the high-profile and fatal attacks expose a large number of crimes targeting victims with learning disability or mental health issues. There is not enough data available to quantify or compare the experiences but anecdotal experience would tend to suggest that this is an area worthy of further research.

Friendship/relationship

One of the most notable common factors in the noted murder cases is the fact that many of the victims were friends or had some other relationship with those who went on to violently abuse them. For some, such as Michael Gilbert, who died in 2009 at the hands of a family who had taken him in as a friend, the relationship was long-standing and domestic. The EHRC Inquiry reported that over a seven year period he was treated as a domestic slave who was tortured over much of that period and ultimately murdered.

Other victims, such as Fiona Pilkington, suffered years of abuse from neighbours but some, like Brent Martin, sought out friends who quickly abused his trust and friendship, in a rapidly escalating violence that ranged from financial abuse to physical, torturous and eventually fatal attacks.

This 'friendship' element is anecdotally recognised by many commentators to be a common factor in the more serious disability hate crimes and it presents real challenges for professionals. It is easy to imagine the challenges faced by Brent Martin as he sought friendship on an estate where he had not attended school with the other people of his age. If you add to this the challenges that some people with learning disability may have in social interactions, it is not difficult to envisage why Brent returned to his abusers over the three-month period before his death.

Some charities and commentators have referred to these types of crimes as 'mate crimes' which they believe helps to alert victims or potential victims to the dangerous situations in which they could find themselves. Such charities, for example the Association for Real Change, have developed material and training designed to help those at risk to have strategies to deal with friendships that become abusive.

Serious degrading abuse

Perhaps one of the most distressing traits of some of the crimes discussed is the process of 'dehumanisation' and torture that has preceded the murder of the victim. Such treatment was noted in the EHRC Inquiry (2011) in several of the cases considered. Their examples included the murder of Steven Hoskin, which is perhaps one of the most graphic portrayals of such abuse. As we have heard, he suffered an escalating level of degrading treatment which included some common factors such as: being treated like an animal; being 'tried' in a 'kangaroo court', often accused of being a paedophile; being forced to ingest harmful materials and ultimately dying in some sort of depraved 'game'. Many of the offenders will record their behaviour on video, almost like they are collecting a trophy of their dominance over the victim who they have dehumanised and held in such disdain.

References

Crown Prosecution Service (2012) 'Winterbourne View abusers sentenced' (blog) *CPS News Brief,* 26 October, 2012. Available at blog.cps.gov.uk/2012/10/winterbourne-view-abusers-sentenced.html, accessed on 28 January 2015.

Equality and Human Rights Commission (EHRC) (2011) *Hidden in Plain Sight: Inquiry into Disability-Related Harassment.* London: EHRC. Available at www.equalityhumanrights.com/uploaded_files/disabilityfi/ehrc_hidden_in_plain_sight_3.pdf, accessed on 17 October 2014.

EHRC (2012) *Out in the Open: Tackling Disability-Related Harassment – A Manifesto for Change.* London: EHRC. Available at www.equalityhumanrights.com/publication/out-open-tackling-disability-related-harassment-manifesto-change, accessed on 17 October 2014.

Iganski, P (2008) *Hate Crime in the City.* Bristol: The Policy Press.

Mind (2007) *Another Assault.* London: Mencap.

Quarmby, K (2008) 'Unequal before the law.' *Disability Now.* Available at www.disabilitynow.org.uk/article/unequal-law, accessed on 17 October 2014.

Quarmby, K (2011) *Scapegoat: Why We are Failing Disabled People.* London: Portobello Books.

Smith, K., Lader, D., Hoare, J. and Lau, I. (2012) *Hate Crime, Cyber Security and the Experience of Crime Among Children: Findings from the 2010/11 British Crime Survey.* London: Home Office.

CHAPTER 4

PERPETRATORS OF DISABILITY HATE CRIME

JEMMA TYSON AND DR NATHAN HALL

For us, criminology is about seeking answers to seven basic questions. What is the problem? When is it occurring? Where is it occurring? How much of it is there? Who is involved? Why is it occurring? And what should we do to make the problem better? Of course, whilst the questions are simple, the answers are anything but. Moreover, there are countless inherent complexities within the hate crime paradigm per se that fundamentally constrain our efforts to formulate even the most basic of answers to each of these questions. Whilst this book collectively furthers our understanding of disability hate crime in many areas relating to these seven questions, this particular chapter will primarily concentrate on just two – who are the perpetrators of disability hate crime and why do they do it? (More comprehensive discussions of each of these areas can be found in Hall 2013.) For reasons that we shall explain in due course, anyone reading this hoping to find definitive answers to these two crucial questions is likely to be disappointed. There are no certainties in these areas, particularly the latter. Rather, it is our intention to examine a range of potential explanations for the phenomenon we have only relatively recently come to know as disability hate crime.

Background and context – the significance of impossible questions

Although we do not wish to tread on the toes of colleagues who have contributed to this book by revisiting ground that has already been covered, the complexities associated with each of the seven questions posed above are important in understanding why it is that we know so little either about perpetrators or the causes of their offending behaviour.

As such, before we can begin to examine any of the other issues relating to the subject of hate crime it is, of course, crucial that we have a clear understanding of what it is we are talking about. The question 'what is hate crime?' may seem straightforward, but providing an accurate answer is fraught with difficulties. Like any other crime, hate crime is a social construct, but there isn't too much by way of consensus amongst academics, policy makers or practitioners about what hate crime actually is. Definitions proffered from these different sources often variously include terms such as bias, prejudice, hostility, oppression, stigmatised, marginalised, power, inequality, discrimination, vulnerability, group affiliation, and so on (see Hall 2013, for a discussion of definitions of hate crime and their implications). Fortunately for those of us in the UK, there is at least now a common definition accepted across the criminal justice system (ACPO 2014):

> Hate crimes and incidents are taken to mean any crime or incident where the perpetrator's hostility or prejudice against an identifiable group of people is a factor in determining who is victimised… So any incident or crime, which is perceived by the victim or any other person to be motivated because of a person's disability or perceived disability will be recorded as such.

Whilst defining hate crime remains both difficult and open to a degree of controversy, for our purposes here these issues are less important than the value the definitions hold in providing some clues as to what might motivate someone to target another in this way. In particular the term 'prejudice' points towards the world of psychology and, together with 'hostility', implies that a real 'hatred' of selected others, at least in layman's terms, is not necessarily the sole (or even the main) motivating factor behind the offender's behaviour.

These broader terms, which necessarily include a much wider range of human emotions beyond just 'hate', marry nicely with the use of the term 'incidents' to illustrate the point that hate crime generally, and disability hate crime more specifically, can (and does) include a range of behaviours that are what we might crudely term 'low level' and not necessarily criminal, and motivated by factors other than a 'true' hatred of the victim. Indeed, Hollomotz (2012) suggests that the victimisation of people with disabilities is best viewed as a continuum. Such violence, she suggests, should not be understood as singular acts of physical or sexual assault because these simply represent the more severe expressions of bigotry on a spectrum of routine intrusions that include social exclusion, name calling and other hurtful language, derogatory treatment, and so on. Akin to Bowling's (1999) conceptualisation of racist hate crime as a process rather than a series of unrelated incidents, Hollomotz states that:

> the notion of a continuum seeks to draw attention to the fact that boundaries between incidents of mundane intrusions, derogatory treatment and violence are blurred, which can make it difficult for an individual to distinguish that which is seen to be 'acceptable' as part of the everyday from that which is seen, even by others and the law, as an act of violence. (2012, p.54)

In addition, the terms used in other definitions of hate crime also offer clues about why certain types of victims are specifically selected by offenders, which may lie in notions of power differentials, stigmatisation, scapegoating and blaming, vulnerability and so on. We shall return to the use of some of these concepts as explanatory frameworks for understanding hate crime offending shortly.

Our relative lack of knowledge about the perpetrators of disability hate crime is also a product of some of the answers to the question – when is hate crime occurring? Whilst societal interest in hate crime generally (and disability hate crime specifically) may only be contemporary, in reality examples of behaviours, some of them very violent indeed, that we would now label as hate crimes are littered throughout history. The juxtaposition of a 'relatively old problem' and 'relatively new concern about it' therefore presents us with an interesting supplementary question – why is it that we have only relatively recently taken an interest in (disability) hate crime as a problem in need of comprehension and of resolution?

The emergence of disability hate crime as a social and political concern is discussed in Chapter 1 and elsewhere in this book (see also Roulstone and Sadique 2013, for an interesting discussion on disabled groups' fight for legal recognition), and it is not hard to identify a number of key historical and contemporary milestones that have played important roles in shaping political, and scholarly, interest today. Nevertheless, the relatively recent appearance of disability hate crime in the political and academic arenas means that, inevitably, our search for answers is also relatively new. Consequently our depth of knowledge in this area is fairly shallow.

The third question – where is it occurring? – and aspects of the fourth – how much of it is there? – further limit our ability to understand perpetrators. Searching for the answers to these questions is far from straightforward, not least because of the complexities associated with the various ways in which hate crime is defined and conceptualised, and therefore understood, in different parts of the world, and the different levels of political priority afforded to associated 'hate' issues. An examination of the various reports from the Organization for Security and Co-operation in Europe (OSCE 2012) reveals a very mixed picture around the world, from countries where hate crimes seemingly occur with worrying regularity, to others where, officially at least, none occur at all.

With reference to disability hate crimes, 14 out of 57 participating OSCE States claim to have recorded data on such crimes against people with disabilities in 2012, but when the report was published, in November 2013, only Finland, Germany and the UK had provided data, recording 19, 29 and 1853 cases of disability hate crime respectively (OSCE 2012).

As such, the comparative position of the UK is particularly interesting with regard to disability hate crime. The official figures reported above represent the most ever recorded by the police. Despite this, it is apparent from the research undertaken by various disability-related organisations and others that disability hate crime remains vastly under-reported to the authorities (see for example, EHRC 2011; Mind 2007; Quarmby 2008; Smith *et al.* 2012).

The statistics recorded by the authorities are therefore important for a number of reasons. For our purposes, the fact that there were just 643 cases referred to the Crown Prosecution Service by the police in 2011/12, and only 480 cases that resulted in a successful prosecution, means that statistically at least, the perpetrators of disability hate crime are scarce (CPS 2012). In turn, the low number of individuals formally labelled as perpetrators means that researching them for the purpose of understanding their offending behaviour becomes extremely difficult.

Nevertheless, the data from the CPS (2012, p.26) gives us a small insight into the answer to the fifth question – who is involved? The information relating to those prosecuted for disability hate crimes demonstrates that:

> Most defendants are men (77.0%), but there were a significantly higher proportion of women (22.9%) compared to other strands of hate crime (16.9% in racially and religiously aggravated hate crime and 15.7% in homophobic and transphobic hate crime). Most defendants were White British (82.0%) and those between 25 and 59 accounted for 53.3% and a further 26.7% were between 18 and 24. Of interest is the fact that the proportion of both 10–13 year olds and 14–17 year olds involved as defendants has declined from 4.9% and 23.5% respectively in 2007/08 to 0.8% and 15.0% in 2011/12.

Whilst interesting, this of course tells us little, if anything, about what is going on in the lives of these offenders. And nor can we be certain about the generalisability of the information we derive from official sources. For example, Iganski and Smith's (2011) examination of hate crime offender rehabilitation programmes in different parts of the world identified hate perpetrators predominantly (but obviously not exclusively) as young, male, white, socio-economically marginalised, with a tendency towards violence and aggression, and as being generalist rather than specialist in their offending behaviour. But they rightly acknowledge that data on offenders in different countries is severely limited and inconsistent, and although the not uncommon use of convicted offenders (or those otherwise coming to the attention of the authorities) as a research sample allows for a degree of certainty about their misdemeanours, the activities of the agencies of different criminal justice systems may well play a part in shaping the characteristics of the offender sample. Indeed most perpetrators of crime fit Iganski and Smith's description.

Beyond trying to identify the basic characteristics of perpetrators per se, the question of who is involved in this type of offending is also hindered by other gaps in knowledge, many of which were lamented well over a decade ago by Bowling (1999), who referred to hate offenders as 'devilish effigies' about which criminology can claim to know very little. Whilst some progress in the field as a whole has been made in respect of issues such as the relationship that offenders have with their victims (see Iganski 2008; Mason 2005; Walters and Hoyle 2012), the social milieux in which prejudice and hostility are fostered, the extent to which offenders are 'ordinary' or 'extreme' (Iganski 2008), and the role of gender and masculinities (Blee 2004; Treadwell and Garland 2011, for example), our ability to now refute Bowling's claim that criminologists operate with scant evidence about what is going on in the lives of offenders remains more limited than we would ideally like, particularly in the area of disability hate crime.

Nevertheless, the relatively limited research that has been conducted into disability hate crime has been particularly illuminating in this rather shady area of our knowledge base. For example, the Disability Rights Commission found that:

> Strangers, either individually or in groups, are most likely to be responsible for the attacks, but one in five disabled respondents have experienced an attack by a friend or colleague and the same proportion have been frightened or attacked by a teacher or carer. Under 16 year olds are most likely to be seen as responsible for attacks in urban areas, whereas in rural areas 16–44 year olds are viewed as the perpetrators…[others include] schoolchildren, doctors, nurses, and drivers. (2004, p.19)

Clearly, the latter groupings, although relatively small in number in terms of those identified by the research, highlight the difficulties in relying on official data to identify who perpetrators might be. The recognition of children, doctors, nurses and others acting in a 'caring' capacity as being responsible for disability hate crimes does not, to our mind at least, sit comfortably with stereotypical images of offenders as 'young, male, white, socio-economically marginalised, with a tendency towards violence and aggression'.

Echoing these notions, Quarmby (2008) suggests that hate crimes against disabled people are common and widespread, and range from low-level harassment, name calling, bullying, intimidation and vandalism to more serious crimes (often escalating in seriousness), but that they are often 'hidden' and their prevalence 'concealed'. She also argues that 'disablist' hate crimes are different from comparable crimes motivated by other forms of prejudice, most notably because the perpetrators of 'disablist' hate crimes are often 'friends' or carers, as opposed to strangers – a situation not normally associated with other forms of hate crime.

More recently, and in a statement that neatly sums up the position that we have taken in this chapter, the Equalities and Human Rights Commission (EHRC) inquiry into disability-related harassment noted that:

> Incidents of harassment recounted by disabled people involved a wide range of perpetrators: complete strangers as well as family, friends and acquaintances; men and women; younger and older people; and people from all social classes and cultures. In general, no one group was singled out as more or less likely to be involved in disability-related harassment, although there was some perceived correlation between certain groups and harassment situations. There is however, a distinct lack of evidence on both the motivation and the profile of perpetrators. (EHRC 2011, pp.86–87)

So, whilst we may now be able to say a little more about who offenders are in terms of identifying some of their basic characteristics, the search for a satisfactory answer to the why? question remains elusive. We should not forget though that ours is a relatively new area of scholarly interest and although there is relatively little by way of applied research on, or theorising about, hate crime offenders either generally or specifically in relation to disability hate crime and the factors that cause such offending to occur, a degree of progress in both of these endeavours has nevertheless been made in recent times.

Hall (2013) has noted the increasing engagement of the social sciences with the problem of hate crime, both in those branches that you would perhaps expect to have an interest (such as psychology and criminology) and encouragingly those that are arguably less obviously related (such as geography and cultural studies). This has produced what Iganski (2008) and Chakraborti (2010) have both described as a 'welcome surge' in scholarly interest in our subject area. This 'welcome surge' is producing a 'welcome flurry' of research and other scholarly activity, bringing with it 'an astounding diversity of methodologies...to more fully document and comprehend the problem' (Perry, 2010, p.19). As such, it is our view that there are reasons to be optimistic about edging closer to finding the answers to the why? question, and it is to this that we shall now turn.

Why?

Before we can explore the various issues associated with hate crime offending, it is important that we understand the foundations of hatred, namely the psychological concept of prejudice and its relationship to discriminatory behaviour. As Stangor (2000) points out, there are few if any topics that have engaged the interests of social psychologists as much as those of prejudice, stereotypes and discrimination. Indeed, as Paluck and Green (2009) note, the 'remarkable volume' of literature on prejudice ranks amongst the most impressive in all of social science. This, Stangor suggests, is a consequence of the immense practical importance that such studies hold for understanding the effects of these issues on both individuals and societies, particularly given the increasing diversity of the world we live in. However, Jacobs and Potter (1998) point out that whilst prejudice has long been an object for study, sociologists and psychologists have been unable to agree on a single definition for it, nor agree on where it comes from, or exactly what purpose it serves – a position that still holds true today. Instead, a number of competing theories each seek to explain the phenomenon in different ways, but none of them it would seem are either definitive or conclusive.

The departure point for modern research into prejudice is generally attributed to the seminal and encyclopaedic work of Gordon Allport (1954). According to Allport (1954) prejudice is a normal and rational (that is to say, predictable) human behaviour by virtue of our need to organise all the cognitive data our brain receives through the formation of generalisations, concepts and categories whose content represents an oversimplification of our world and experiences therein. This process is essential to our daily living and the forming of generalisations, categories and concepts based on experience and probability helps us to guide our daily activities and to make sense of the world around us. As a result, when we categorise, we think of things in terms of groups, rather than as unique individual entities, and we assume that these categories are informative and salient.

Similarly, Allport suggests that in order to further simplify our lives human beings naturally homogenise, often for no other reason than convenience, which in turn creates separateness amongst groups. According to Allport, humans tend to relate to other humans with similar presuppositions for the purpose of comfort, ease and congeniality. However, it is this separateness, coupled with our need to form generalisations and categories, and therefore stereotypes, which lays the foundations for psychological elaboration and the development of prejudice. Allport argues that people that stay separate have fewer channels of communication, are likely to exaggerate and misunderstand the differences between groups and develop genuine and imaginary conflicts of interests. It is this, according to Allport, that contributes largely to the formation of 'in-groups' and 'out-groups' and therefore to the potential formation and development of in-group loyalty and out-group rejection and the subsequent potential expression of prejudice and discriminatory behaviour towards those out-groups. This contributes to the development and maintenance of our social identity and therefore to our feelings of well-being. From the situation Allport describes, numerous theories of prejudice have been proffered (see Hall 2013, for a more comprehensive discussion of the psychology of prejudice and hatred). However, three that are perhaps most relevant to us are:

- Social Identity Theories – these suggest that the need for individuals to enhance their self-esteem by identifying themselves with specific social groups is significant in the development of prejudice. This identification inevitably leads people to view their social group (their in-group) as superior to other, competing social groups and, since all groups form and develop in the same way, prejudice can arise out of the resulting clash of social perceptions. For example, whites may see themselves as superior to blacks, men as superior to women, the able-bodied superior to people with disabilities, one nationality superior to another, and so on.

- Realistic Conflict Theories – these propose that conflicting interests develop through competition into overt social conflict and that these conflicts create antagonistic intergroup relations whilst simultaneously increasing identification with and positive attachment to the in-group. Thus, prejudice can stem from a sense of relative deprivation derived from competition between social groups for valued commodities (such as, for example, jobs, land, power, welfare benefits, and so on) or opportunities, and as the competition for these scarce economic resources intensifies members of competing social groups will come to view each other in increasingly negative terms that if permitted to foster will develop into emotion-laden prejudice.

- Social Learning Theories – these suggest that attitudes are learned in childhood through contact with older and influential figures who reward children for adopting their views. Children and adolescents also adopt and conform to the social norms of the group to which they belong, resulting in the development and expression of prejudicial attitudes towards others. Social learning and stereotype formation can also occur via other avenues, most notably through the media. As Blaine (2008) points out, the influence of television is of particular interest given the amount of time many people, including children, now spend absorbing information from that source, and whose cultural education might be limited to what they see and hear on television. He suggests that whilst programmes on television have become more racially diverse in recent years, portrayals of other groups have largely failed to follow suit to the same degree, thereby potentially feeding a range of stereotypes about these groups.

Despite the fact that the concept of prejudice marks the starting point for theorising about the perpetrators of hate crime, the existing literature, as vast as it is, tells us remarkably little about how prejudice transforms into actions that would constitute hate crimes. Indeed, as Green, McFalls and Smith suggest:

> It might take the better part of a lifetime to read the prodigious research literature on prejudice…yet scarcely any of this research examines directly and systematically the question of why prejudice erupts into violence. (2003, p.27)

So what then can criminological research add? An examination of existing criminological literature suggests that there is a range of answers to the why? question. Of course there is only the space here to scratch the surface (but see Hall 2013, for a more comprehensive discussion of the application of criminological theory and research to hate crimes) of what criminology has to offer and as such we shall concentrate on a few pieces of research that have specifically focused on disability hate crime.

McDevitt, Levin and Bennett (2002) have suggested a typology of hate crime perpetrators that identifies four distinct categories of motivation. The first and most common category relates to those motivated by a desire for thrill or excitement; the second is the defensive perpetrator; motivation for retaliatory reasons is the third; and the final category within the typology, and the rarest form of hate crime offending, relates to 'mission' offenders. Whilst this research was not explicitly about disability hate crime, the typologies have since been applied to this area, aiding in part our understanding of why people commit disability hate crime.

In applying the original typology to disability hate crime, Levin (2012) points to the importance of cultural sources of hate. Here, negative perceptions of people with disabilities are learned from an early age and are a reflection of the prevailing cultural position of 'disabled' as 'inferior' (note the link here to social learning theories, and see Perry (2001) for a discussion of hate crime as a tool by which power is expressed and social hierarchies are maintained). Once these early prejudices have been forged, it becomes easier for what might simply be an aversion to become 'hatred' later in life. For example, Levin cites a number of cases from the US where young, bored individuals, often operating in a group, commit thrill attacks that have few practical benefits other than to enable them to 'look cool' in front of their peers and to strengthen their group cohesion through shared offending behaviour (note here the links to social identity theories).

Levin also cites a number of cases where a defensive motivation can be identified. In line with realistic conflict theories, he suggests that some perpetrators will view an out-group (in this case people with disabilities) as a threat to their economic well-being, health, neighbourhood composition, educational opportunities and so on. To illustrate this, apparent recent increases in the occurrence of disability hate crime in the UK are, in part, being attributed to what is perceived to be irresponsible political rhetoric from the British government in relation to statements concerning the numbers of people claiming incapacity benefit who are 'faking' disabilities (Riley-Smith 2012). Research by ComRes (2012) on behalf of the disability charity Scope, for example, found that disabled people identified the small number of people falsely claiming disability benefits and the way the actions of this minority of claimants are reported (for example in the tabloid press) as primary causes of public hostility. Scope concluded that it was impossible to ignore that the results came at the same time as the government continued to focus the welfare debate on a few benefit 'scroungers' as part of efforts to make the case for more radical reform to the welfare system. Indeed, as Perry (2001) points out, perceptions of social strain have long been identified as a cause of hate crimes generally, where competition for scarce resources can fuel hostility towards out-groups considered to be inferior and/or undeservedly usurping resources at the expense of the in-group.

The final two categories, retaliatory and mission, are arguably less directly relevant to our purposes here. Levin discusses cases where disabled victims have retaliated as a result of their own victimisation and have found themselves on the wrong side of the law, and notes the extreme nature of 'mission' offending by members of organised groups, particularly in relation to the potential influence that such groups can have in inciting others to commit hate crimes against people with disabilities.

Gerstenfeld (2011) has also drawn on the work of McDevitt, Levin and Bennett (2002), with a primary focus on stereotypes and their internalisation. When stereotypes are left unattended, they are then more likely to be assumed to be true. As a result, a prejudice is formed which consequently influences the behaviour towards a member of the targeted group, purely due to their association with that group. Gerstenfeld also suggests that hate crimes are committed because of a lack of the appropriate education in schools and in the home (again note the link to social learning theories). For some, the institution of the family actively promotes such hostile thinking. If an individual is surrounded by people favourable to negative attitudes towards those with disabilities, this way of thinking is likely to become entrenched within that individual. Indeed this view fits neatly with the criminological theory of differential association (Sutherland 1947), which holds that a person is more likely to offend via a process of social learning if they have associations with individuals engaging in similar activities, or who hold similar beliefs.

The recent emergence of the term 'mate crime' to illustrate the differential nature of disability hate crime is also reflected in recent research into offending behaviour. Thomas (2011), for example, suggests that some 'hate crimes' are indeed better understood as 'mate crimes', whereby the perpetrator is viewed as an 'insider' with some form of relationship or connection to the victim (note the links to research into who offenders are, above). This could be that of a friend or even a carer, where there is (or is supposed to be) an element of trust. Perpetrators that fall under this category have the opportunity to exert a level of control or power over the victim by abusing their relationship with them. As a result the experience of victimisation can be compounded because the victim may be more reluctant, or less able, to inform the authorities. The perpetrator may (threaten to) knowingly leave items out of reach, withhold medication or take advantage for a personal gain in order to ensure the victim does not expose their behaviour. Such behaviours may not be considered crimes and may consequently be overlooked, but may be a precursor to other, more serious events (note the link to Hollomotz's continuum of violence, above). If nothing else, the use of the term 'mate crime' illustrates that in order to understand why disability hate crimes are committed, we may need to look past the 'traditional' notion of 'stranger danger' (see Mason (2005) for an interesting discussion of this issue).

Furthermore, Grundy (2011) also comments on the notion of 'mate crime', with particular reference to the victimisation of those with learning disabilities. Again it is a 'friend' of the victim who is the opportunistic perpetrator, rather than an unfamiliar individual. Grundy's research importantly highlights the opportunity for the perpetrator's personal gain that disability hate crime can provide. For example, the research discusses cases where people with disabilities are exploited in order to unwillingly hide stolen goods or be involved in drug dealing. The assumption that disabled people are 'vulnerable' (Roulstone and Sadique 2013) further fuels this exploitation.

In addition, there are other theoretical offerings that can further aid us in understanding the why? question. For example, Mason *et al.* (2004) apply the theory of enhancing the self-concept as one such explanation for disability hate crime. This suggests that through committing a disability hate crime, the perpetrator is able to reaffirm their own self-worth and feel superior to others, but also protect their own self-concept. This correlates with the typology of 'defensive' and indeed 'thrill' perpetrators and the notion of power that we highlighted earlier. Out-group homogeneity suggests that people with disabilities are viewed as not fitting with the 'normal' characteristics of society (note the link to Levin's concern with cultural norms, and Perry's identification of social hierarchies), reinforced by a lack of understanding and limited or no exposure to disabled people. People with disabilities are therefore viewed as anonymous members of the out-group on the fringe of society.

Implications for practitioners

So what, then, does all of this mean for the practitioner? Of course much will depend upon the professional setting and the nature of the practitioner's work, which may vary greatly, but here we suggest some common issues that may well have relevance across a range of professional and practical settings.

Although we have addressed this topic in a fairly academic manner, for practitioners, abstract knowledge about why offenders do it is perhaps less important than the knowledge that they are doing it, given that the latter may very well present the need to do something to stop it. Despite being largely theoretical and research-based, the literature considered here, exploring who offenders might be and why they might do it, allows us to draw some inferences about the potential practical implications these may have on the practitioner working in areas where victimisation of this nature may well be encountered.

Arguably the most obvious issue concerns the potential identity of the perpetrators. The literature suggests that disability hate crime offenders often defy 'traditional' conceptions of both criminals more generally, and hate offenders more specifically. Indeed, anyone could be an offender, including those assuming the role of 'the good guy/girl' who may normally be beyond suspicion. An awareness of this possibility may well be crucial for practitioners seeking to find explanations for things 'that just don't seem right' when engaging with people with disabilities.

The diversity of potential offenders similarly gives rise to the possibility of a broad range of offending behaviours that similarly may defy traditional conceptions of 'victimisation'. As we discussed above, some forms of disability hate crime may not appear to the casual observer to be criminal at all, yet can be more subtle forms of wider patterns of abuse. Again, an appreciation of the possibilities here may well prove to be a valuable part of the practitioner's toolkit in this regard.

The points noted above give rise to similarly valuable clues concerning the possible location of disability hate crime offending. Traditional notions of crimes occurring in 'dangerous' or 'risky' places (i.e. in public spaces) committed by 'strangers' have the potential to be turned on their head to include supposed places of 'care' and 'safety' (i.e. private spaces – homes, schools, hospitals, the workplace, and so on) committed by people known and/or trusted by the victim. In turn, this may have significant implications for whether or not the victim actually knows that they are a victim, necessarily placing the burden of recognising such abuse on others, including practitioners.

Of course, all of this means that recognising patterns of both offending and victimisation may require the practitioner to think beyond stereotypes of what 'offenders', 'victims' and 'criminal behaviour' more generally 'look like'. But all of these issues, potentially at least, come with an extra layer of complexity for the practitioner, particularly where these traditional notions are broken completely. Deciding what action to take when one suspects abuse, by trusted individuals, in 'safe' settings, can be a very different prospect to deciding what to do when the 'local troublemakers' abuse someone as they go to the shops. Actions taken in relation to the former may result in unintended consequences such as, for example, the removal of 'support networks'. That said, fear of 'making things worse' shouldn't be an excuse for not responding to a problem. Indeed, as Elie Wiesel once perceptively noted in a speech at the White House in 2000, 'indifference is always the friend of the enemy'. So for the practitioner, indifference and ambivalence should be avoided at all costs. Indeed, the very nature of disability hate crime means that practitioners need to think more holistically and perceptively about the issues that may present themselves.

Concluding thoughts

It would be wrong for us to propose that the issues we have raised here provide a complete answer for comprehending why disability hate crimes are committed, nor what the practitioner should do where such behaviour is suspected. That, sadly, remains elusive. Instead, we have demonstrated just some of the reasons that might lie behind the actions of perpetrators, and what the implications for professional practice might be. Within the offender–victim context the term 'vulnerability' frequently appears, and whilst clearly important it can be misleading in terms of understanding disability hate crime. Victimisation because of an offender's 'hatred' is fundamentally different from victimisation because of the perceived 'vulnerability' of the victim. The latter is situational and can occur without any 'hatred' on the part of the offender. Disability hate crimes, though, always involve hostility towards a person's disability as a motivating factor. Just where that hostility comes from, and how and why it manifests itself in criminal behaviour, remains a mystery that really needs to be solved if our final question – what can be done to make the problem better? – is ever to be properly answered.

References

Association of Chief Police Officers (ACPO) (2014) True Vision website. Available at www.report-it.org.uk, accessed on 17 October 2014.

Allport, G. W. (1954) *The Nature of Prejudice*. Massachusetts, MA: Addison-Wesley Publishing Co.

Blaine, B. (2008) *Understanding the Psychology of Diversity*. London: Sage.

Blee, K. (2004) 'Women and organized racism.' In A. Ferber (ed.) *Home Grown Racism*. New York: Routledge.

Bowling, B. (1999) *Violent Racism: Victimisation, Policing and Social Context*. New York: Oxford University Press.

Chakraborti, N. (ed.) (2010) *Hate Crime: Concepts, Policy, Future Directions*. Oxon: Routledge.

ComRes (2012) *Scope Disability Survey*. Available at www.comres.co.uk/poll/712/scope-disability-survey.htm, accessed on 17 October 2014.

Crown Prosecution Service (CPS) (2012) *Hate Crimes and Crimes Against Older People*. London: CPS.

Disability Rights Commission (DRC) (2004) *Hate Crime Against Disabled People in Scotland: A Survey Report*. Edinburgh: Capability Scotland.

Equality and Human Rights Commission (EHRC) (2011) *Hidden in Plain Sight: Inquiry into Disability-Related Harassment*. London: EHRC. Available at www.equalityhumanrights.com/uploaded_files/disabilityfi/ehrc_hidden_in_plain_sight_3.pdf, accessed on 17 October 2014.

Gerstenfeld, P. B. (2011) *Hate Crimes: Causes, Controls and Controversies (Second Edition)*. California: Sage Publications.

Green, D. P., McFalls, L. H. and Smith, J. K. (2003) 'Hate crime: an emergent research agenda.' In B. Perry (ed.) *Hate and Bias Crime: A Reader*. New York: Routledge.

Grundy, D. (2011) 'Friend or fake? Mate crimes and people with learning disabilities.' *Journal of Learning Disabilities and Offending Behaviour 2*, 4, 167–169.

Hall, N. (2013) *Hate Crime (Second Edition)*. Oxon: Routledge.

Hollomotz, A. (2012) 'Disability and the continuum of violence.' In A. Roulstone and H. Mason-Bish (eds) *Disability, Hate Crime and Violence*. Oxon: Routledge.

Iganski, P. (2008) *Hate Crime and the City*. Bristol: The Policy Press.

Iganski, P. and Smith, D. (2011) *The Rehabilitation of Hate Crime Offenders: An International Study*. Research Report. Available at www.equalityhumanrights. com/scotland/research-in-scotland/the-rehabilitation-of-hate-crime-offenders-an-international-study, accessed on 17 October 2014.

Jacobs, J. B. and Potter, K. (1998) *Hate Crimes: Criminal Law and Identity Politics*. New York: Oxford University Press.

Levin, J. (2012) 'Disablist violence in the US: unacknowledged hate crime.' In A. Roulstone and H. Mason-Bish (eds) *Disability, Hate Crime and Violence*. Oxon: Routledge.

Mason, A., Pratt, H. D., Patel, D. R., Greydanus, D. E. and Yahya, K. Z. (2004) 'Prejudice towards people with disability.' In J. L. Chin (ed.) *The Psychology of Prejudice and Discrimination: Disability, Religion, Physique and Other Traits*. Westport: Praeger Publishers.

Mason, G. (2005) 'Hate crime and the image of the stranger.' *British Journal of Criminology 45*, 6, 837–359.

McDevitt, J., Levin, J. and Bennett, S. (2002) 'Hate crime offenders: an expanded typology.' *Journal of Social Issues 58*, 2, 303–317.

Mind (2007) *Another Assault*. London: Mencap.

Organisation for Security and Co-operation in Europe (OSCE) (2012) *Hate Crimes in the OSCE Region – Incidents and Responses. Annual Report for 2011*. Warsaw: OSCE.

Perry, B. (2001) *In the Name of Hate: Understanding Hate Crimes*. New York: Routledge.

Perry, B. (2010) 'The more things change…post 9/11 trends in hate crime scholarship.' In N. Chakraborti (ed.) *Hate Crime: Concepts, Policy, Future Directions*. Oxon: Routledge.

Paluck, E. L. and Green, D. (2009) 'Prejudice reduction: what works? A review and assessment of research and practice.' *Annual Review of Psychology 60*, 339–367.

Quarmby, K. (2008) *Getting Away With Murder: Disabled People's Experiences of Hate Crime in the UK*. London: Scope. Available at www.scope.org.uk/Scope/media/Images/Publication%20Directory/Getting-away-with-murder.pdf, accessed on 17 October 2014.

Riley-Smith, B. (2012) 'Disability hate crime: is 'benefit scrounger' abuse to blame?' *The Guardian*, 14 August, 2012.

Roulstone, A. and Sadique, K. (2013) 'Vulnerable to misinterpretation: Disabled people, 'vulnerability' and the fight for legal recognition.' In A. Roulstone and H. Mason-Bish (eds) *Disability, Hate Crime and Violence*. Oxon: Routledge.

Smith, K., Lader, D., Hoare, J. and Lau, I. (2012) *Hate Crime, Cyber Security and the Experience of Crime Among Children: Findings from the 2010/11 British Crime Survey*. London: Home Office.

Stangor, C. (ed.) (2000) *Stereotypes and Prejudice*. Philadelphia, PA: Psychology Press.

Sutherland, E. H. (1947) *Principles of Criminology (Fourth Edition.)* Philadelphia, PA: J.B. Lippincott.

Thomas, P. (2011) '"Mate crime": ridicule, hostility and targeted attacks against disabled people.' *Disability and Society 26*, 1, 107–111.

Treadwell, J. and Garland, J. (2011) 'Masculinity, marginalization and violence: A case study of the English Defence League.' *British Journal of Criminology 51*, 621–634.

Walters, M. A. and Hoyle, C. (2012) 'Exploring the world of everyday hate victimization through community mediation.' *International Review of Victimology 18*, 1, 7–24.

PART 2

DISABILITY HATE CRIME – THE IMPACT ON VICTIMS

CHAPTER 5

A DIFFERENT REALITY

MARK BROOKES AND DAVID CAIN

Introduction

For those of us who do not face the daily risk of targeted hostility, because of a hostility to our personal characteristics, it is often difficult to imagine how debilitating it can be. It is not a problem faced by all disabled people, many people with disabilities will never experience hostility and indeed the public will sometimes not recognise some as being disabled. However, for those whose disability is more visible, through physical characteristics or mannerisms, the reality is often very different. They, in the same way as people with a minority ethnicity, are unable to 'fade into the background'. For many reasonable people this difference would engender compassion and empathy but all too often it identifies them as 'The Other' and makes them a target for indifference, discrimination or even hostility.

Contributors in this book have attempted to describe the reality of this hostility and the nature of the perpetrators but in this chapter we hear the very real experiences of this hostility, first hand from two individuals who have been directly impacted by it. In this chapter Mark Brookes and David Cain powerfully describe the burden this places on such victims and the way it can alter lives.

Part 1 – An Everyday Experience
Mark Brookes

This chapter is about people's experiences of being victims of hate crime and hostility. I have thought about my own experiences, which has made me curious about whether other people have had the same experiences and felt the same as I have. I have run many workshops with people about hate crime, where I talk to them about how they felt when they were targeted and what they did afterwards to keep safe. I have heard stories about people's experiences of specific incidents, but I haven't really talked about or focused on the kind of daily hostility that people experience. These are some of the things that I want to explore in this chapter and with other people with learning difficulties.

When I first started thinking about this, I thought of the examples I knew about and realised that I hadn't heard many 'serious' stories about hate crime recently. I remembered a story from years ago: a friend of mine got off a bus and a gang of youths were laughing at him and calling him names. The next thing he knew he had a lit firework in his pocket. He went to the police who, at first, said that they couldn't do anything because he couldn't identify any of them; it was too dark for him to provide a description. He then went to the local papers who published his story and, the next thing he knew, the police came back to see him. I don't know if the perpetrators ever got caught, but as a result of the newspaper story the police took more notice of him.

I also thought about my own experiences. Over the years, as I have been walking home from work in the evening, some youths in cars call me names such as 'mong' or 'idiot' and throw eggs and tomatoes. When I first thought about it, I guessed that it happened four or five times over the past ten years. When I talked it through with a friend, I realised that it probably happened a lot more than that. I had been underestimating how often I had been a target.

Of course I don't like the eggs or name calling, but I often just try to ignore it and move on, because it is over so quickly. Unfortunately for me they often have quite a good aim. I was annoyed because instead of covering myself in food, like getting ketchup on my jacket, someone else was doing it instead. Also egg is quite a lot smellier, especially if it is rotten. I have never reported it.

I know from my own work that this is an attack, that it is wrong and possibly criminal. I am being assaulted. People are calling me names connected to my perceived disability, so the police could treat it as a hate crime. But every time it happens, I think, is it something I can report? Maybe it's not serious enough because it happens so quickly? Anyway, I never have time to take down the licence plate or notice the type of car. Will I be taken seriously?

I also experience staring in public, on the street, in the tube and in trains when travelling around the country. Sometimes I imagine myself saying, 'Do you want a picture? Am I that fascinating? What is your problem? Maybe you should look in the mirror some time.' But I don't because I don't want a confrontation and it can wear me out. Most of the time, I feel not nice for a second, but then just walk on because it is their attitude that is the problem, not mine.

I have noticed when I get on a train and people see me in a suit, that at first they think I am normal, a normal guy. Then I see that something has changed and they look at me differently. I don't know what it is but I have seen people's expressions change when they see a very overweight woman or man and it is the same expression, especially from the younger generation.

I don't report staring either. Even if it is not nice, you can't do anything about it. Is this an issue that should be looked at more? What can be done? I can't see us bringing in a law that says after two minutes you've got to look away. I smile when I imagine a police officer on the train with a stopwatch, arresting people for staring for more than two minutes.

Sometimes I get asked, 'What are you doing on this train? Why aren't you accompanied by someone?' and this is just another member of the public! I have witnessed it with other people as well. To be honest, I think that this person is being an idiot, but I don't say anything. I ignore them. I would never confront someone or risk upsetting them, as I worry that this will lead to a confrontation. I wish I had the courage to say, 'Do you mind not being rude?' But I just don't have the confidence to do that right now. I have seen confrontations become nasty and I don't want that for myself.

People are beginning to understand people with disabilities, but I don't trust that they are going to stick up for us. I am happy to see that now society is, generally speaking, behind the fight against racism but I don't think we are there yet with disability. I feel that if I stick up for myself, even politely, I will be on my own.

I have changed my behaviour because of what has happened to me. I won't go out after 8 o'clock at night, because of what might happen. Sometimes I need to go out and get something. I might have forgotten to buy milk, but I will not go out after 8. If I really have to, I rush there and back and don't stop for anything. If I see youths hanging around outside the shop, I cross to the other side of the street.

When I get on the bus, I look out for groups of young people and if I think I can see a person who might protect me, I will get on the bus. If not, I will wait for the next one. I never go upstairs on a bus.

I hope that what I write will help children and parents to be aware of the issues that have happened, and are happening, to people with learning difficulties and to be aware of the impact of such behaviours. This is a topic that as children grow up they might experience, especially if they are visibly different. One person's story about this type of hostility may not have an impact, but many stories could. Some incidents are not criminal, but still damage people's confidence and feeling of inclusion in society. Is there something we can do to address this? If not, then how do we reduce this feeling of exclusion and put an end to these experiences?

Part 2 – The Sibling's Story
David Cain

I am the triplet brother of Paul who was disabled at birth with cerebral palsy. We are three boys born in 1958 to working-class parents in Lancashire. We have two older sisters and we come from a strong Catholic tradition. It was some months after birth that Paul was categorised as a spastic (this term was in use for several years during the late 1950s and 1960s). He was the middle child and as I was born after him I always have with me the thought of how lucky I was not to have had to face the challenges in life that he has had. In short, I am so fortunate to be able bodied, successful and able to resolve most, if not all, of life's problems. He is not so fortunate.

During our early years we did not notice as such the difficulties that Paul was to face, apart from the fact that he was not chosen to play sports and was often 'left behind' in any selection. My lasting memory was mostly about being stared at in our handmade pram, being dressed identically all through childhood. Paul has a physical disability, he wears a calliper and has a withered right hand. It was unusual for someone with Paul's disability not to be kept indoors; he was allowed to play just like the rest of us. We were always told to look after Paul and he enjoyed his early childhood years, being generally accepted. Our father was chairman of the local Spastics Society and we used to go with him to his disabled classes and on pantomime trips.

There were happy times in early childhood but very quickly prejudice, discrimination, lack of opportunity and fear began to feature more strongly in Paul's life. We all passed our 11-plus examinations but the local grammar school would not take Paul because of his physical handicap, so that avenue was denied and we enrolled in our local comprehensive school as the only available option. Of interest, this particular issue with Paul's handicap caused problems at primary school level as Paul again was not accepted in mainstream education. My father paid for our private education (actually paid for two not three) and as such had to work seven days a week and take on a second job running his own joinery business.

Our teenage years were generally uneventful, other than the usual scraps and scrapes that go on, until the age of 16. When Paul and I left school he joined the local council as a clerk and I, after a false start as an articled clerk for a local firm of solicitors, joined the NHS as a clerical officer, rising through the ranks during the next 30 years to hold office as a Chief Executive in a number of NHS Trusts. Paul, by comparison, had to take early retirement at 26 because he was seen as incapable of fulfilling the role of a clerk despite his best attempts to do so. There were a series of events during his employment within which he sought help and support – it was not forthcoming. Paul had obtained a Higher National Diploma (HND) in Business Management and so had the intellectual capacity but not the physical endurance needed to fulfil the role.

Our collective passion was, and still is, Burnley Football Club, who over the years have had many highs and lows but have always managed to survive. We shared activities together. Paul loved to go out and liked to dance (he cleared many a dance floor in his attempts to follow the steps).

The first awareness of a difference between us started to materialise during these years. I felt sad and disappointed that people were not accepting Paul, on the street, at the bar and in the community. He did and does have friends, but has to work hard to get them. As a family we didn't talk about it much, brushed it over, moved on and sort of ignored it; he was falling behind emotionally and we hardly noticed. The rest of the family had busy professional lives in public health, management, nursing and teaching, so our own focus was on our own professional and personal lives. We all married and had children, and we visited Paul alongside our ageing parents. I used to attend home football games as his companion, but had time for very little else because of my own family commitments.

At an early stage, I became worried about Paul's personal safety. He was mugged at 18 whilst walking to the football ground for his scarf. He was with my father at the time who struggled to prevent this from happening. Paul became angry and tried to fight back and my father was angry and humiliated. I wanted to take revenge but I wasn't sure how to.

Paul retired from employment at 26 on the grounds of ill health caused by the stress and lack of support in employment. At this particular period in the early 1980s, there was very little available to assist by way of disabled access adaptations. Training would have helped his colleagues understand better and be able to help resolve the many difficulties he faced.

As the years unfolded, Paul was active in his Church, outgoing to the point when he would go to the local pub and mix with people and generally had a reasonable quality of life. It was better in the summer than the winter as the dark nights kept him in more and my parents were finding it more difficult to cope with Paul's needs. It could be argued that this was a pivotal stage in his life when we should have asked for more help. In the latter stages of my father's life he was constantly checking his welfare. He passed away at 94 years of age and my mother was left in sole command. She has helped Paul with his personal care and Paul became more dependent.

As he got older there was an increasing number of incidents when he felt worried, frightened and at risk. His local pub/ hotel closed which had been his main place for relaxation and, regrettably, he lost a lot of his social contact. On his journey to and from the pub from his home he has been approached on a number of occasions, asked for money, been on the receiving end of verbal abuse and propositioned by a local prostitute. On the first occasion this happened he asked for my advice and I have to admit that I tried to find humour and said, 'Ask her if she takes a credit card.' He quickly put me right with my poor attempt at a resolution and we had a more sensible conversation about him crossing the road and trying to ignore her approaches. In recent months a different prostitute has approached him whilst out walking several times, seeing him as easy prey. He has had to develop strategies to deal with this. He mentioned it to a local police detective who he met in the pub who, as far as I know, took it upon himself to warn the individual to stay clear as '…she is still working the area.' For someone who just wants a normal loving relationship this is like a slap in the face.

One particular unpleasant event was when a group of youths surrounded him early one summer evening outside the park opposite his house and took his walking stick away whilst laughing and making fun of him. The immediate problem was that he needed his stick to stand up so he was wobbling about, having to beg for it back. He tried to stand up to them and shouted out and they, eventually having had their fun, gave him his stick back. That night when he rang me I was particularly angry at hearing his story. Paul was wary of Asian youths from that day and still is. I fail to understand and can never accept that young people of any race or background could do something like this. I shared the experience with my own two sons, both of whom were mortified that their generation could act in such a way. I always now look out for small groups when I see a disabled person, just in case a situation were to develop. It will come as no surprise to learn that I would be in the middle of that group preventing this from happening, whatever the personal consequences. I like to think that the vast majority of our population would do exactly the same, but unfortunately the cowards tend to pick their moment when the vulnerable people are on their own and without support.

Paul became more in need of his medication and was a frequent visitor to his GP as he became more anxious and depressed. Interestingly, old school friends used to say that, without exception, Paul was always so pleased to meet them and reflect on the past.

Apart from collecting his surgical shoes, visits to the chiropodist and visits to the GP there has been very little help and support. Paul has frequently been in contact with the police regarding attempted break-ins to his garage, access to his back yard and other disturbances – there will be a log of a significant activity from him.

As we get older we try to be in contact with Paul as frequently as possible, but he has a feeling of isolation. In recent weeks Paul has made a decision to look into continuing care (which is provided in the community by the NHS), partly resulting from our mother's admission to hospital and subsequently nursing care as she now has dementia. We hope to put plans in place to secure Paul's long-term future in a more protective environment.

CHAPTER 6

DISABILITY HATE CRIME – THE PARENT'S PERSPECTIVE

DAME PHILIPPA RUSSELL DBE

In Greece, I saw a tombstone – a tribute from parents to a daughter called Athene. Athene died five centuries ago and my son translated the epitaph because we could see from the carvings that she was disabled. The Ancient Greeks valued physical perfection and we were keen to see how they had clearly honoured a disabled child. The epitaph made me cry because it said that Athene was loved and loved life. She died young but the parents praised the Gods for taking her whilst still a child and they could protect her. Clearly Ancient Greek parents (like their twenty-first-century British counterparts) had little faith in the wider world respecting and protecting their daughter. As my son said, the Olympics have celebrated much in the lives of disabled people. But they haven't stopped the school kids picking on Jon[1] (who has Autism and learning disabilities), taking his phone, calling him names, jumping out and frightening him. The school and the police do what they can, but it's the community, isn't it? I heard another parent say that disabled children 'cost too much' the other day. One actually said to me that 'kids like yours keep our kids back at school – why can't they go to a special place? And I have heard other parents like us talking like Athene's parents too – are we the only parents who hope that our children don't outlive us? It's a lonely world out there but it could be so much better. (Parent, personal contribution to focus group, 2013)

---

1   Jon is not his real name.

The deaths of Fiona Pilkington and her daughter were in many respects a wake-up call to police, communities, schools and (perhaps) to those families who had not prevented their children from tormenting the family. Like Jon's mother quoted on the previous page, we have also encountered hostility and name calling in the street, and our adult son (now living with support in his own home) has had the 'friends' he craved come into his house, steal, put lit cigarettes in drawers, take his food and mock him. Reluctantly, we put in CCTV and the disrespect and bullying took to the street. We were fortunate. Our son lives on a pleasant road in a pleasant area. There are good community policing services and he has his Telecare surveillance and CCTV. He also has family round the corner. But two years ago, some young people went further than name calling and set fire to the bins and fence at the back of his house. It was a dry summer and the fire spread along the fence to the wooden conservatory at the back of the house. The CCTV faithfully recorded the young people (very drunk on vodka stolen from the local Tesco); the surveillance system alerted the police, the fire brigade and us. The fire was put out, and the kind local police patched up the fence.

But what next? We had the CCTV images of the young people and they were identified. Friends and neighbours wanted the courts involved, some kind of retribution, not least to discourage others who thought it 'fun' to hurt and harm disabled people. The police suggested restorative justice, that is, the young people being cautioned, required to work with school and the police and to come and say sorry. I had mixed feelings about the idea of an apology. But they came, sheepishly, with a box of plants for the garden which had been well and truly trampled over by the emergency services. I then learnt an important lesson – disabled people (of all ages) are not only at greater risk of being bullied, but may also themselves become bullies. One of our assailants had a major hearing impairment and a moderate learning disability. As it turned out, he in his efforts to fit in, had 'gone with the lads' who lived in his road and gave him some sort of protection. As for our son, he was very reluctant to leave his house for many months 'in case they came back and burnt it down'. As a neighbour commented, if he did go out, 'he was always looking over his shoulder, not his old confident self'.

The incident described above is now over and has not been repeated. The new fence is untouched and, unlike the Pilkington family, I am confident that the local police, and indeed the local community, are on my side. But the incident also gave us as the family much food for thought. Could we as parents (and could our son's school and college) have done more to make him more resilient and better able to cope with bullying and hate crime? Could we be sure that he would be safe in future? We found no easy answers except the kindly and well-meant comments of friends that maybe we should be looking at 'safer solutions' for our son in a care home or sheltered community. Thinking of Winterbourne View and the evidence of bullying and abuse within an expensive specialist residential unit, we doubted that this option would bring any real security.

Our own thoughts were further stimulated by the experiences of our seven-year-old grandson – a bright, gentle and lovely child with Asperger's Syndrome. He managed to cope through the nursery and reception years at school (where all children got close supervision and personal attention). The advent of the junior school was a different matter. Children's break times were much busier and more loosely supervised. The children formed their own networks and circles and made their own games. Our grandson wanted to join in the groups. But each time he tried – without, we later realised, the skills to make an entry – he was rebuffed. A kind dinner lady on playground duty would sometimes try and help but he often sat on his own and of course the teasing and bullying started.

The school was good; they had an active anti-bullying policy and they introduced a buddy scheme and a circle of support. They also explored different ways of developing the skills that all of us need in order to make good relationships and friendships. They encouraged our grandson to join the choir, the school band and the athletics clubs. Everybody is good at something and vulnerable children (particularly those with communication difficulties) need to be encouraged to develop and show their skills. The buddying helped and we feel that we are on the right path. But schools are to some extent sheltered and controlled environments. What happens on the bus or walk home, at the local shops or in the leisure centre can be a very different matter. As Professor Wolke (2013) commented in a new report, parents themselves have an important role in tackling bullying and hate crime by creating resilience and giving coping skills to their children.

If we want to change attitudes and prevent our own family's bad experiences (both happily resolved for the time being in our case but with no guarantees about resolution in the wider community), we need to understand the context of bullying and disability hate crime. Bullying may be low level but it is insidious and it can escalate. It erodes self-confidence and encourages vulnerability. Most importantly, we need to see the development of personal confidence and resilience (and the skills for communication) as a high priority for all children and a 'must' for those who are most vulnerable.

We know that certain groups of children and young people are particularly vulnerable to bullying. A study from the Anti-Bullying Alliance (2013) found that children and young people with disabilities were substantially more likely to be bullied and harassed than other young people. Seventy per cent of parents of children and young people with an autistic spectrum disorder or Asperger's Syndrome felt that their child's condition attracted negative attitudes and bullying from peers, with 73.5 per cent of parents saying that school play times and lunch breaks were particularly 'difficult and frightening' periods in the school day.

A survey by Contact a Family and the Anti-Bullying Alliance (2011) found parents often frustrated by not being believed; by inertia on the part of the school; by penalising of the bullied child and found parents being made to feel as if they were making a fuss. As one parent commented:

> Very quickly we were made to feel a nuisance… Some instances necessitated the need for the involvement of the police. We became desperate after our last meeting with the Head, he admitted that he couldn't guarantee our son's safety whilst at school. (p.28)

From the parent perspective, a particularly worrying aspect of bullying and hate crime is the nature of the perpetrators. A study on loneliness and cruelty found that:

> the perpetrators in the main are not strangers, but local people, neighbours, often young people and schoolchildren. Incidents happen when people are out and about but also in and around their homes. There is little that is subtle about these acts. They are often opportunistic, crass and vulgar. They can also be targeted and cynical. It is the loneliness of some people with learning and other disabilities – their search for friendship within a selfish society and within deeply fragmented communities – that is putting them at particular risk, leading them to frequent alone hostile and permissive public spaces and bringing them to the attentions of the cold hearted and criminal few. (Gravell 2012, p.4)

The perpetrators in the case of Fiona Pilkington, Steven Hoskin and other high-profile victims were certainly local, often known to family as well as the victim. Worryingly they were often young (whether or not the victim was a child or an adult). Equally worrying, as the Equality and Human Rights Commission (EHRC) (2011) found, cyber-bullying and instant communication played an important part in the harassment and bullying behaviours with images often shared and 'enjoyed'. As one police officer commented:

> It almost seemed as if the harassment and constant hate crime directed at this young man were carried out in order to put something amusing up on YouTube. Of course the evidence on their smart phones was not in the least amusing but neither they nor their parents took our concerns sufficiently seriously. One parent even voiced the opinion that 'people like him shouldn't live where there are young kids, they're all a bit "you know"'. I said did they mean paedophile and they nodded. Of course I told them their views were ridiculous, no evidence whatsoever, but I knew the harassment was likely to continue unless we took legal action. The parents didn't wish to take it further, they thought things would get worse. They managed

to get a housing transfer and I hope they found a better area. (Personal communication)

From a parent's perspective, the attitudes of others are particularly hard to bear. We want (and need) inclusive communities. As a family we have always lived in neighbourhoods which were friendly and intrinsically safe. Our son suffered from the young people who followed and filmed him on their mobile phones and stole his possessions. I know that our neighbours now look out for him. But life is not necessarily like that for all families with a disabled child and if we want to build safe communities, then we need to understand the key factors that so often contribute to bullying and hate crime. We also need to start with schools. As parents commented in the Contact a Family and the the Anti-Bullying Alliance Survey (2011), schools must review their anti-bullying policies regularly and involve parents and pupils, including disabled children and parents, in the reviews. One parent in the survey noted that:

> The most useful thing they [the school] did over the next couple of weeks [after the bullying was reported] was to ensure that his self-esteem was not damaged in any way. They made sure that they praised him for all the good things he did. (p.7)

Another parent emphasised the importance of whole school policies, commenting that:

> They did an education session with the rest of the class on autism to increase awareness and make sure everyone was aware of appropriate behaviour. (p.7)

All professionals need to be more aware of the long-term impact of bullying and harassment. As the Francis Report of abusive care of older people in the Mid-Staffordshire Hospital noted, all health and social care (and by implication education) professionals must have and demonstrate a duty of care (Department of Health 2013). As the Law Commission (2014) noted when launching its review of hate crime (including disability hate crime), we need to start by accepting that:

- Disabled people of all ages are at greater risk of experiencing violence than non-disabled people.

- Disabled children and young people with special educational needs (particularly those with learning disabilities) are particularly at risk.

- On-going low-level incidents are widespread and often go undetected or reported. But these may escalate and are often ignored by public agencies even though they have a significant impact on disabled people and their families.

- Many disabled people (of all ages) and their families restructure their lives to minimise real harm even if they have not experienced targeted violence personally. A study from the EHRC (2012) showed that many disabled people and children consistently avoided parts of their town; limited their time spent in public spaces; and often travelled circuitous routes because of the risk of abuse in some areas.

Parents are often asked why they themselves do not take more action in raising instances of abuse or bullying with schools, the police or community leaders. We know that disability hate crimes recorded by police forces in England and Wales for 2011/12 increased by 24.1 per cent on the previous year. This might suggest an encouraging rise in the number of citizens confident enough to make a complaint. However, other figures show that less than three per cent of disability related hate crime is reported or recognised as such. In Fiona Pilkington's case, we know that the family repeatedly reported incidents and asked for help. Other families, reflecting on her death, commented that:

> Most of us have experienced hate crime of some kind, ranging from name calling to stone throwing and sometimes theft. Some of us have had kids come round to our house shouting, ringing the doorbell, putting nasty things through the letter box sometimes. It's as if we're somehow the scapegoats for all the things that aren't right for them, poor housing, no jobs, parents not interested somehow…we're frightened to say much because the police come round and then go away and the kids

come back and they're all wound up then. It's worse. I blame the parents, they know what they are up to and they don't care. Where's the Olympic effect they all talk about? I think it will get worse with all the welfare stuff, we get older and we and our children are seen as scroungers, cheats – it's hard to be positive. (Parent of a 16-year-old son with learning disabilities and Asperger's Syndrome, at parent carer workshop, March 2013. Personal communication)

Changing attitudes and expectations

Notwithstanding the anxiety about hate crime, the past decade has seen changing attitudes and expectations towards disabled people. The government's strategy for children and young people (and their parents) as set out in the Children and Families Act is optimistic and progressive. But the reality is that many families are more vulnerable because of the wider impact of having a disabled child has on their lives. Evidence from the Office for Disability Issues (2013) confirms that:

- Families with a disabled child are less likely to be living in a decent home compared to families with a non-disabled child (2003/4 English Housing Conditions Survey). They are 50 per cent more likely to live in overcrowded accommodation and to rate their home as being in poor repair.

- Where people live can have a profound impact upon their perceptions of personal safety; supportive neighbours and the development of social networks and friendships make a great difference in their lives. Disabled children and young people spend more time at home than non-disabled children and often lack opportunities to develop friendships and social skills. They are much less likely to take part in sport or leisure activities in and out of school and are much more likely (28% more likely as opposed to 9% of those without a disability) to experience barriers in accessing play and leisure activities. One of the key causes for these barriers are the negative attitudes of others (34% compared to 8% of children and young people without a disability)

(Office for Disability Issues 2010–12). 20 per cent of the children and young people with a disability participating in the survey (as compared to 1% without a disability) reported problems and barriers in relationships and anxieties about the safety of public places like playgrounds and shopping precincts. Transport was seen as a particular problem because of the opportunities it offered for bullying, name calling and aggressive behaviour.

As one parent commented:

> If we could afford it, we would live in such a different area. Nobody feels safe round here. My daughter doesn't go out on her own at all because of the name calling. We've found a club for her, she is making friends, but it's the other side of town. She can't just go out and meet friends. We've got her a wonderful whizzy wheelchair, the Rotary Club bought it for her and it's fantastic. But she doesn't like to use it round here because the kids shout 'spazzy' and one tries to jump on the back for a ride. So she never goes out in it unless she gets a lift in the school bus or Dial-A-Ride. Our local bus is wheelchair accessible. But she's been harassed and bullied so much, she won't go on a bus now without an adult with her. The drivers do speak up for her, but what can they do? They get threatened too. She's a teenager, she needs to be out and about. She's so over-protected I don't know what she would do if we were not around. Is there a Kung-Fu or self-defence class she could go to? But that wouldn't help her, it's the words that really destroy her self-esteem and make her vulnerable. (Personal communication from the parent of Sophie[2], a 16-year-old girl with cerebral palsy, 2014)

Finding solutions to Sophie's challenges will require joined-up solutions and group action. The Tizard Centre at the University of Kent initiated a multi-agency research project (2013) which is working with people with learning disabilities and autistic spectrum disorders, families, support staff and police officers to improve reporting and subsequent action and to consider factors

---

2   Sophie's name has been changed.

in community development to reduce incidents of hate crime and harassment. As Sophie's mother noted:

> Hate crime and harassment hurt everyone. The bus driver is scared by these big lads and their nasty behaviour. If Sophie can't live safely in her community, then maybe she will opt for residential care in the future. That will cost everyone a lot of money and will be a waste of a life. I am going to tell our new Health and Well-Being Board that safe streets and buses for everyone should be number one priority!

The context for hate crime – influencing public attitudes

A number of recent surveys have shown that attitudes towards disabled people are changing. 81 per cent of people thought that the Paralympics had a positive impact on the way in which disabled people are viewed by the British public (Ipsos MORI 2012).

However, although we have this encouraging evidence that people who are disabled and thereby at risk of being seen as 'different' are being viewed more positively, other surveys suggest otherwise and remind us of the context in which abuse and hate crime are most likely to occur. In 2011 almost 1 in 10 people thought of disabled people as 'getting in the way, most or some of the time' (ODI 2013; Staniland 2011). 79 per cent of people in a 2011 survey (Staniland 2011) thought that prejudice towards disabled people had increased rather than reduced. Even more worryingly, Briant, Watson and Philo (2011) note that whilst there has been a significant increase in the reporting of disability issues in the media over the past five years, this has been coupled with an increase in the number of articles documenting the claimed 'burden' that disabled people are alleged to place on society and economy. As one parent of a young adult with learning disability, newly moved into his own flat, commented:

> We can't properly tackle bullying and hate crime unless we tackle negative attitudes to disabled people. I was told by another parent in my son's class that it would be better if we went elsewhere, as he was taking too much of the teacher's

time! If our children are seen as 'scroungers', non-productive, taking resources from those who can better use them, then we won't stop hate crime. We need to work the other way and to remember that ALL of us benefit from safe, welcoming and inclusive environments. I wish I could trust my son's new neighbours, but I can't. (Personal communication)

A series of focus groups of disabled people and parent carers run by the Office for Disability Issues as part of the development of a new strategy for disabled people on 'Fulfilling Potential' emphasised the need for schools, communities and the media to promote more positive role models for disabled people and to also to put disability on a par with wider equality issues around race, religion, gender and age. As one parent put it:

We need new attitudes to disability. I think people are aware of hate crime around race and religion. I don't think we have achieved full equality around disability, particularly around disability and hate crime. Mental health issues in particular are just not understood. We are very intolerant of difference when really we should celebrate it! (Personal communication)

From a family perspective, it is also important to remember that young people can be bullied and abused because they are the carers of an adult family member with a disability. There are estimated to be around 175,000 young carers in England and Wales, many providing high levels of support for relatives (usually parents) who are disabled or have a long-term condition. A study by the Princess Royal Trust for Carers and the Children's Society (Frank 2002) found that two-thirds of the young carers had been bullied at school, noting that:

Many young carers are enduring bullying, mental health problems and lack of support from the school, all because they are caring for a family member with a disability who cannot cope without their help. (p.32)

The young carers, like the young people with autistic spectrum disorders in the Anti-Bullying Alliance Report (2013) felt that their situation and challenges were not well understood. They thought that schools in general did not understand disability (whether in pupils or in wider family relationships) and they felt challenged in maintaining both school work and family roles. As one young carer commented at a focus group of young carers in North London:

> My mum's disabled, she's got MS and some days she can hardly move. She's really depressed too and I know the neighbours think she's a bad mother because the house doesn't look right. The other kids tease me because I am always checking my phone. Sometimes she sends me texts every few minutes and I get told off for not doing my work. I've been pushed and shoved and called the 'kid with the funny mother.' It hurts when they say things about my mum and sometimes I am frightened. I told my teacher but nothing happens. (Personal communication)

But another boy at another school in the area had a very different experience:

> My mum and I are both hearing impaired – I can hear a bit but I miss things and so does she. I got a lot of name calling when I went to secondary school. They used to hang about waiting for me to start walking home and then they'd start. I told the teacher and they took it really seriously. They had a special day and I talked to the other kids about what it was like not hearing well. The school got some other people along to talk about being disabled and we talked about difference and then we talked about bullying. I was surprised when other kids said they got bullied too and hadn't spoken up. We're going to set up a buddy system now. Funny thing is the boy who treated me real bad, he now wants to be a buddy. Suddenly it's a cool thing to do! I am really pleased too because I know my mum was upset, felt it was her fault. Things were getting really bad at home before I spoke up. (Personal communication)

Solutions – from a family perspective

Families of course want justice for their children whenever hate crime and bullying takes place. But we are well aware that even if the criminal justice system becomes more accessible and responsive, prevention will always be better than punishment.

First, we need to ensure that vulnerable children and young people (and adults) are adequately valued and supported throughout their lives. The tragic deaths of young men like Steven Hoskin remind us all that communities are not always safe places and 'friendships' are not always what they seem. People of all ages with learning and other disabilities yearn for friendships and relationships (just like everyone else). But we need to be much better at:

- helping children from an early age to develop friendships and relationships and to have the appropriate social and communication skills to not only make but to sustain the social networks which are a good first line of defence against hate crime

- raising awareness in schools, health, and social care and education services about the real risk of hate crime and ensuring that the relevant staff and professionals understand how to identify, report and pursue action on a potential hate crime

- promoting self-esteem and confidence – we need to cherish what our children can do and encourage the sense of self-worth that helps us all to cope with difficult situations and decisions; many disabled children and young people have very low self-esteem – we need to identify and nurture their talents

- encouraging interests and participation in activities which will enable children and adults to make community connections and widen networks; the personalisation agenda offers new opportunities to move from very traditional views of 'services' to supporting 'participation'.

Families need support too. It is very easy to over-protect disabled children (and adults) rather than managing risk. Many disabled young people are very isolated, heavily dependent on family members for any social or other activities. Parents of disabled children (and disabled adults) are bad at risk taking. We have seen the risks and we are reluctant to take them. But we need to be proactive, to encourage our children to get engaged and to accept that we ourselves as families have to be part of the wider challenge of:

- working with the local authority, schools, the police and the community to identify and target the local 'hot spots', the public spaces, transport, streets, underpasses and shopping centres where hate crime is most likely to take place; making communities safe for disabled people makes them safe for older people, parents with young children and for the local business community

- using the new opportunities with Health and Well-Being Boards and Joint Strategic Needs Assessments to link personal safety to wider improvements in personal health and well-being

- helping to develop proactive approaches to reporting incidents when they occur and tracking the outcomes of any investigation; as the EHRC (2012) advise in *Out in the Open: Tackling Disability-Related Harassment*, we must also ensure that Safeguarding Boards and Community Safeguarding Partnerships provide sufficient accessible information and advocacy services to enable disabled people of all ages and their families to know and to exercise their rights; support for witnesses is vital – even the bravest parent or disabled person will quail at giving evidence against people living in their local community without adequate support

- exploring ways of helping people feel safe – for example the West Midlands 'yellow cards'[3] for people with an autistic

---

3   In the West Midlands, families were concerned that young people and adults with autistic spectrum disorders were reporting bad experiences with the local police. They reported that the police often misinterpreted behaviour which was due to autism as being aggressive or anti-social. The local branch of the National Autistic Society offered training for the police and people with autistic spectrum disorders were issued with special 'yellow cards' explaining why autism might make them behave differently and who to contact if there was a problem. The yellow cards were very successful and the police and the various autism groups in the area now actively work together.

spectrum disorder – and recognising that disability hate crime is often associated with other areas of hate crime around race, religion etc.

• helping to create positive attitudes towards disabled people – schools are the first line of defence but bullying, hate crime and discrimination can take place anywhere.

Most challengingly, we parents have to play our own role in ensuring that our potentially vulnerable children are as resilient as possible and have the skills necessary to survive in a sometimes very hostile world. We (and they) have to learn to manage risk rather than always to avoid it. As Professor Wolke (2013) notes, overprotective parenting can lead to bullied children. In reviewing over 70 studies involving more than 200,000 children, he concluded that parents who try to buffer their children from all negative experiences may actually prevent those children from learning effective ways of dealing with bullies and thereby make them more vulnerable. In effect, disabled children in particular need the chance to develop and practice coping skills.

A final reflection – using equality legislation

Finally, we have to consider whether the current legal framework is fit for purpose in protecting children and adults from disability-related harassment and hate crime. The Equality Act (2010) protects citizens from discrimination on grounds of race, disability, religion, gender, sexual orientation and age. At present, a crime is recorded as a hate crime if the victim or anyone else believes it to have been motivated by hostility or prejudice based on one of these personal characteristics.

The criminal justice agencies monitor hate crimes related to the five main characteristics set out in the Equality Act (currently omitting age) but not all the existing legislation actually protects victims in the same way. The Public Order Act (1986) makes it an offence to intentionally stir up hatred on grounds of race, religion and sexual orientation. The Crime and Disorder Act (1988) creates racially and religiously aggravated offences. The Law Commission is currently carrying out a review (reporting in

2014) to consider whether these two Acts should be reformed to extend similar protection to all five characteristics and in effect to give disability-related hate crime parity of esteem with other protected areas.

Disability hate crime is almost invariably part of a pathway of discrimination against disabled and sometimes other vulnerable people. Casual bullying may seem very far removed from the murders of young men like Steven Hoskin and Brett Martin. But it is part of a pathway of indifference, disrespect and anti-social behaviour that can escalate into attacks that damage lives and affect whole families. As the parent of an adult son with a learning disability (and as a parent determined to give my son as ordinary a life as possible), I realise that we are all part of a process of change and development. Communities need to be more proactive in valuing all their citizens. The police and the criminal justice system have important roles to play but they in turn must learn to operate in a society where disrespect for disability is often widespread. Sadly, Time to Change, a £40 million campaign to reduce discrimination against people with mental health problems, has reported that the campaign has missed key targets in its first four years because of harsher and hardening attitudes to disability during the recession. Therefore, families like my own must be champions of change and recognise our collective responsibility in creating safe communities which benefit all their citizens.

Most importantly, if we wish to change attitudes towards disabled children and adults, we have to look to our schools and the mental health and well-being of all pupils. As a Department for Education (2014) report on mental health and behaviour in schools notes:

> Schools offer important opportunities to prevent mental health problems by promoting resilience. Providing pupils with inner resources that they can draw on as a buffer when negative or stressful things happen helps them to thrive even in the face of significant challenge. Having a 'sense of connectedness' or belonging to a school is a recognised protective factor for mental health.

Throughout the literature on bullying and hate crime, there is a common thread of isolation; of vulnerability (even in the bullies and perpetrators); and a strong reminder that change happens when families, schools, communities and police work together to create communities that are safe and good to live in. Safe communities require confidence and resilience in all their citizens.

References

Anti-Bullying Alliance (2013) *Annual Report*. London: Anti-Bullying Alliance.

Briant, E., Watson, N. and Philo, G. (2011) *Bad News for Disabled People: How the Media Reports Disability*. Glasgow: University of Glasgow, Strathclyde Centre for Disability Research.

Contact a Family and the Anti-Bullying Alliance (2011) *Bullying of children with disabilities and special educational needs in schools: briefing paper for parents on the view and experiences of other parents, carers and families*. Available at www.cafamily.org.uk/media/395239/reports_and_research_bullying_of_children_with_disabilities_2011_parents_briefing.pdf, accessed on 17 October 2014.

Independent Police Commission (IPC) (2011) *Report into the Death of Fiona Pilkington*. London: IPC.

Department for Education (DFE) (2014) *Mental health and behaviour in schools: departmental advice for school staff*. London: DFE.

Department of Health (2013) *Report of the Mid-Staffordshire NHS Foundation Trust Public Inquiry Chaired by Robert Francis QC*. London: HMSO.

Equality and Human Rights Commission (EHRC) (2011) *Hidden in Plain Sight: Inquiry into Disability-Related Harassment*. London: EHRC. Available at www.equalityhumanrights.com/uploaded_files/disabilityfi/ehrc_hidden_in_plain_sight_3.pdf, accessed on 17 October 2014.

EHRC (2012) *Out in the Open: Tackling Disability-Related Harassment – A Manifesto for Change*. London: EHRC. Available at www.equalityhumanrights.com/publication/out-open-tackling-disability-related-harassment-manifesto-change, accessed on 17 October 2014.

Frank, J. (2002) *Making it Work: Good practice with young carers and their families*. London: The Children's Society with The Princess Royal Trust for Carers. Available at www.youngcarer.com/pdfs/MAKING%20IT%20WORK%20Vol%201.pdf, accessed on 28 January 2015.

Ipsos MORI (2012) *Ipsos MORI Paralympics Poll: Topline Results*. Available at www.ipsos-mori.com/Assests/Docs/Polls/Paralympics%20topline.pdf, accessed 28 January 2015.

Law Commission (2014) *Hate Crime: Should the Current Offences be Extended?* London: Law Commission.

Gravell, C. (2012) *Loneliness and Cruelty: People with Learning Disabilities – Their Experience of Harassment, Abuse and Related Crime in the Community. Ongoing Inquiry*. London: Lemos & Crane.

Office for Disability Issues (2010–12) *Life Opportunities Survey*. London: DWP.

Office for Disability Issues (2013) *Fulfilling Potential: The Discussions So Far*. London: DWP.

Staniland, L. (2011) *Public Perceptions of Disabled People: Evidence from the British Social Attitudes Survey 2009*. London: Office for Disability Issues.

Tizard Centre (2013) *Living in Fear: Better Outcomes for People with Autism and Learning Disabilities Living in Medway*. Canterbury: Tizard Centre, University of Kent.

Wolke, D. (2013) *Child Abuse and Neglect*. Warwick: University of Warwick.

CHAPTER 7

ABSENT PRESENCE

KATHRYN STONE OBE

In our lounge, on a shelf, we have a picture of my husband's mum, Edie: I'm reliably informed that she always – always – told her three children: 'I'm not your mother, I'm your mum!'

In the photo, she is 20; she is smiling, in a blurred enlarged reprographic of a badly damaged, small, poor quality, black-and-white photo taken in 1954. She gave the picture to her boyfriend, later her husband (my husband's father). On it she scratched in struggling ink: 'All my love, Ede x'. It is now framed in a beautiful, simple, elegant silver surround. It is all my husband has of her. She died in 1992. She looks out upon us each day: a dashing, fleeting moment of her life captured beautifully.

I never knew her. Nor did our daughter: she never sat in her Nan's lap, never hugged her, never kissed her, never moaned about her over-salted potatoes, never had the chance to raid the posh biscuit tin in the kitchen. But Edie is with us in our lives, in that room, on that shelf, in that picture.

She is with us. But, of course, she isn't. She is gone, lost, absent. But she is also, always, here, with us, present.

Her picture, her 'absent presence' is a warm, fond, and occasionally sad, daily reminder. But for victims of disability hate crime an absent presence can have a more sinister and damaging effect. Unwelcomed and uninvited, the daily reminder of someone crawling around in the very fibre of your daily life can be emotionally paralysing, physically frightening and potentially traumatising.

I would suggest that our ability to empathise (to share and understand another person's feelings) is an indicator of our humanity. Empathy – unlike sympathy – is not an instant and uncontrolled emotional response but rather a learned, developed skill. It enables us to attempt to see the world through another's eyes; to be in their shoes; to see, experience and feel situations as they see, experience and feel them. Of course, it is highly unlikely that we can ever really know for sure how another person feels, but it is surely part of our role as skilled practitioners to imagine those experiences as best we can.

When it comes to disability hate crime, we can offer a better service to victims if we can draw on empathy. We need to better understand what it must feel like to be those people who are victims. In doing so, we need to better understand the concept of absent presence. We need to put ourselves in the shoes of the person who was kicked because they use a wheelchair in which to get around. We need to see for ourselves through the eyes of the person with Down syndrome who was made to look while someone urinated on them because they were a 'Spaz'. We need to try and experience what that must have felt like and, critically, continues to feel like.

We need to try and experience what it must feel like to be targeted – not because someone is after your bag, purse or wallet and not because you happened to be in the wrong place at the wrong time; but because you are you; because of what you look like; because of what you sound like; because of the way you walk. You are targeted because of who you are.

The man who nicks your car or the drunken woman who smashes your window is unlikely to come again. He hasn't taken your car because it's you; he just wanted your car. It just happened to be yours. She didn't smash the window because it was you; she was drunk and wanted to smash a window. It just happened to be yours.

However, being sworn at, being called hateful names ('sticks and stones may break my bones, but names will break my heart'), being ridiculed, being attacked, being humiliated because you can't see or can't hear or can't walk or can't think quickly or don't look like everybody else – that abuse, those crimes are because you are you. That abuse is born of hate; those crimes are born of hate; a hatred of who you are. And the deadly outcome of hate is fear.

And that hate, and that fear, does not go when the perpetrator stops, goes or is taken away. That hate and that fear is buried in you.

What they did and what they said and what they think remains. The perpetrators have an absent presence.

That is why hate crime in general and disability hate crime in particular is important.

A senior police officer for North Wales Police once told me this story relating to race hate crime but the lessons for disability hate crime are clear: 'Some twenty years ago I was patrolling the shopping precinct of a Lancashire mill town when I came across two middle-aged and drunken white men running a tape measure across the back of an elderly Pakistani. In the full glare of passing shoppers, they were pretending to measure him up for a coffin. I will never forget the look on the victim's face. I arrested the louts and took them to a police station. I remember a few raised eyebrows amongst colleagues in the charge office, but this was nothing compared to the indifference shown by prosecutors and magistrates when the case arrived at court. I ended up feeling guilty for making the arrest.'

Thankfully, things are now different. The same officer says: 'Officers sometimes ask me why we should treat race hate crime so seriously. In response I ask them to imagine their reaction should they wake up next morning to find their car had been damaged overnight. They would be annoyed and a little angry; but once the insurance had paid out the incident would be quickly forgotten. I then ask them to think about their reaction if, in addition to the damage, 'I hate coppers' had been sprayed on the car. They would wonder who hated them. They would fear for their family. They might even consider moving house. This is the plight of far too many vulnerable, isolated and scared individuals who are abused simply for who they are. We owe them our best efforts.'

We do, indeed, owe them our best efforts. We owe John-Paul Nathan[1] our best efforts. John-Paul (JP) is 25 and has a moderate learning disability and verbal communication difficulties. JP's mother died soon after his birth from unforeseen but unavoidable complications. He lived at home with his father, step-mother and two step-brothers. His two older sisters live abroad – they both blame JP for their mother's death and haven't spoken to him for

---

1   Not his real name.

over 15 years. Unsurprisingly, JP himself feels that he was the main cause of her death.

JP's youngest step-brother, Ronnie, 14, regularly fails to attend school. Ronnie's educational welfare officer (EWO) referred JP to social services. When he visited the family home, the EWO was concerned that JP had seemingly no services or support. The local younger adults social work team took the case and carried out an assessment of JP's needs, albeit amid some hostility from the family. Although JP had attended a special school, there has been no contact with social services since he left over seven years ago. Given the family's opposition and veiled aggression, two social workers carried out the assessment of JP's needs.

The family, who had a history of conflict with authority, were deeply suspicious of the social workers' intentions: why were they there: why do an assessment of JP's needs now?

The assessment concluded that JP was socially isolated and lacked independent living skills. His life appeared to be just ticking along – watching TV or going out to the local supermarket to shop or collect the evening paper. The workers linked JP up with a local day service: one day a week initially; and then increasing gradually to three days a week.

JP appeared transformed; staff noted his improved demeanour – he relished getting stuck into activities and even started going to college. He did some metalwork classes and made a frame for his mum's photograph – his most-treasured possession.

It was at college that JP alleged his family often physically hurt him – and scared him by turning off his light at night (he likes it kept on and is very scared of the dark). JP told his tutor that his step-brothers would make him watch horror movies – scaring him so much that he would, at times, wet himself. His step-brothers would laugh at him uncontrollably, pointing at him, calling him a scare-baby and asking him where his nappy was. He showed his tutor and staff at the day service some scratches along his back and bruising on his chest. He also said he had cigarette burns on his armpits.

Raising the alarm as a safeguarding issue, JP was accommodated in a community care home while the allegations were investigated.

However, he returned home about five days later as police were unable to uncover any evidence. His step-mother had been saying that because of his learning disability JP didn't know what he was saying and that no one should listen to him. She added that nobody in the house smoked – so the cigarette burns story was clearly made up. She said that JP was a fantasist and could not be trusted.

Workers were dissatisfied that no action was taken – and resolved to keep an extra eye on the situation. They involved advocates, a psychologist and a speech and language therapist. When JP again disclosed at the day service that he was being humiliated, frightened and beaten, workers acted swiftly. JP refused to leave the day service and would not go home. Although lacking evidence there was a strong suspicion that if he returned home he would be at risk of physical abuse. The workers' view was that while there was no proof that it hadn't happened, there was just no evidence that it had.

However, once again police could not turn up evidence and took no further action. With no criminal investigation, the workers shifted the focus: what did JP now want? Did he want to go back home? Did he want contact with the family?

Over the past months, JP had grown in confidence. He had support networks at the day services, and through advocacy services and speech therapy he was beginning to articulate what he wanted rather than what everyone thought was best for him. JP made a very clear choice not to go home.

It was important for the staff that despite the collapse of the police investigation they didn't lose sight of the adult protection issues; in the past they had relied on police and if that fell through they just felt there was nothing else they could do.

Having refused all contact with his family, JP was placed in an adult placement scheme (adult fostering). He had his own room in his carers' terraced house. JP had a framed photograph of his mum in his room. His carers made a copy for him and put one downstairs in the front room on the mantelpiece. JP felt like he and his mum were part of the family.

He would go and fetch the evening newspaper just like he used to – but this time he could go alone. JP enjoyed this. He felt really independent. He was taking control of his life.

On one occasion someone coming out of the shop jostled him, knocking him back a pace or two while muttering something under his breath. JP didn't think much of it – just thought the boy was a rude teenager. On his way back out of the shop another youngster seemed to spit at his shoes but missed. Maybe, thought JP, he was just spitting – as some boys seem to. He had missed, after all.

On another walk around the area he heard someone – a female voice – shouting something – names, maybe – but wasn't too sure: the traffic was too noisy. JP shrugged his shoulders and carried on walking.

One night during his second week in his new home, his carers left for an evening out: every second Wednesday was Bridge night. Proudly being trusted with having the house to himself, JP settled down to watch *Midsomer Murders*. He likes Barnaby and his fun, waltz-like theme tune – it was JP's favourite. There was a knock at the door.

Frustrated, he opened the door quickly intending to confront whoever it was disturbing his best programme; only to be confronted himself by two people with scarves around their faces and hats over their heads – he could only see their eyes. They pushed him in and began shouting at him: 'We don't want any 'Spackos' living here.'

A terrified JP ran to the other side of the room – only to realise he was now trapped as the youths blocked his way to the doors out. Shaking he instinctively picked up his mum's photograph and tried to place it under his sweatshirt.

One of the youths grabbed it off him. He dropped it ceremoniously onto the floor and stamped on the glass shattering it. The other youth then punched and kicked JP to the floor. 'Get out, mong – or we'll burn you out,' they screamed and then they left as quickly as they arrived. JP, hunched in a ball on the floor, looked up. He could smell burning. His mum's photograph was on fire.

Despite investigating, the police again could find no evidence of the perpetrators. As far as JP could figure it – the police never seem to help him. Not even DCI Barnaby any more. All those little events that happened when he was out now took on more significance: had he been targeted before?

Just the night before, he recalled how happy he felt at fetching the paper on his own, taking control of his life. Now all that control has been lost with each flame across his mum's photograph. Now he doesn't want to fetch the paper. Now he doesn't want to go out. If he did go out, he is scared they will see him. 'They' are everywhere and everyone. They see him but he cannot see them.

He stays in. He will only watch television if his carers are watching. The theme tune to *Midsomer Murders* now makes him cry. He is frightened to go downstairs alone. Will they come in again and hurt him? Will they burn his other photo of his mum: the one in his bedroom? That is now hidden from view. Each time he sees his mum's face he doesn't wish her 'night, night, kiss, kiss'; he just sees her image melting in flames.

Each time he sees his mum's face he worries someone will come and smash her again. And take her away again.

The thugs only came in for three minutes on one night – but, for JP, they have never left; nor will they ever leave.

That is the destructive power of the absent presence.

In my recent role as Commissioner for Victims and Survivors in Northern Ireland, I saw the concept and reality of absent presence every day. The memorials and commemorations to those killed, the suffering of the bereaved and seriously injured and the constant reminders in murals of the Troubles here.

In 2012 in his speech to the 8th European Day in Remembrance of Victims of Terrorism, the EU counter-terrorism co-ordinator, Gilles de Kerchove, said:

> More attention has to be given to the victims and their fate. We always have to remember: while public life gets back to normal some time after an attack, there is no normal life any more for survivors, families of victims, their relatives and friends. The suffering of victims does not stop with the end of the attack.

This would be my message to policy makers and those working as investigators of hate crime. Please understand the suffering does not stop with the end of the attack. Please make sure you don't just walk away. Arrange ongoing support; take time. These victims are worth your time. They expect nothing more from you and deserve nothing less.

CHAPTER 8

DISABILITY HATE CRIME IS EVERYONE'S BUSINESS

DR ROBINA SHAH MBE

This chapter will explore what we think about how some organisations work in the context of 'protection' and the interrelationship that should exist between them to recognise that 'disability hate crime is everyone's business'. Such an approach requires an open mind and the ability to consider this issue outside our comfort zone. This may in turn make the difference between life and death, mental well-being and physical injury.

The picture that I am referring to will only emerge from a shared data system that is owned by organisations who have responsibility for protecting disabled people from all forms of harm including hate crime. The journey must begin with an honest conversation about us, 'the professionals', our roles, our practice, our values and the living environment which shapes them.

My father once told me 'to live my life in the way that I wish to be remembered by others', so that when people looked back and reflected on what they knew about me they would be able to say something about who I was, my values, my aspirations, my hopes, my fears, my dreams, my loves, my hates and what I stood up for in a world full of opportunities and challenges.

This was great advice spoken from a wise man who I admired for his honesty, compassion, humility and integrity. True to his word, this is how he is described by others since he passed away more than 28 years ago.

Our values shape our behaviour and inform our working and personal relationships with others. They are not only a core feature of our professionalism, and therefore fundamental to the way we practise, but they also define who we are on a personal level. In the context of disability hate crime and our subsequent response to it, we need to feel confident that we have demonstrated professionalism at a high standard and shown compassion when it is most needed, in order to support people who have been targeted because of their disability.

Throughout our professional working lives we progress our knowledge, skills and expertise using standards of best practice as benchmarks. We pride ourselves on our ability to reflect on our professionalism, so that we can continuously improve our practice. We also nurture our professionalism by creating a safe learning environment so that when 'critical incidents' occur professionals can respond appropriately. This is why greater awareness of the risk factors, early identification of the harm indicators and better understanding of the circumstances that contribute to a pattern of 'critical events' is important.

This proactive approach is vital in the war on hate crime generally, yet the personal stories about victims who have been hurt, harmed, abused or killed simply because they have a disability suggests that we have failed to optimise the opportunity to work collaboratively, to prevent hate crime from escalating into serious harm and to ensure that the poor experience of others is not ignored or devalued.

So what have we learnt about disability hate crime? What have we understood about why it happens? What have we discovered about ourselves and how it feels to experience it? And once we have become more aware, what changes have we put in place to address it?

Some of the harrowing accounts of disabled people who have experienced hate crime have been mentioned in other chapters but for the purpose of making a point, what action have we taken to prevent it from happening in the first place?

Holding up the mirror

The poem on the next page captures my personal reflection and learning from the findings of various serious case reviews discussed in Parts 2 and 3 of this book. I hope it sets the scene for further consideration of some of these questions and the challenges related to them in more detail.

Disability hate crime – where was the help?

They didn't hear the pangs of pain from a broken soul where words unspoken are louder than thunder, where was the help?

They didn't see the abuse that I lived again and again, in my sleep and wide awake, where was the help?

They didn't touch me emotionally, when I needed to know they cared, that I mattered, where was the help?

My humanity left blackened, soiled and cracked from the charred wreckage of a life debased by prejudice and hate, where was the help?

My desperation, my fears, my misery received no comment, why did they not understand the urgency to make it stop?

The poem illustrates the web of 'entanglement by ignorance' that can mask our senses to see, hear, smell and touch the lives of others who cannot reach us through a common language. The Pilkington findings are a stark reminder about how the routine sufferings of people with a learning disability went unnoticed, unrecognised and sometimes ignored by the very agencies whose job it was to protect them, such as the police, social services and the NHS. This failure to act may have been due to a series of factors ranging from a lack of focus and attention given to incidents, which may begin at a low level but can escalate very quickly unless they are checked, or because of a lack of training to raise awareness about learning disability and understand the impact of bullying, abuse and harm. Sadly, in the case of the Pilkington family, their vulnerability was not recognised and more worryingly the information held by different agencies about their circumstances was treated in isolation and not linked to form an overall picture of their experience, a link and a picture that might have potentially saved their lives.

Since 2005, disability hate crime has been recognised in law and yet some authorities and the professionals who work in them have failed to recognise disability as a possible incitement for abuse. This lack of awareness and ignorance permeates public opinion too and only serves to exacerbate the difficulty of poor identification and the adequate collection and recording of disability hate crime. This ignorance or lack of awareness must be overcome by society and by organisations as together they can influence a sea change in the way we identify and understand disability hate crime.

It is our shared values and behaviour that can alter public opinion thereby making our communities safer and our public services more effective. This can be achieved by organisations supporting their staff through awareness training, designing multi-agency teams that understand the causes and symptoms of disability hate crime and valuing the experience of people who are its victims. Senior managers should also provide safe and supportive environments for staff to discuss the emotional and psychological impact in situations where they may have been involved directly or indirectly, especially in cases of poor standards of care. Staff should be valued and supported to raise concerns and encouraged to speak out.[1]

Leadership with a purpose

Effective leadership on this issue from organisations such as the police, NHS, social services and education is a major concern that must be addressed. Collaboration and shared leadership underpinned by a joint strategic approach will facilitate a trajectory for disability hate crime that is multi-agency focused. Establishing such a trajectory can create a working environment that leads to greater staff awareness and understanding about the wider causes of hate crime both within and outside their specific areas of expertise. This in turn may also lead to a wider application of the definition of harm used in safeguarding to a generic set of characteristics that indicate the possibility of a disability hate crime being committed which requires further investigation.

However, laudable as this approach may sound, one must also appreciate the difficulty and complexity that surrounds it because of the different service and personal environments in which harm, abuse and violence may take place. Prior to the Care Act (2014) the legal framework for the protection of adults was fragmented and lacked a co-ordinated and systematic approach. This has been

---

1   The appointment of 'freedom to speak out ambassadors' in the NHS is one of the recommendations in *Freedom to Speak Up – An Independent Review into creating an open and honest reporting culture in the NHS* (Department of Health 2015).

addressed in law and means that for the first time key organisations and individuals responsible for adult safeguarding should agree on how they must work together and what roles they must play to keep adults at risk safe.

The Care Act (2014), safeguarding and disability hate crime

Safeguarding is the process of protecting adults with care and support needs from abuse or neglect. It is an important part of what many public services do, and a key responsibility of local authorities. Safeguarding is mainly aimed at people with care and support needs who may be in vulnerable circumstances and at risk of abuse or neglect by others. Since this definition also includes disability then why is it that disability hate crime is not considered within the same context as safeguarding?

The Care Act (2014) sets out a clear legal framework for how local authorities and other parts of the health and care system should protect persons at risk of abuse or neglect. This means, for the first time in law, key organisations and individuals responsible for safeguarding can agree on how they must work together and what roles they must play to keep at risk adults and children safe. This presents an excellent opportunity for organisations to work together to develop a common framework that aligns hate crime to safeguarding children and vulnerable adults.

By adopting a process of association, it is possible to show that terms such as 'harm' used in the safeguarding process have shared domains with the characteristics that also evidence disability hate crime. If we accept that the shared characteristics of 'harm' include: harassment and bullying, physical, emotional or sexual abuse, neglect and violence that can lead to physical and emotional trauma and even death, then it is possible to agree that safeguarding and disability hate crime are close relatives.

This analysis may appear far too simplistic to address the 'blurred lines' that exist to separate safeguarding from hate crime. However, recent changes in law now provide a legal framework for police, health and social workers to produce that clarity leading to a clear picture of the situation in which suspected abuse and neglect takes place that is shared and owned by them.

The characteristics that underpin harm become the trajectory that captures information about suspected disability hate crime within the safeguarding process rather than treating it as an isolated issue. So when an adult with care and support needs is suspected to be at risk of abuse or neglect this also prompts a key line of inquiry that includes suspected disability hate crime. This means that it is the person's disability that is the primary factor that incites acts of hatred towards them and by default this behaviour must be considered a safeguarding concern and attributed to a disability hate crime.

The trajectory should be used in the NHS and in primary care to help staff reframe certain events and acts of suspected 'harm' into suspected acts of disability hate crime. So if a disabled person presents at the accident and emergency department with an unexplained injury or bruising, staff need to feel confident that this injury was not sustained as an act of abuse, neglect or hate. Any suspicion should trigger an alert for safeguarding but also a red flag to explore a suspected hate crime. In general practice, if a looked-after person presents with distressing behaviour that appears different from their normal behaviour, this may also alert the GP to suspect a safeguarding concern, once again the same protocol may trigger a similar red flag alert. One of the key challenges here for staff to recognise is that some people with intellectual disability may find it difficult to communicate what has happened to them and may also not realise that such behaviour is a crime. It is important that NHS Trusts and general practices identify a main lead who can deal with hate crime and provide access to a psychiatrist or psychologist trained to assist in the disclosure process and trained to interview them appropriately.

This function is built into the new role of the Safeguarding Adults Board (SAB) which should involve regular meetings between the local authority, the NHS and the police to discuss and act upon local safeguarding issues; it should develop shared plans for safeguarding and working with local people to decide how best to protect adults in vulnerable situations. Importantly, it should publish a safeguarding plan and report to the public annually on its progress, so that different organisations can make sure they are working together in the best way. In the future this collaboration will ensure that safeguarding and disability hate crime is 'everyone's business'.

Greater awareness of the alignment between safeguarding policy and hate crime and the pooling of information between key organisations may also lead to better personal outcomes for disabled people and their carers through a needs assessment or a timely review of an existing care plan.

This approach may have prevented the unforgivable treatment and abuse by uncaring staff towards people with a learning disability at Winterbourne View. The harm inflicted upon them through routine abuse and violence is characteristic of the trajectory of harm. In this situation Safeguarding Adults Reviews (SARs) will also provide robust tools that can protect vulnerable people from hate crime, abuse or neglect by responding strongly when there is a failure in safeguarding. They also provide a context for mutual learning between key organisations by presenting a forensic approach to understanding what went wrong. This is important because evidence suggests it is the failure to deconstruct the warning signs from previous inquiry recommendations about the treatment and care of people with learning disability in the NHS and social care settings that may explain why lessons have not been learnt.

In 2007, following the deaths of six people with a learning disability in the care of the NHS, Mencap published their report *Death by Indifference*. It provided an insight into the differential care and treatment of people with learning disabilities and their experience of poor standards of care, which ultimately led to their premature death. The report illustrates the 'invisibility' of people with learning disabilities and provides a useful context to explore a wider debate about institutional discrimination and its relationship to disability related hate crime through neglect, abuse and patient harm.

The Mencap report suggests that these cases represent a systematic failure, where institutional discrimination and neglect have led to premature and avoidable deaths. In response to this report an independent inquiry, chaired by Sir Jonathan Michael, was set up to investigate access to healthcare for people with learning disabilities. Its findings (2008) concur with those identified by Mencap with regard to patient safety and also some more general concerns such as the fact that people with learning disabilities have higher levels of unmet needs and receive less effective treatment despite the legislation. People with learning disabilities find it harder to access treatment and assessment for health problems. It also found that there is insufficient adjustment to support equal treatment, and communication problems and anxieties are not addressed appropriately. Carers also experienced poor treatment and found that their opinions were ignored and complaints about the care received by the cared-for person were not heard.

Fundamentally, the NHS and social services are perceived to be failing disabled people and there remains widespread concern that this lack of focus is increasingly compromising the health and well-being of disabled people being cared for in these institutions.

The report recommendations by Sir Jonathan Michael (2008) were the catalyst for the confidential inquiry into the premature deaths of people with learning disabilities (CIPOLD). Its aim was to review the patterns of care that people received in the period leading up to their deaths, to identify errors or omissions contributing to these deaths, to illustrate evidence of good practice and to provide improved evidence on avoiding premature death.

The CIPOLD findings were reported in March 2013 and in its foreword the inquiry team said that they 'hoped that the lessons from *Death by Indifference* will have been learnt and that the recommendations of Sir Jonathan Michael will have been implemented'. NHS staff, students and trainees work to the highest standards to deliver safe and high-quality care for all patients. However, the serious care failings at Mid-Staffordshire NHS Foundation Trust and at the residential care home for people with learning disabilities, Winterbourne View, have shown that the NHS and other social care organisations still have some way to go before public confidence in the ability of caring institutions to provide effective, safe, personal and equitable care can be restored.

Caring with compassion in the NHS

Concerns about the lack of pace and motivation in the NHS in particular to implement the inquiry's recommendations continue to be aired. While there has been a specific focus on patient safety and quality improvement in response to the Francis Report (Department of Health) (2013) and Berwick (2013) overall, here remains a significant gap about what needs to be done regarding the protection and safety of disabled people in health and social care institutions.

Sir Robert Francis QC, has provided a powerful insight into a culture of a 'care system which ignored the warning signs and put corporate self interest and cost control ahead of patients and their safety' (Clwyd and Hart 2013, p.5). His challenge has been resolutely clear that:

> If there is one lesson to be learnt, it is, that people must always come before numbers. It is the individual experiences that lie behind statistics and benchmarks and action plans that really matter, and that is what must never be forgotten when policies are being made and implemented. (Francis 2010, p.4)

The NHS Constitution: 'Our values are our behaviour'

The NHS Constitution is a legal document that consists of a common set of principles, values and responsibilities that bind together organisations that provide NHS services with the community and people it serves, with patients, with the public and its staff. In its opening statement it says:

> The NHS belongs to the people. It is there to improve our health and wellbeing, supporting us to keep mentally and physically well, to get better when we are ill and, when we cannot fully recover, to stay as well as we can to the end of our lives. It works at the limits of science – bringing the highest levels of human knowledge and skill to save lives and improve health. It touches our lives at times of basic human need, when care and compassion are what matter most.

'Every one counts', 'dignity and respect' and 'care and compassion' are three of the core values that the NHS Constitution commends. It is when we are at our most vulnerable, often described as the 'defining moment for patients', that we rightly expect to be treated with dignity and respect, care and compassion, to have our voices heard and to feel confident that the people providing care are trained, qualified and supported to do so in an environment that puts the needs of its patients first.

Ensuring healthcare professionals are trained not only to treat and cure, but also to show empathy and compassion is absolutely critical to our experience. This is especially true for patients with disabilities and in the context of this chapter, this is essential to understanding the impact of hate crime on the psychological well-being and personal safety of disabled people in the care-giving environment.

Knowledge transfer and learning through practice

We need to see greater organisational leadership that visibly and proactively seeks alignment to the social model of disability, safeguarding and the trajectory of harm. This can be achieved by staff engagement that encourages learning through knowledge transfer between health and social care organisations including education, the police and the criminal justice system. The ability of government agencies to recognise the harm caused by the harassment of disabled people is supported by the findings from the EHRC Inquiry mentioned in Chapter 2. The Care Act (2014) also suggests that government departments need to work much more collaboratively to optimise their ability to communicate and assess risk and implement prevention strategies that significantly reduce harm. The checklist below identifies some of the key areas that require further attention and focus:

- Improve awareness of disability hate crime; understand what it is and its impact on the well-being of disabled people through staff training and education.

- Use leadership for a purpose to promote the social model of disability with the trajectory of harm and the process of safeguarding.

- Use existing safeguarding partnership arrangements and involve disabled people in service redesign, service improvement and other interventions designed to improve overall care.

- Provide appropriate support to staff and service users/carers/patients at the time of disclosure; enhance existing procedures to support this change.

- Raise staff and patient awareness, with advice on how to stay safe.

- Challenge public attitudes and tolerance for violence against people with disabilities.

- Use the opportunities provided by the Care Act (2014) to align safeguarding with disability hate crime.

- Culture change – encourage reference to the NHS Constitution as an important signpost to get the values and behaviours right.

- Be sensitive and provide support for staff who may be victims themselves by improving workplace safety.

- Embed disability hate crime into CQUIN[2], PROMs[3] and QUIPP[4] standards.

- Integrate and co-ordinate 'care pathways' to identify early warning signs of disability hate crime.

---

2   CQUIN is the commissioning for quality and innovation payments framework set up in 2009/10 to encourage care providers to share and continually improve how care is delivered and to achieve transparency and overall improvement in healthcare and the patient experience.

3   PROMs (Patient reported outcome measures) is a common set of measures used in the NHS to assess and compare through peer review the impact of healthcare on a patient's health and experience.

4   QUIPP (Quality, Innovation. Productivity and Prevention initiative) is an umbrella term to describe the approach the NHS is taking to provide high quality, person-centered and safer care for all, delivered with greater efficiency.

- Enable better tracking of cases across the system by introducing early warning indicators and flagging disability hate crime related incidents.

- Provide an open transparent learning environment that encourages the reporting of hate crime.

- Develop the safeguarding infrastructure to accommodate the standards expected from the Care Quality Commission and its new duty to investigate failing caring institutions.

- Use complaints and positive stories to improve support services and the overall quality of care experienced by disabled people, carers and families.

This discussion has shown that some organisations and the staff who work within them have been slow paced or absent in acknowledging that disabled people in their care may have experienced hate crime. This may have occurred either directly through mistreatment and poor care from a staff member or indirectly, from someone outside of the service. Whatever the explanation, much more needs to be done to identify and recognise disability hate crime when it is occurring and to provide staff with adequate training and support to reduce the risk of disabled people becoming victims, suffering harm, abuse or neglect and experiencing poor standards of care.

Raising awareness about disability hate crime alone will not be enough to prevent it from happening again. However, all journeys begin with the first step and it will be the learning from tragic deaths such as Francecca Hardwick and Fiona Pilkington that will make a difference to our professional practice, our understanding about disability hate crime and why it is our collective professional responsibility to recognise that 'it's everybody's business' to do something about it.

To conclude this discussion a framework for action in the form of an aide memoir is provided. It is hoped that organisations and professionals will use this information to take forward some of the key questions and challenges discussed in this chapter.

The vision

Understanding a disability hate crime – a framework for action

- Disability hate crime is a safeguarding issue – Commit to reduce avoidable harm, neglect and abuse by showing zero tolerance to disability hate crime.

- Holding up the mirror – Ensure your organisation is held to account for highlighting risks, acting on the feedback from disabled people, carers and by constantly measuring, monitoring and reporting how safe services are.

- Honesty – Encourage staff to raise concerns, promote a transparent environment, tackle disability hate crime in the same way as patient safety issues and support staff to be candid with patients and their families if something goes wrong.

- Motivation – Lead through collaborative models of learning, so that conditions constantly improve to redress reporting incidents and improvements are made across all of the local services that disabled people and their families use.

- Leadership – Help staff understand why things go wrong and how to put them right at times of disclosure. Give staff the time and support to improve professionalism and feel valued.

The action framework
PREVENTION

- Raise public awareness, with advice on how to stay safe.

- Encourage, value and support staff to speak out and raise concerns.

- Co-design a culture of safety and learning with staff, patients, carers and families.

- Challenge attitudes and tolerance of violence against disabled people.

- Improve access to treatment for victims and also offenders.

- Improve collaboration through multi-agency working and multi-professional learning.

IDENTIFICATION AND TRAINING

- Provide a supportive disclosure process for staff trained to work with people with intellectual disability.

- Embed a red flag or trigger for disability hate crime as part of the safeguarding protocol and procedure in accident and emergency departments and in primary care.

- Link this to Crime and Disorder Reduction Partnerships to enhance public safety (red flags), consider other entry points, such as 'True Vision' (see Chapter 16).

- Consider and plan for implications such as capacity and informed consent.

- Raise awareness about crime and abuse in care settings.

  ◦ Provide staff training and education to understand how to identify victims of violence and know how to offer appropriate interventions, including disclosure and onward referral.

  ◦ Include disability hate crime in core curricula for all health and social care staff including undergraduate and postgraduate training.

WORKING WITH KEY PARTNERS

- Arrange multi-agency conferences.

- Work with Safeguarding Adults Boards.

- 'Nothing about us, without us' – involve victims of disability hate crime and relevant key stakeholders to improve design and planning of services.

- Consult with and build on existing partnership arrangements with Learning Disability Partnership Boards.

- Promote collaborative partnerships and share learning between the Department of Health, Public Health England, NHS England and the Care Quality Commission.

PROFESSIONALISM AND WORKFORCE

- Acknowledge professionalism in the context of values based practice and support the commitment made by Health Education England to recruit for an NHS workforce with the right values and behaviours.

- Identify a named person to lead on reporting disability hate crime.

- Improve recognition of staff discomfort due to a lack of knowledge of the issues around violence, and of practical ways to support victims.

- Provide staff training and education to understand how to identify victims of violence and know how to offer appropriate interventions, including disclosure and onward referral.

- Include disability hate crime in core curricula for all health and social care staff including undergraduate and postgraduate training.

- Standardise crisis management, violence and abuse training, for health workers and student doctors, nurses and others.

- Update professional practice and (also legal) guidance.

- Define roles and responsibilities, with follow-up procedures.

DEVELOP KEY SERVICES AND CARE PATHWAYS

- These should include evaluation of interventions based on outcomes.

- Translation of good practice and effective tracking systems should be in place.

- Staff need support and time to understand issues surrounding disability hate crime.

- They should feel empowered, aware and trained in how and when to act.

INFORMATION SHARING (A CROSS-GOVERNMENTAL OUTLOOK)

This should involve:

- safety planning and risk management

- multi-agency conferences

- agreed and robust information-sharing protocols

- a third party reporting function to improve disclosure

- systematic analysis of informational trends

- learning from raising concerns reported regularly, to improve practice and develop a safety culture that generates change across all agencies.

References

Berwick, D. (2013) *A Promise to Learn – a Commitment to Act*. London: Department of Health.

Clwyd, A. and Hart, A. (2013) *A Review of the NHS Hospitals Complaint System: Putting Patients Back in the Picture (Final Report)*. London: Department of Health.

Department of Health (DH) (2009) (revised March 2013) NHS Constitution. London: Department of Health.

DH (2012) *Transforming Care: A National Response to the Winterbourne View Hospital Review. Final Report*. London: DH.

DH (2013) *Report of the Mid Staffordshire NHS Foundation Trust Public Inquiry Chaired by Robert Francis QC*. London: HMSO.

Disability Rights Commission (DRC) (2007) *A Formal Investigation into Physical Health Inequalities Experienced by People with Learning Disabilities and/or Mental Health Problems*. London: DRC.

Francis, R. (2010) *Independent Inquiry into care provided by Mid Staffordshire NHS Foundation Trust, January 2005–March 2009 Volume 1, Chaired by Robert Francis QC*. London: HMSO.

Francis, R. (2015) *Freedom to Speak Up – An independent review into creating an open and honest reportning culture in the NHS*. London: DH.

Mencap (2007) *Death by Indifference*. London: Mencap.

PART 3

DISABILITY HATE CRIME – LESSONS FROM OTHER DISCIPLINES

CHAPTER 9

RAPE AND SEXUAL ABUSE

DR CATHERINE WHITE OBE

Case studies

Clara is 53 years old with learning disabilities. She lives in a residential home. Her sister visits her every week and has noticed that Clara seems more distressed than usual when she leaves her at the end of a visit. When questioned, Clara becomes upset. She tells her sister that she doesn't like Derek, one of the care workers. She gives no reason why except that he does 'bad' things to her 'front bottom'. Clara is reluctant to undergo a forensic examination as she is frightened of doctors.

Stephanie is 19 with learning difficulties and lives with her mother. They are out shopping when Stephanie argues with her mum and storms off. Mum reports Stephanie as missing to the police. She is reunited with her mum after presenting in a chemist asking for tablets to stop her having a baby. Police investigations uncover that a stranger had found Stephanie upset in the street, taken her to his home and raped her before dropping her back off in the city centre. The male claimed all sexual activity was consensual. No prosecution followed as a decision that Stephanie would not be a strong witness was made by the lawyers.

Martin is a 44-year-old man with long-standing mental health problems and alcohol misuse. He has been in and out of state institutions including prison most of his life. He is currently living in a hostel. After a night of heavy drinking he presents with rectal bleeding and soreness. He has no memory of events. The two men he shares a room with are found to have images on their phones of themselves engaging in sexual activity with Martin. Martin does not wish to make a report to the police as he says he has had poor experiences in previous interactions with them.

Introduction

The above cases, whilst not real, are based on actual cases that have happened. They highlight some of the issues such as consent for sexual activity, disclosure, consent for examination, safeguarding issues and progress through the criminal justice system. From the cases above it can be seen that not only was the victim targeted because of their disability, they also face particular difficulties as a result. This chapter covers sexual violence with particular emphasis on instances where the victim has a disability.

There is no legal definition of disability hate crime. The criminal justice agencies use the following: 'Any criminal offence, which is perceived, by the victim or any other person, to be motivated by hostility or prejudice based on a person's disability or perceived disability' (True Vision n.d.).

In this chapter, sexual assault, sexual violence and sexual abuse are used interchangeably and not necessarily in their technical or legal definitions. In referring to the individual no one term is always correct. For the purposes of this chapter the term 'victim' will be used rather than 'patient', 'client' or 'complainant', 'survivor' etc; although it is acknowledged that false complaints are made.

In terms of the law, the Sexual Offences Act (2003) (England and Wales) is the basis of the legal terms relating to sexual assault referred to in this chapter. This would apply to offences committed (in England and Wales) after 1 May 2004. Prior to that, the Sexual Offences Act (1956) would apply. The 2003 Act covers numerous different offences including:

SECTION 1 (STATUTORY DEFINITION OF RAPE)

1. A person (A) commits an offence if:

    a. he intentionally penetrates the vagina, anus or mouth of another person (B) with his penis.

    b. does not consent to the penetration, and

    c. does not reasonably believe that B consents.

2. Whether a belief is reasonable is to be determined having regard to all the circumstances, including any steps A has taken to ascertain whether B consents.

SECTION 5 (STATUTORY DEFINITION OF RAPE OF A CHILD UNDER 13 YEARS)

1. A person commits an offence if:

    a. he intentionally penetrates the vagina, anus or mouth of another person with his penis, and

    b. the other person is under 13 years.

Sexual activity with a child under 16 is an offence, including non-contact activities such as involving children in watching sexual activities or in looking at sexual online images or taking part in their production, or encouraging children to behave in sexually inappropriate ways.

Prevalence

Governmental statistics published in 2013 provide the following:

> Based on aggregated data from the 'Crime Survey for England and Wales' in 2009/10, 2010/11 and 2011/12, on average, 2.5 per cent of females and 0.4 per cent of males said that they had been a victim of a sexual offence (including attempts) in the previous 12 months. This represents around 473,000 adults being victims of sexual offences (around 404,000 females and 72,000 males) on average per year. These experiences span the full spectrum of sexual offences, ranging from the most serious offences of rape and sexual assault, to other sexual offences like indecent exposure and unwanted touching. The vast majority of incidents reported by respondents to the survey fell into the other sexual offences category. (Ministry of Justice 2013, p.6)

It is estimated that 0.5 per cent of females report being a victim of the most serious offences of rape or sexual assault by penetration in the previous 12 months, equivalent to around 85,000 victims on average per year. Among males, less than 0.1 per cent (around 12,000) report being a victim of the same types of offences in the previous 12 months.

Around 1 in 20 females (aged 16 to 59) reported being a victim of a most serious sexual offence since the age of 16. Extending this to include other sexual offences such as sexual threats, unwanted touching or indecent exposure, this increased to one in five females reporting being a victim since the age of 16.

Around 90 per cent of victims of the most serious sexual offences in the previous year knew the perpetrator, compared with less than half for other sexual offences.

Females who had reported being victims of the most serious sexual offences in the last year were asked, regarding the most recent incident, whether or not they had reported the incident to the police. Only 15 per cent of victims of such offences said that they had done so. Frequently cited reasons for not reporting the crime were that it was 'embarrassing', they 'didn't think the police could do much to help', that the incident was 'too trivial or not worth reporting', or that they saw it as a 'private/family matter and not police business'.

In 2011/12, the police recorded a total of 53,700 sexual offences across England and Wales. The most serious sexual offences of 'rape' (16,000 offences) and 'sexual assault' (22,100 offences) accounted for 71 per cent of sexual offences recorded by the police.

Prevalence of sexual violence against people with disabilities

There have been numerous studies that have shown that people with learning disabilities are more vulnerable to being victims of sexual violence. A 2012 World Health Organisation (WHO) funded systematic review indicated that children with disabilities are 3.7 times more likely than non-disabled children to be victims of any sort of violence, 3.6 times more likely to be victims of physical violence, and 2.9 times more likely to be victims of sexual violence (Hughes *et al.* 2012; James *et al.* 2012; World Health Organisation 2012). Children with mental or intellectual impairments appear to be among the most vulnerable, with 4.6 times the risk of sexual violence compared with their non-disabled peers. Adults with disabilities are 1.5 times more likely to be victims of violence than those without a disability.

There are several factors which result in people with disabilities being at increased risk of sexual abuse:

- stigma
- discrimination
- ignorance about disability
- lack of social support for those who care for them
- placement of people with disabilities in institutions
- communication impairments which hamper their ability to disclose abusive experiences.

Sexual violence and abuse may result in severe and long-lasting harm to victims across a range of health, social and economic factors. In addition it can worsen the impact of inequalities to which people with disabilities are already vulnerable. Long-term effects can include mental health problems such as depression, anxiety, post-traumatic stress disorder, psychosis, drug and substance misuse, self-harm and suicide.

The Duluth Model[1] was developed to help understand and reduce interpersonal violence (domestic violence against women). Studying the Power and Control Wheel (Figure 9.1) it is easy to see how vulnerable any person with a disability would be to abuse.

---

1   See www.theduluthmodel.org/about/index.html for more information.

Figure 9.1 The Power and Control Wheel

Reproduced with permission from the Domestic Abuse
Intervention Project (www.duluth-model.org).

The needs of a sexual violence victim

Each victim will have different needs. This will depend not only upon characteristics relating to a given individual but also the context of the abuse, for example the needs of a victim of a one-off stranger assault are likely to be different from that of a victim of chronic abuse at the hands of a carer, and the needs of a child will differ from the needs of an adult etc.

Not all victims will present directly or immediately (see Figure 9.2).

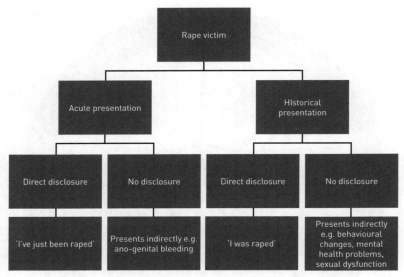

Figure 9.2 Rape victims and their routes
to disclosure/non-disclosure

People with disabilities are more likely to fall into the non-disclosure camps. This may be for a number of reasons including:

- a lack of appreciation that they are actually a victim in terms of either not understanding what is happening to them and or not understanding that it is illegal

- absence or lack of education regarding sexual matters

- lack of opportunities to disclose, for example if in an institution or under the control of an abusive carer such as a family member

- communication difficulties

- dependence on the abuser with conflicting emotions

- fear of retribution, stigma

- lack of awareness of professionals regarding possible presentations of sexual violence.

Even if the victim does disclose they still face many barriers and challenges including:

- inability or unwillingness of others to accept the allegations
- inability of professionals to view the victim as a credible witness meaning that cases are not pursued through the criminal justice process
- communication difficulties.

Should a victim be identified then their needs should be assessed under the following considerations:

- medical
- forensic
- psychological
- safeguarding
- practical.

In addition, consideration should be given to any public interest issues. This is particularly necessary where other vulnerable people may be at risk from the abuser. More detail regarding these considerations follows.

Medical

This would include assessment and treatment where necessary for injuries, emergency contraception, pregnancy, post-exposure prophylaxis for sexually transmitted infections including HIV, Hepatitis B, drug and alcohol issues.

Forensic

Documentation of any injuries, including photo documentation where appropriate, should be carried out. Evidence, including trace evidence such as DNA, should be preserved and allegations should be documented. All this is to be done in a manner that makes any such evidence admissible to a court. The Faculty of Forensic and Legal Medicine has produced *Recommendations for the Collection of Forensic Specimens from Complainants and Suspects* (2014). These are updated twice a year and are available on their website along with numerous other guidelines, proforma and body maps to aid the documentation of injuries. These give guidance regarding samples in terms of what to take, and when to take it, and how to take and store samples.

It should be noted that whilst some rape victims will suffer horrific injuries, the vast majority will not. Most victims will either not sustain any injuries at all or the injuries will be of a minor nature and will heal rapidly leaving no scars. This is true even with chronic repeated abuse. This is an important concept to appreciate as it follows that lack of injury should not necessarily negate any allegation.

Psychological

This should include a risk assessment of mental health including suicide and self-harm risk.

SUICIDE RISK ASSESSMENT

Table 9.1 Suicide risk assessment, high-risk and low-risk factors

High-risk factors
Are you thinking about suicide?
Do you have a specific plan to kill yourself?
Do you have access to any of these methods?
Are you suffering from mental health problems?
Do you feel that the future is hopeless and that things cannot improve?
Have you ever self-harmed or attempted suicide in the past?
Lower-risk factors
What methods have you considered?
Do you have a date or place in mind?
Do you have thoughts about harming yourself?
Has anyone in your family died by suicide?
Have you suffered from mental health problems in the past?

Have you ever had contact with mental health services or seen your GP in relation to psychological or psychiatric problems?

Are you taking any medication for mental health problems?

Do you have a problem with drugs or alcohol?

Have you been drinking in the past few hours?

Are you experiencing particular difficulties in your life or struggling to deal with difficult past events (e.g. bereavement, divorce, running away from home)?

Do you have friends or family you can turn to for help?

Table adapted from The Faculty of Forensic and Legal Medicine (n.d.) *Suicide Prevention and Assessment Aide-Memoire.* Oxford: Oxford University.

Safeguarding

Local safeguarding protocols should be followed. Consideration must be given to both immediate and longer-term safety of the victim. Also there should be consideration as to whether or not others are at risk, for example children or vulnerable adults. Many victims will be victims of other types of abuse as well as sexual abuse. It is also often the case that whilst the presenting assault is due to one offender, the victim is also at risk of abuse by someone else, for example domestic violence in their relationship. This should form part of their assessment with appropriate action where necessary, for example DASH[2] (Domestic Abuse, Stalking and 'Honour'-based violence risk identification checklist) and MARAC (multi-agency risk assessment conference) referrals.

In recent years there has been greater awareness of child sexual exploitation (CSE) with several reports having been published by the Office of the Children's Commissioner.[3] Various tools have been developed to assist professionals to identify CSE. One such is *Spotting the Signs* a proforma produced by BASHH and Brook in 2014.

---

2   See CAADA (Co-ordinated action against domestic abuse) for resources (www.caada.org.uk/index.html).
3   Inquiry into Child Sexual Exploitation in Gangs and Groups (CSEGG) see www.childrenscommissioner.gov.uk/info/content/publications/content_743.

Practical

There may be a need for clothing, housing, care of pets, transport etc.

What a Sexual Assault Referral Centre can offer

An ideal way of taking this holistic view would be for the victim to be seen in a Sexual Assault Referral Centre (SARC). They are able to provide specially trained staff, including forensic physicians, support workers, ISVAs (independent sexual violence advisers) and counsellors as well as having strong links with local safeguarding teams, genito-urinary medicine, witness support and the criminal justice process etc. In the UK contact details for SARCs can be found on the NHS Choices website.[4]

The initial assessment of the victim should bear in mind fundamental principles of care (Table 9.2):

Table 9.2 The fundamental principals of care

What does a victim of sexual violence need?
To be shown respect and compassion
To have their privacy protected as much as possible
To feel safe
To have power and control over what happens to them
To have a voice
To feel listened to and be treated in a non-judgemental manner
To be reassured that they are not to blame; the attacker is at fault, not them
To have their options (for example, any likely procedures) explained to them in a clear and objective manner

Consent and capacity assessment

A key aspect of sexual violence is that, during the assault, power and control has been taken away from the victim. It is important to give back this power and control to the victim as much as possible. Consent is a central tenet of medical treatment and must be

---

4   See www.nhs.uk.chq/pages/2482.aspx.

respected. In cases of sexual violence any medical assessment will tend to have both therapeutic and forensic components. In England and Wales the Mental Capacity Act (2005) (MCA) applies to all victims aged 16 years or over. The MCA is very clear that there should be a presumption that all adults (aged over 16 years) must be assumed to have capacity unless it can be established that this is not the case. For people with a disability, physical as well as mental, there has been a tendency for professionals and the public to underestimate their capabilities and make decisions for them. The MCA sets out to protect against this. It also sets out a framework to provide protection for people who are unable to make decisions for themselves in terms of procedures for making decisions on behalf of people who lack mental capacity. For victims under 16 years old consideration should still be given to whether or not they have capacity and this is often referred to as Gillick competency.[5]

The General Medical Council (2008) has produced guidance on issues of consent and confidentiality. The latter is particularly pertinent where vulnerable victims are concerned as it may be that other vulnerable people are at risk. Disclosure of personal information without the patient's consent may be necessary if failure to do so would leave others exposed to a risk so serious that it outweighs the patient's and the public interest in maintaining confidentiality. The Faculty of Forensic and Legal Medicine (2011) has produced guidance: 'Consent from patients who may have been seriously assaulted'. Many institutions have developed proforma when undertaking a mental capacity and best interest assessment.

The criminal justice process

The attrition rate for sexual violence is often used as a political football and generates much debate and attention. In terms of the care of victims, the outcomes of the criminal justice process should not be the only consideration.

---

5   See www.nspcc.org.uk/preventing-abuse/child-protection-system/legal-definition-child-rights-law/gillick-competency-fraser-guidelines/ for information about Gillick competency.

The Youth Justice and Criminal Evidence Act (1999) (YJCEA)[6] introduced 'special measures' as a series of provisions that help vulnerable and intimidated witnesses give their best evidence in court.

Vulnerable witnesses are defined by Section 16 of the YJCEA as:

- all child witnesses (under 18); and
- any witness whose quality of evidence is likely to be diminished because they:
  - are suffering from a mental disorder (as defined by the Mental Health Act 1983)
  - have a significant impairment of intelligence and social functioning
  - have a physical disability or are suffering from a physical disorder.

With the agreement of the court these special measures can be made available to vulnerable and intimidated witnesses and include:

- screens to shield the witness from the defendant
- live link; this enables a witness to give evidence during a trial outside of the court via a televised link
- evidence given in private; here members of the public and press may be excluded from the court room
- removal of wigs and gowns by judges and barristers
- video-recorded interview; this may be done with the vulnerable witness before the trial and then admitted by the court as the witness's evidence-in-chief
- use of an intermediary to assist the witness giving evidence at court and also to provide communication assistance in the investigation stage; the intermediary is allowed to explain questions or answers so far as is necessary to enable them to be understood by the witness or the questioner without changing the substance of the evidence

---

6   Youth Justice and Criminal Evidence Act (1999) (see www.legislation.gov. uk/ukpga/1999/23/contents).

- aids to communication; these may be permitted to enable a witness to give best evidence whether through a communicator or interpreter, or through a communication aid or technique, provided that the communication can be independently verified and understood by the court.

In addition to special measures, the YJCEA (1999) also contains the following provisions intended to enable vulnerable or intimidated witnesses to give their best evidence:

- Mandatory protection of witness from cross-examination by the accused in person: a prohibition on an unrepresented defendant from cross-examining vulnerable child and adult victims in certain classes of cases involving sexual offences.

- Discretionary protection of witness from cross-examination by the accused in person: in other types of offence, the court has a discretion to prohibit an unrepresented defendant from cross-examining the victim in person.

- Restrictions on evidence and questions about the complainant's sexual behaviour: the Act restricts the circumstances in which the defence can bring evidence about the sexual behaviour of a complainant in cases of rape and other sexual offences.

- Reporting restrictions: the Act provides for restrictions on the reporting by the media, of information likely to lead to the identification of certain adult witnesses in criminal proceedings.

At the time of writing a pilot scheme is underway for pre-recorded cross-examination of vulnerable witnesses. This is Section 28 of the YJCEA (1999). It is hoped that this will improve the court process for vulnerable witnesses as it will allow them to give evidence in surroundings deemed less intimidating than the court room and also be questioned at a time closer to the events in question (Stevenson and Valley 2014).

The CPS has produced guidance regarding all of these special measures for victims, witnesses and professionals.[7]

Myths and stereotypes regarding sexual violence

These are numerous and exist for many reasons, some anthropological, religious or cultural, but many are the result of sheer ignorance. See Table 9.3 for some examples.

Table 9.3 Some myths and truths regarding sexual violence

Myths	Is this true?
Most rapists are strangers	No. Most victims will know their abuser.
Most abuse takes place outside the home.	No. Most abuse takes place where the victim lives. This is especially true of child victims.
Rape victims will have injuries.	No. Most will not, and those injuries that do happen often heal quickly and fully leaving no scars.
Rape victims will disclose the abuse at the earliest opportunity.	No. Many never disclose at all. A significant number of those that do disclose will do so well after the attack and may only give partial details.
Some rape victims must shoulder responsibility for the abuse.	No. The rapist is responsible for his own actions.
Men cannot be raped.	No. Men and boys can be victims of sexual violence.

Key recommendations

There is still much to be done for rape victims in general but by definition vulnerable people need even greater protection.

---

7   Crown Prosecution Service (n.d.) *Special measures: help with giving evidence.* Available at www.cps.gov.uk/victims_witnesses/going_to_court/vulnerable. html.

Acceptance

Society must accept that:

- Sexual violence happens and it is always wrong.

- Vulnerable people are at higher risk than others of becoming a victim.

- Vulnerable people have the same rights as others and are deserving of protection and advocacy.

Prevention

Sexual violence is endemic in all societies. Measures to reduce the opportunities and circumstances that abusers require to commit these crimes should be maximised. This may include enhanced thorough vetting for those with access to the vulnerable.

There should be transparency of systems of recording and reporting allegations of and also suspicions of abuse. Many offenders are repeat offenders and therefore apprehending them for one crime will help prevent future offending.

Given some of the recent high-profile disclosures of historical abuse there is currently a debate about whether there should always be mandatory reporting. The evidence base around the benefits and pitfalls of mandatory reporting is lacking but what is clear is that the answer is unlikely to be simple (Wallace and Bunting 2007).

Campaigns such as PANTS[8] by NSPCC and Mencap try to encourage parents to protect children by talking to them about keeping safe.

NSPCC: THE UNDERWEAR RULE

PANTS stands for:

- **P**rivates are private.

- **A**lways remember your body belongs to you.

- **N**o means no.

---

8   See 'The Underwear Rule' by the NSPCC at www.nspcc.org.uk/preventing-abuse/keeping-children-safe/underwear-rule/.

- Talk about secrets that upset you.
- Speak up, someone can help.

Awareness of abuse

Professionals should have:

- a greater understanding of the prevalence and presentation of sexual abuse

- a high level of suspicion (and should include sexual violence in the differential diagnosis of a wide range of presentations rather than relying on direct disclosure)

- greater confidence in identifying individuals with learning disabilities and then improved skills in communicating with those identified

- knowledge of safeguarding referral processes, reporting systems and resources for victims and carers (such as SARCs)

- greater understanding of disability hate crimes and how they impact on victims and society.

Accessibility of services

Professional responses and local resources should be accessible and suitable for all victims. Vulnerable victims may be unable to read, unable to access the internet or access websites etc. in order to obtain the help that they require. Organisations such as CHANGE, a national human rights organisation led by disabled people, have produced clear guidelines on how organisations should produce documents and information in accessible, easy-to-read text with pictures.[9]

Vulnerable victims may not have the means to physically access resources, for example they may not be able to access public transport independently. When providing any resource these barriers should be considered and removed or minimised.

---

9   See www.changepeople.org/downloads/CHANGE_How_to_Make_Info_ Accessible_guide_2009.pdf.

Police and prosecutors must cease to concentrate on the perceived weakness of witnesses' credibility but focus instead on case building and the characteristics of the suspect.

Sexual violence is a pervasive problem in all strata of society but is especially a problem for the vulnerable such as those with disability. It is incumbent upon a civilised society to protect this group and respond appropriately and with vigour when necessary.

References

BASHH and Brook (2014) *Spotting the Signs: A National Proforma for Identifying Risk of Child Sexual Exploitation in Sexual Health Services.* Compiled by Dr Karen Rogstad and Georgia Johnston. Available at www.fsrh.org/pdfs/SpottingTheSignsNationalProforma.pdf, accessed on 17 October 2014.

Crown Prosecution Service (CPS) (2010) *CPS Policy for Prosecuting Cases of Disability Hate Crime.* London: CPS.

CPS (2014) *Special measures – help with giving evidence.* Available at www.cps.gov.uk/victims_witnesses/going_to_court/vulnerable.html, accessed on 24 October 2014.

Faculty of Forensic and Legal Medicine (2011) *Consent from patients who may have been seriously assaulted.* Available at http://fflm.ac.uk/upload/documents/1311675189.pdf, accessed on 24 October 2014.

Faculty of Forensic and Legal Medicine (2014) *Recommendations for the Collection of Forensic Specimens from Complainants and Suspects.* Available at http://fflm.ac.uk/upload/documents/1404142708.pdf, accessed on 24 October 2014.

Faculty of Forensic and Legal Medicine (n.d.) *Suicide Prevention and Assessment Aide-Memoire.* Available at http://fflm.ac.uk/upload/documents/1383570602.pdf, accessed on 24 December 2014.

General Medical Council (2008) *Consent: patients and doctors making decisions together.* Available at www.gmc-uk.org/guidance/ethical_guidance/consent_guidance_index.asp, accessed on 24 October 2014.

General Medical Council (2014) *Confidentiality guidance: disclosures to protect others.* Available at www.gmc-uk.org/guidance/ethical_guidance/confidentiality_53_56_disclosures_to_protect_others.asp, accessed on 24 October 2014.

Hughes, K., Bellis, M. A., Jones, L., Wood, S., *et al.* (2012) 'Prevalence and risk of violence against adults with disabilities: A systematic review and meta-analysis of observational studies.' *The Lancet 379,* 9826, 1621–1629. Available at www.thelancet.com/journals/lancet/article/PIIS0140-6736(11)61851-5/abstract, accessed on 17 October 2014.

Jones, L, Bellis, M., Wood, S., Hughes, K. *et al.* (2012) 'Prevalence and risk of violence against children with disabilities: A systematic review and meta-analysis of observational studies.' *The Lancet 380*, 9845, 899–907. Available at http://dx.doi.org/10.1016/S0140-6736(12)60692-8, accessed on 17 October 2014.

Ministry of Justice, Home Office and the Office for National Statistics (2013) *An Overview of Sexual Offending in England and Wales.* London: Office for National Statistics. Available at www.gov.uk/government/uploads/system/uploads/attachment_data/file/214970/sexual-offending-overview-jan-2013.pdf, accessed on 4 December 2014.

Stern, V. (2010) *The Stern Review: A Report of an Independent Review into How Rape Complaints are Handled by Public Authorities in England and Wales.* London: Home Office.

Stevenson, M. and Valley, H. (2014) 'Pre-recorded cross-examination.' *Criminal Law and Justice Weekly 178*, 21. Available at www.25bedfordrow.com/news-pdfs/crime-bulletin-june-2014.pdf, accessed on 17 October 2014.

True Vision (n.d.) *The Agreed Definition of 'Monitored Hate Crime' for England, Wales and Northen Ireland.* Available at http://www.report-it.org.uk/files/hate_crime_definitions_-_v3_0.pdf, accessed on 12 February 2015.

Wallace, I. and Bunting, L. (2007) *An Examination of Local, National and International Arrangements for the Mandatory Reporting of Child Abuse: The Implications for Northern Ireland.* NSPCC NI Policy and Research Unit. Available at www.parliament.nz/resource/mi-nz/49SCSS_EVI_00DBHOH_BILL 10599_1_A193838/81b970577b60456ba029626e2187d5912da5b50d, accessed on 17 October 2014.

World Health Organisation (2012) *Prevalence and Risk of Violence against Adults with Disabilities: A Systematic Review and Meta-Analysis of Observational Studies.* Geneva: WHO. (Summary also available: 'Violence against adults and children with disabilities'.) Available at www.who.int/disabilities/violence/en, accessed on 17 October 2014.

CHAPTER 10

COMBATTING HOSTILITY THROUGH EDUCATION – THE SOPHIE LANCASTER FOUNDATION

SYLVIA LANCASTER OBE

My name is Sylvia Lancaster although these days I am more often than not called 'Sophie's mum'. It is a strange tautology that once again I become validated through my daughter's name. I suppose my story starts in 2007. I worked as a Connexions adviser, a service that grew out of the careers service. I was an 'intensive adviser' who worked with young people from the age of 13 up until 25, if the person had 'special needs'. My caseload was mostly made up of young offenders, drug users, the homeless, those excluded from school and teenage pregnancies. I also worked in three local high schools providing one-to-one support for young people who were having difficulties in school.

It became very apparent to me that young people who belonged to Alternative Subcultures were in the majority when it came to problems. Alternative Subcultures is a term used to cover Goths, Emos, Metallers, Moshers, Skaters, Punks etc. They would tell me about the bullying they received, not just from their peer groups but also from teachers. Comments such as 'Well, if they didn't dress like that they wouldn't get bullied' were often bandied about, particularly by teachers. I had two 'Alternative' young people at home and it used to upset me that Alternatives were often seen as 'other'.

The other section of young people in schools would often use the term 'Dirty Mosher' which was seen as a derogatory term. I would challenge their use of language and would question them about the meaning of this term, often being told that Alternatives didn't wash, always wore black, looked scary and one young person even told me that he didn't like them because they drank babies' blood. It became patently obvious to me that something needed to be done to help young people overcome what seemed to me to be irrational and groundless prejudice. I thought about the issues, probably for six months, and then decided that perhaps the best way of combatting this would be to take my daughter Sophie into youth clubs and let young people see her for what she was, a lovely, kind, funny, intelligent young woman, certainly no one to be scared of.

The Connexions centre in which I was based became a third party reporting centre for hate crime. As part of this procedure I attended a training session on hate crime and I remember whilst sitting there listening it suddenly struck me that Alternatives fitted into these categories. They had a shared communality, shared norms and values, history of intolerance and prejudice, so why shouldn't they be covered as well? I obviously needed to think about work that in my own mind needed to be done.

My daughter Sophie and her partner Rob were attacked in a park in Bacup on 11 August 2007. Sophie was a little dot of a girl, five foot one and she weighed about eight and a half stone. Sophie and Rob had been out to a friend's house and on their way home they called into a local garage to buy some cigarettes. Whilst there they met two young men, one of whom they had met previously and one who stated that he didn't want anything to do with them because, in his words, 'They looked a state.'

Sophie and Rob were chatting happily and went with this young man to meet other friends of his, mostly young females. They went into Stubbylee Park with this group of young people, chatting happily, and a group of five teenage boys came into the park; they did not know Sophie and Rob nor did they speak to them. One of the boys said 'let's bang the Moshers' and so they attacked Rob. They jumped and stamped on his head and face and Sophie went to help him. Two of the five then attacked Sophie.

Whilst in hospital with Sophie, I decided that 'enough is enough' and that I needed to do something about the situation, obviously not wanting anyone else to have to go through what she and Rob had been through. My first thought was to set up a charity using Sophie's name. My friend Odette Freeman was supporting me during the time I spent in hospital with Sophie. Odette was obviously not allowed into the Intensive Care Unit and so spent many hours sat outside. She came up with a strapline 'Stamp Out Prejudice Hatred and Intolerance Everywhere (S.O.P.H.I.E.)'. This has become our logo and our 'mission statement'.

The Foundation are very proud of our logo and our supporters from all over the world send us pictures of the tattoos they have created from it.

My view is that young people are not naturally intolerant to people who are different; they learn intolerance or have it instilled in them. I genuinely believe that if we get to young people, using compelling messages and demonstrating the human tragedy of such hostility, we can work to reverse this hostility, at least some of the time. It is clear to me that our work has benefit for all of the groups of 'others' including young disabled people.

It took 13 days for Sophie to die and the important message to get out there to young people is 'you choose to jump and stamp on people's head and face, they don't just slip away, it is a disgusting and totally undignified process'. Our message to young people is to stop and think before they act, because next time it could be them, their sister or girlfriend.

My main aim after Sophie's death was to campaign to get her case tried using the existing hate crime legislation. I went to speak to an old friend Kate Conboy-Greenwood and discussed the position with her. We then started working towards 'Making a Noise'. Whitby Goths, an annual gathering of Alternatives, sent messages of support and put an e-petition on the internet stating that in their opinion, Sophie and Rob's attack was a hate crime. At that time we managed to get 7500 signatures, always being aware that we needed 150,000 to force a parliamentary debate; it was a start.

I decided that family and friends needed to get together and celebrate Sophie's life. In order to achieve this, it had to be done in a way that she would have loved and approved of. We decided to have a gig where local bands would play and carry on the theme of 'Making a Noise'. We set up a 'MySpace' internet site so that the bands could talk to each other. Kate monitored this quite closely and started to answer people who left messages of support and condolences. Interspersed with these messages, people also came and told their stories of how they had been attacked because of their appearance and they told of the bigotry and hostility they faced. It seemed to me that it was imperative that we, as a Foundation, develop an educational process in whatever form that takes, to go into schools, prisons, colleges etc. and get the message out there to as many young people as possible.

During this early phase of working out what our aims and objectives would be, we received an email from a company based in Leeds called Propaganda. They explained that the director of the company was setting up a makeup company and he felt that our ethos and theirs merged together and therefore he would like to talk to us. We went to meet Julian Kynaston in a hotel in Huddersfield and he told us about his makeup company called Illamasqua. Illamasqua is makeup with a difference, it is about celebrating your inner beauty, celebrating who you are and being proud to stand out from the crowd…exactly the message our Foundation had started to promote.

Julian is obviously a business man first and foremost and recognised that we could work together and build a brand loyalty. He has been a stalwart support for us ever since.

The Foundation developed our aims and objectives:

1. To create a lasting legacy to Sophie.

2. To provide educational group-work that will challenge the prejudice and intolerance towards people from Alternative Subcultures.

3. To campaign to have the UK hate crime legislation extended to include people from Alternative Subcultures, lifestyle and dress code.

Julian helped us create our branding: for instance our posters, leaflets based on our logo and Sophie's image. We always use red and black when we undertake our work, to create a strong identity. Our office is also the same colours. It is important that people by a mere glance can recognise who and what you stand for. In

London when in taxis and chatting to people, explaining why I am in London, I very often get comments from people about 'the Goth girl' or 'the girl in red'. That shows the importance of brand – they may not always recognise our name but our posters and image sticks in their minds.

When we were developing our approaches we also discussed our hopes of developing some form of educational resource to enable us to work in schools. Julian put us in touch with Tony from Huthwaites International; they are an international 'blue-chip' training company. Meetings were held and after discussion the format was decided. Huthwaites wrote the content that was extrapolated from their research into verbal behaviour and used the lessons learned from many years' experience in handling behaviour change projects.

We developed the S.O.P.H.I.E. game which includes two packs of 30 cards, the first with images only of 'different' people, around a third being 'Alternative', the others including disabled people, covering the other 'hate crime strands'.

Once again Julian and Propaganda helped and produced for us an animation depicting the events of the night of 11 August. The result is a beautifully crafted film. The art work was undertaken by a French graphic designer called Fursy T with Mark Williams as the director. The film was premiered on MTV and caused a sensation. It ramps up empathy levels particularly when used with young people in schools and you can actually feel the temperature in the hall or classroom drop when using it. The film is called *Dark Angel* and the music was very kindly given to us by Portishead.

We offer schools a choice of presentations usually done by myself or using the S.O.P.H.I.E. game as a workshop, usually undertaken by Kate and Stacey Elder, the third member of staff to join the Foundation. The resource can be used flexibly in tackling issues around bullying, body image, equality and diversity. We always try to encourage teachers to develop the game further. It has been used across the curriculum in various subject areas including drama, English, Personal, Social, Health and Economic Education (PSHE) and 'off timetable' curriculum days where it has been used during Anti-Bullying and Holocaust Remembrance days. We are also asked into schools and colleges as part of the work being done on equality and diversity.

We are finding that within schools young people know not to talk inappropriately about race, disability or homosexuality; this is obviously due to the work that has been undertaken in schools around these subjects and that has to be applauded. Kate and Stacey use the game by getting young people to pick two people out of the pack of 30 cards who they do not want to spend time with. They then write their thoughts down on a roll of wallpaper. What they do comment on are the pictures that show the Alternatives. Initially using terms such as: 'evil', 'freaks', 'self-harm', 'ugly', 'scary', 'creepy' and 'horrid clothes'.

We then show the videos to introduce Sophie's story and then work with the young people to overcome their preconceptions and to value rather than fear difference. I have been heartened by how successful the training is and how well it is received by staff and young people whether they feel themselves to be an 'other' or not.

The short-term impact of the work when using the resource can be seen from the comments from various schools:

@sophie_charity since the assembly, I have thought a lot about how I judge strangers. This will never happen again # [name of school] academy #thanks

Stacy. Everything is fine miss has sorted it out and i have u to thank.

Thank u for being there xxxxxxxx

I'm part of one of the 'Emo' groups of the year 10s in [name of school], and we're very thankful to the message that was given to our year today, hopefully it opened the eyes of the people who like to skit us for being 'Emo' and thinking that self harm is a joke.

Thank you had a brilliant hour listening, made me think and change.

We know from comments from teachers that the impact we have after delivery is impressive; many young people come and join our Facebook page and help fundraise for us. Recently we have worked extensively with Greater Manchester Police and have presented in many schools in their area. Garry Shewhan, an Assistant Chief Constable said, 'The work of the Foundation in our schools has been both impactful and impressive and has led us to become the first force in the UK to monitor hate crime on Alternatives.'

The Foundation's work is currently being evaluated by Dr Stephen James Minton CPsychol AFBPsS from Trinity College, Dublin to ascertain long-term impact.

We have a Facebook page with over 62,000 likes and our success can be seen on this page. Whenever we work in a school many of the young people come to us afterwards and thank us for the work we are doing, many of them telling us that they feel safer now. That can only be positive.

Work surrounding hate crime is not and should never be seen as a tick-box exercise, but an area of work that needs to be delivered with passion and a clear message to people that hostility and bigotry is not acceptable and that there is a will within society to deal with these crimes seriously.

Statistics show that hate crime is vastly under-reported, particularly disability hate crime, and we always urge people to report incidents. I believe that the way forward for all strands is for our resource to be embedded within the curriculum. We know that our input in schools works, not just for 'Alternaphobia' as we can and do get the message across for all types of hate crime. It may have different stories in the background but the message is the same: we all have a right to live our lives free from abuse, whether you are disabled or an Alternative.

The work of the Foundation has always been based on my previous experiences. Whilst working for Connexions and the Youth Service I saw too many agencies working in areas that they had no understanding of, spouting statistics at young people, and it was apparent to me that this approach was not working. In order to impart information to them in a relevant and meaningful way it has be presented in an engaging and interactive manner.

A criticism to be levelled at governments regardless of who is in power is their short-term viewpoint. They seem to be enthusiastic about certain issues, for example NEETs (young people not in education, employment or training), gender, Entry to Employment programmes, and they bombard agencies working in these areas with lots of money then suddenly cut funding and then move on to the next development, often not giving projects the time needed to work effectively or pushing masses of funding to agencies, but where is the accountability?

Hostility and bigotry in all forms have to be eradicated within society. I believe that the hatred shown to people who are disabled, in whatever form that takes, preys upon some of the most vulnerable within society. Government has a role to ensure that initiatives to combat this are the norm, rather than the exception.

I believe that charities, or 'civil society' as some people call them, have a key role to play in helping to educate out hostility from young people. Maybe in a perfect world programmes like ours would be part of the curriculum, but even if they were, I don't think there are many teachers, who have no direct experience of hate crime, who could get the message over to young people the way that a well-motivated individual can when they have a direct experience to share. Key to winning over the 'hearts' of the young people is to make them emotionally moved by the horrors suffered by the victim and to help them realise the harm such hostility causes to people. I believe the best way of achieving this is to have a genuine partnership between the educators and foundations such as ours.

As I mentioned above, one of our key objectives is to try to change legislation and criminal justice policy. In practice we lobby for change at a national and local level. My message to similar charities is that they need to make the links where decisions are made. We sit on the government's Hate Crime Independent Advisory Group which provides an influence over national policy but we recognise that school governance is largely held at local or county level. We have to make the links and form relationships wherever it makes a difference, whether that is a single youth club or a cross-government programme.

The Sophie Lancaster Foundation has shown that we can combat hostility from young people and whilst we will never know the number of people who are prevented from the horrors suffered by Sophie and Rob, we know it works and we can not ease up in our efforts.

More details of the Sophie Lancaster Foundation can be found at www.sophielancasterfoundation.com.

CHAPTER 11

UNIVERSITY LIFE
A TIME OF CHANGE

BOB MUNN

Going to university or college is a time of significant change for young people – going away to university or college even more so. Familiar people, surroundings and practices are replaced by new ones, and young people have to find their place in their new environment or, more accurately, construct their place in it. For example, they may choose to be known by a new name or a new form of their old name as they explore and develop their identity. Meanwhile, they may find that their old environment changes too, which can contribute to feelings of insecurity.

All of these factors apply with extra force to disabled students. They move from a home environment where support systems have been built up over a lengthy period, to an environment where support may have to be developed from scratch. Informal support from family and friends who are used to them as individuals is no longer readily available.

University and college students typically constitute a large and identifiable group that may not always enjoy good relations with the communities where they live, reflecting the 'town and gown' division. Students may experience hostility and, in an unwelcoming environment, disabled students may be subject to additional pressures and even hate crime.

Disabled students in higher education

Fortunately, universities and colleges take seriously their responsibilities to disabled students. They have professional support staff who provide or facilitate access to specialist resources and, as educational establishments, they are conscious of the need to make teaching and learning materials fully accessible. They make special arrangements for academic assessments and they work hard to make the whole academic community aware of how it should support disabled students. Disabled students are typically offered priority access to shared accommodation, where the other residents provide a built-in community for students that can help to replace the one they have moved from.

The UK Quality Assurance Agency for Higher Education (QAA) has issued advice on provision for disabled students, initially as Section 3 of its *Code of Practice for the Assurance of Academic Quality and Standards in Higher Education* (QAA 2001) The whole Code of Practice has now been superseded by the Higher Education Quality Code (QAA 2012), in which advice on provision for disabled students is now embedded in every section, rather than being hived off into a separate section where it risked being overlooked. For the benefit of the steering group overseeing the introduction of the Quality Code (of which I am a member), a detailed mapping was prepared showing where each clause from Section 3 of the Code of Practice is reflected in the Quality Code, thus confirming that nothing has been lost and that everything is presented in the most relevant place or places.

Support in the UK specifically for disabled students used to be provided by Skill: National Bureau for Students with Disabilities. Unfortunately, Skill closed in 2011, but some of its functions including work on policy and campaigns have been taken over by Disability Rights UK, formed in 2012.

All this is fine, but all students take time settling in and things can go wrong. Disabled students are of course not obliged to declare their disability and some may arrive with an undeclared but visible impairment for which the university or college is obliged to make provision, and that may take time. Sometimes students may decide not to declare an invisible impairment (even though that is necessary for them to receive the Disabled Students' Allowances) so as to avoid being labelled as disabled (Department for Innovation, Universities and Skills (DIUS) 2009). This can reflect a typical wish to make a new start, encouraged by self-confidence based on good support previously experienced at home – but students may not fully appreciate how much they have relied on such support and still need it. An example is the student who left his assessment of dyslexia at home, thinking he had somehow left his dyslexia at home as well; he struggled to cope with his academic work until eventually he told his tutor about his dyslexia and was offered the support he needed to demonstrate his full ability.

Experiences of disabled students in higher education

There are certainly positive stories from disabled students in higher education, for example the wheelchair user who said she had had not experienced any hate crime, having found students and staff to be very helpful, friendly and inclusive (Bond 2011). Her college and university had been very supportive and had made adjustments to her needs where necessary. However, not all disabled students report so favourably on their experiences. The higher education community accepts its legal responsibilities and certainly tries to provide a caring environment for all students, but even if most people are well-meaning, they may be unthinking.

The experiences of disabled students among others in higher education are a frequent subject of study and such studies typically report not only on immediate educational questions, but also on social ones. Even so, an early detailed study had little to say that might bear on the question of hate incidents and quoted a student who had at first been nervous about fitting in, saying, 'I think if anyone turned round and shouted at me I would say it was because of me and not because of any disability' (Hall and Tinklin 1998, p.63). A later broad study (Jacklin *et al.* 2007, p.31) did quote a student with mental health issues who had experienced a 'lack of understanding among students and staff, and obnoxious, snooty or rough students who see people like me as too weak, pathetic and inferior to be worthy of them.'

The National Union of Students (NUS) invites disabled students to submit articles to it about their experiences. One such article (NUS 2008) describes a student's 'huge shock' at being diagnosed with dyslexia, dyscalculia and dyspraxia in his second year at university. He became president of the students' union, but felt that on the whole the university management dismissed his passion and commitment because of what he saw as a few mistakes in written materials: 'To be looked down upon instead of listened to is wrong'. Because reading and following papers for meetings took him a long time, he had to develop the confidence to ask people to slow down and respect his needs. He felt that if the university examined its approach it might understand why disabled students didn't always disclose their disability. He didn't want sympathy, just respect and tolerance, and for people to realise that barriers could be dismantled within institutions through educating those who – he was willing to concede – might simply not understand.

This account chimes with the experience of a student who strongly resisted a diagnosis of dyslexia in her second year because of the stigma she felt it would bring. When eventually and reluctantly she accepted the diagnosis and the support offered, her grades went from mediocre to very good. Incidentally, what these stories illustrate is the important role that academic and professional support staff in higher education institutions play in monitoring students' academic performance. As part of their role in helping all students to succeed academically, they should identify when poor performance may be attributable to disability and point the students concerned towards relevant specialist practitioners.

National Union of Students report

Recently NUS, supported by the Home Office, has published four reports based on a comprehensive survey that explored the experiences of hate incidents and crime among students (National Union of Students 2011). The report on disability hate was based on responses from 1001 students who identified themselves as disabled among the total sample of 9229. About two-thirds of the respondents were at university, most of them in England. The rest of this section is based on information extracted from the NUS report.

A third of respondents with a physical impairment and a quarter of those with a sensory impairment were worried about being subject to abuse. This was higher than for other groups of disabled respondents, presumably because physical and sensory impairments are often immediately apparent. Over 40 per cent of disabled students altered their behaviour or personal appearance in an attempt to avoid hate incidents. This often meant going out less, which could lead to social isolation. Some tried to conceal their impairment (for example by doing without walking aids), even though that could cause them actual pain.

Eight per cent of disabled respondents said that they had experienced at least one hate incident that they believed was motivated by prejudice against their disability. Respondents with physical and sensory impairments were significantly more likely to experience disability-related prejudice than respondents with other impairments, again presumably because their impairment was more visible.

A quarter of students with a physical impairment and 15 per cent with a sensory impairment stated that they had experienced anti-social behaviour or crime motivated by a prejudice against their disability; for respondents with a mental health condition or a learning disability, the proportions were both 12 per cent. Verbal abuse was the most common incident reported in the survey, although students had also been subject to physical abuse, material loss or offensive written materials. Abuse was commonest in and around the place of study, whereas material loss tended to occur near the place of residence.

Students who experienced disability hate incidents were more likely to be repeatedly victimised than those who had experienced incidents unconnected with disability. This is consistent with other findings that many disabled people experience repeat harassment (Equality and Human Rights Commission (EHRC) 2011).

Unfortunately, reporting levels of disability hate crime and hate incidents were low. Only a fifth of disability hate incidents were reported to an official at the university or college and only 12 per cent to the police. The response of the institution could be very positive, whereas that of the police could sometimes be rather dismissive. Students who did not report an incident to the police mostly thought that they would be ineffective or that it was not serious enough. Other reasons for not reporting included shame and fear of reprisals.

The perpetrators of the crimes were typically of student age but not known to the student and in two-thirds of cases acted with others. Over half were identified as students, of whom 85 per cent were students at the same institution as the disabled student. This obviously presented particular problems when the disabled student might meet them subsequently.

Victims of harassment and crime often suffer beyond its immediate effects and the proportion of disabled students affected was several times greater than for other students in the survey. Disabled students were four times as likely to suffer from mental health issues such as depression and symptoms of post-traumatic stress such as panic attacks – half of them had such issues – and six times more likely to become less accepting of other groups. They were three times as likely to have experienced financial problems and four times as likely to have suffered academic problems – which affected a quarter of them. Many thought of leaving their studies or transferring to another institution.

The smaller picture

The low level of reporting of disability hate crime incidents in higher education means that the problem has a low profile. For example, no such incidents came to my attention during the five years when I was Dean of University of Manchester Institute of Science and Technology (UMIST) and later during the three years when I was Vice-President for Teaching and Learning at the University of Manchester and therefore in each case was specifically concerned with the student experience.

Since the University of Manchester is the largest campus university in the UK, situated near the centre of a city that is not obviously more virtuous than any other large city, one would not expect a particularly small number of disability-related hate crimes against students. Perhaps the incidence has grown significantly since I retired in 2007. However, the experienced head of the disability support office at the University of Manchester does not recall any later incidents of hate directed towards students because of disability (private communication). I am confident that no one in that position would be complacent about the experiences of disabled students and perhaps there were incidents that were reported elsewhere in the university (for example, at a hall of residence), but if there were problems, they seem not to have come to the attention of the disability support office.

However, it is worth noting that the absolute numbers could be quite small even at a large university. In the NUS survey (NUS 2011), 11 per cent of students reported themselves as having some disability; at the University of Manchester, with some 40,000 students, 11 per cent is about 4500 students. Of the 11 per cent in the survey, eight per cent had experienced a disability-related hate incident at some time during their study, which would correspond to 360 students out of 4500. Of that eight per cent, only 20 per cent had reported the incident to the institution, which would correspond to 72 students out of 360. So, if the proportions in the whole NUS survey applied to the large student body at the University of Manchester, there would only be a relatively small number of reports. Note that the NUS survey asked students about their experience while they were at their current institution, so that these reports of incidents would be spread over a period of three or four years. Of course, each separate incident is one too many, because it represents a significant adverse experience for the disabled student. Nevertheless, it is easy to imagine that this number of incidents – at most one report a week – might not be noticed in aggregate, especially if they were encountered as isolated incidents by different people in various locations across a whole large university.

Conclusions

It may be hoped that the measures taken by universities and colleges are effective, not only in supporting disabled students in their educational and social needs as intended but also, incidentally, in shielding them from some of the less attractive aspects of the external environment. Living in accommodation shared with other students who provide a ready-made social group is a help and study is generally experienced in an intelligent and generally supportive group. Nevertheless, students report that they do experience disability-related hate crime and incidents both where they live and where they study and that other students are often the perpetrators.

However, disabled students are reluctant to report incidents and so the evidence available to institutions is more limited than it might be. As the NUS survey (NUS 2011) shows, an absence of evidence is not evidence of absence. The external environment can be uncomfortable for any students, and not least for disabled students, but systematic under-reporting of hate incidents and crime against disabled students makes remedies harder to seek.

Both the EHRC report (2011) and the NUS report (NUS 2011) make a large number of recommendations. From among these, three broad priority areas are identified below for practitioners in universities and colleges to consider. However, although practitioners whose special responsibility is support for disabled students need to raise many of these matters – and to keep raising them if they feel the response is inadequate – many others need to be aware of the same matters and accept responsibility where they can make improvements. A further consideration is that universities and colleges are large institutions, the size of small towns, and they are complex institutions that operate differing administrative and academic structures within which some roles may be extensively devolved. Therefore it is often not possible to specify exactly which post-holder needs to take action: in one institution it might be the Director of the Student Experience and in another the Dean of Students. With that caveat, the priority areas are as follows:

Increased awareness

Leadership teams in institutions need to take systematic steps to make the whole academic community aware of disability hate crime and the disproportionately severe adverse effects it has. Apart from how they affect the disabled students, these effects are also directly important for institutions, given that adverse academic and other consequences can feed through into poorer retention, progression and graduation statistics.

These performance indicators reflect on the effectiveness of office-holders such as heads of department and deans, who therefore need to take ownership of the problem and make it clear to everyone that they will not tolerate any level of disability hate crime.

To back this up, those responsible for regulations and student charters should ensure that such documents make this zero-tolerance approach clear. Correspondingly, staff in departments of student affairs, those with pastoral responsibility for student accommodation, and students' union leaders need to actively foster good relations among all students so that they look out for each other.

Governing bodies of institutions should also ensure that disability hate awareness is explicitly covered within the structures through which they address their responsibilities under the Equality Act (2010). Those who organise induction for students should ensure that printed and electronic materials make it clear to disabled students where in the institution or in the students' union they can easily access help and support if they experience hate incidents.

Increased reporting

Disabled students and those who represent them such as students' union officers need to encourage reporting of even minor incidents. Otherwise, the scale of the problem is masked and therefore the scale of the response is likely to be inadequate. In particular:

- Those responsible for the student experience should ensure that reporting is made easy through a variety of channels where students are reassured that they will be treated sensitively and effective action will be taken.

- Those who operate these channels need to be committed to the task and held to account by their managers for how well they perform it.

- Leadership teams in institutions should also designate a central office where information on all incidents is collated, wherever and however the initial report was received. Monitoring the resulting improved statistics can then help to suggest what further action may be needed and where.

• Governing bodies of institutions should expect regular reports on these statistics and the actions taken in response to them as part of the way in which they and the leadership team reflect on the institution's performance in relation to the Equality Act (2010).

Increased response

Given that nearly half of the perpetrators of these crimes were students at the same institution as the disabled student, those responsible for regulations should check that their internal disciplinary codes for students explicitly mention sanctions against disability hate incidents.

Leadership teams in institutions need to establish and publicise clear protocols designed to make the response to any such incidents consistent, prompt and effective.

Senior staff in institutions responsible for liaison with the local police should alert them to the issue of disability hate crime, either directly in relation to specific matters or perhaps through the police and crime commissioner in relation to police policy, and emphasise their concern that all reports of incidents should be treated sensitively and pursued vigorously. Otherwise, students will continue to doubt whether reporting is worthwhile and efforts to increase it will be negated.

Overall, disability-related hate crime against disabled students is, like that against all disabled people, *Hidden in Plain Sight* as the EHRC report (2011) puts it. It is like text printed in a pale colour on a pale background, easy to overlook and hard to read. A wide range of people in universities and colleges need to turn up the contrast and bring the issue into sharp relief so that it is more visible. Then it can be tackled more effectively and disabled students can flourish academically and socially in tolerant and inclusive higher education communities.

References

Bond, J. (2011) 'Quarter of physically disabled students are victims of hate crime.' *The Oxford Student* (online), 27 December, 2011. Available at ocfordstudent. com/2011/12/27, accessed on 9 February 2015.

Deparment for Innovation, Universities and Skills (DIUS) (2009) *Disabled Students and Higher Education.* DIUS Research Report 09-06. London: DIUS.

Equality and Human Rights Commission (EHRC) (2011) *Hidden in Plain Sight: Inquiry into Disability-Related Harassment.* London: EHRC. Available at www.equalityhumanrights.com/uploaded_files/disabilityfi/ehrc_hidden_in_ plain_sight_3.pdf, accessed on 17 October 2014.

Hall, J. and Tinklin, T. (1998) *Students First: The Experiences of Disabled Students in Higher Education.* SCRE Research Report No. 85. Edinburgh: Scottish Council for Research in Education.

Jacklin, A., Robinson, C., O'Meara, L. and Harris, A. (2007) *Improving the Experiences of Disabled Students in Higher Education.* York: The Higher Education Academy.

National Union of Students (NUS) (2008) *A day in the life of Darren Batey.* London: National Union of Students. Available at www.nus.org.uk/en/news/ a-day-in-the-life, accessed on 26 November 2014.

NUS (2011) *No Place for Hate. Hate crimes and incidents in further and higher education: disability.* London:NUS. Available at www.nus.org.uk/ PageFiles/12238/2011_NUS_no_Place_for_Hate_Disability.pdf, accessed on 9 February 2015.

Quality Assurance Agency (QAA) (2001) *Code of Practice for the Assurance of Academic Quality and Standards in Higher Education.* Section 3: Disabled students. Revised February 2010, updated March 2010. Gloucester: QAA.

QAA (2012) *The UK Quality Code for Higher Education: A Brief Guide.* Gloucester: QAA.

CHAPTER 12

REGULATING HEALTH AND SOCIAL CARE

PAUL FREDERICKS

Are lessons learnt?

How could this have happened? This is the question that is so often asked in the aftermath of a serious case, or cases. Far too commonly we hear a spokesperson offer a 'sincere' apology for an organisation's failings to act to protect the vulnerable. This apology is followed by a commitment to 'learn the lessons' to ensure that such a failing does not happen again. All too frequently cases do happen again either involving the same organisations or others that have not picked up on the lessons to be learnt. Why is this?

To obtain an answer we will turn to the findings of two recent high-profile cases, Winterbourne View and the Mid-Staffordshire NHS Foundation Trust. These cases highlight where there have been system failures and as a consequence some of the most vulnerable in our society have suffered abuse and neglect.

The outcomes from these cases have implications that should influence and impact on the way individuals and organisations identify and prevent cases of disability hate crime.

Winterbourne View

Winterbourne View opened in December 2006 and was a private hospital operated by Castlebeck Care Limited. It was registered with the Healthcare Commission and from May 2009 with the Care Quality Commission (CQC), with the stated purpose of providing assessment and treatment and rehabilitation for people with learning difficulties.

In May 2011 the BBC *Panorama* programme reported on the abuse of patients at Winterbourne View. A journalist, Joe Casey, spent five weeks filming covertly at the hospital, and said:

> The hitting, slapping, bullying, dousing with water, cruel and often pointless use of physical restraint on people – many with a child-like understanding of the world – all happened in front of my eyes.
>
> On a near-daily basis, I watched as some of the very people entrusted with the care of society's most vulnerable targeted patients – often, it seemed, for their own amusement. They are scenes of torment that are not easily forgotten.[1]

The CQC's internal report, *Internal Management Review of the Regulation of Winterbourne View*, identifies over a dozen regulatory engagements with the hospital between December 2006 and May 2011, of these nine involved announced and unannounced inspection visits by the Healthcare Commission, Mental Health Act Commissioner and the CQC.

In September 2007 the Mental Health Act Commissioner visited Winterbourne View and spoke to eight detained patients, as well as the Responsible Medical Officer and other staff at the hospital. Nine recommendations were made as a result of this visit.

The CQC's internal report identifies that in the year April 2009 to March 2010 there were seven notifications made to the regulator under Section 28 of the Private and Voluntary Health Care (England) Regulations (2001). This regulation provides for the notification of events or incidents which may have directly affected the safety of patients. Of the seven reports, five related to complaints about abuse to patients including a report of an incident that was witnessed by a consultant psychiatrist when a member of the care staff was seen to 'yank a patient forcefully, forcefully push a patient and then shout at them'.

For a number of these incidents referrals and notifications were made to the police and/or the South Gloucestershire Adult

---

1   'Undercover reporter "haunted" by abuse of patients' (May 2011). Available at http://news.bbc.co.uk/panorama/hi/front_page/newsid_9501000/9501531. stm.

Safeguarding Team. Alarmingly, the CQC failed to follow up the outcomes of these alerts and therefore failed to formally sign off any agreed actions.

This lack of co-ordinated action by the regulators, adult safeguarding team and police resulted in missed opportunities to intervene and protect vulnerable patients. The need for such co-ordination has been recognised for a number of years, the Commission for Social Care Inspection 2008 report *Raising Voices* states:

> The systematic nature of effective safeguarding practice and the importance of co-operation between agencies and their staff are understood and increasingly central to effective practice. (2008, p.13)

One of the outcomes of the Winterbourne View case is a report from the Department of Health, *Transforming Care: A National Response to Winterbourne View* (2012). This report outlines a number of actions for health, local authority commissioners and regulators to work together to protect some of the most vulnerable people in our society. For example it asks for joint working between regulators:

> Ofsted, CQC, Her Majesty's Inspectorate of Constabulary (HMIC), Her Majesty's Inspectorate of Probation and Her Majesty's Inspectorate of Prisons will introduce a new joint inspection of multi-agency arrangements for the protection of children in England from June 2013. (2012, p.36)

Mid-Staffordshire NHS Foundation Trust Inquiry

During the same period that regulators were failing to respond to the warning signals at Winterbourne View there was an even more alarming situation occurring at Mid-Staffordshire NHS Hospital. In February 2013 Robert Francis QC published the *Report of the Mid-Staffordshire NHS Foundation Trust Public Inquiry*.

The Francis Report contains 290 recommendations and in the Executive Summary identified that: 'Between 2005 and 2008 conditions of appalling care were able to flourish in the main hospital serving the people of Stafford and its surrounding area' (p.7).

One of the most concerning aspects identified in the Francis Report is the failure of the system of regulation and the oversight by service commissioners who did not identify at an early stage the significant failings at Mid-Staffordshire. Indeed Francis attributes the identification of serious concern to the persistent complaints by patients and those close to them.

The failure of the regulatory system was not a consequence of lack of regulatory contact. The Inquiry report evidences frequent interaction from 2006 onwards, on a wide range of issues, between Mid-Staffordshire NHS Trust and the Healthcare Commission, and later the CQC. Other regulatory and supervisory bodies including Monitor, the Strategic Health Authority, the Primary Care Trusts (a commissioner of services) also interacted with the Trust and failed to identify or sufficiently address concerns over a prolonged period.

Francis identifies the failings of each regulatory and supervisory body and makes a number of recommendations pertinent to the way regulators operate in the future. Of particular interest are the recommendations relating to the way regulatory bodies gather and analyse information and how this is then used to inform engagement with other regulators.

The interaction between regulatory bodies is a common theme in Inquiry reports, for example the Shipman Inquiry[2] and the Victoria Climbié Inquiry.[3] Francis highlights the need for effective communication between regulators:

> Communication of intelligence between regulators needs to go further than sharing existing concerns identified as risks, and it should extend to all intelligence which when pieced together with that possessed by partner organisations may raise the level of concern. Too many assumptions were made that others

---

2   See http://webarchive.nationalarchives.gov.uk/20090808154959/http://www.
    the-shipman-inquiry.org.uk/reports.asp.

3   See www.dh.gov.uk/prod_consum_dh/groups/dh_digitalassets/documents/
    digitalasset/dh_110711.pdf.

would be aware of important information. (Para 1.67 summary report)

If the sharing of concerns is to be effective in identifying and tackling disability hate crime, regulators need to create an environment where individuals, friends, carers and the public have confidence that raising a concern will result in positive action.

A significant challenge to anyone wanting to raise a concern about potential or actual abuse is knowing the correct organisation to turn to. If regulators work more effectively together to respond to concerns, it would enable the 'regulatory system' to ensure that the correct agency was alerted to an issue.

Berwick Report

In August 2013 the National Advisory Group on the Safety of Patients in England, chaired by Professor Don Berwick, published their report *A Promise to Learn – A Commitment to Act*.[4] The role of the group was to study the recommendations from Francis and others to distil for government and the NHS the lessons learned and the changes that are needed to improve patient safety in the NHS.

A number of recommendations emanating from the report are equally relevant to tackling disability hate crime in the NHS and elsewhere. In particular the following:

- The NHS should continually and forever reduce patient harm by embracing wholeheartedly an ethic of learning.

- All organisations should seek out the patient and carer voice as an essential asset in monitoring the safety and quality of care.

- Supervisory and regulatory systems should be simple and clear. They should avoid diffusion of responsibility. They should be respectful of the good will and sound intention of the vast majority of staff. All incentives should point in the same direction.

---

4   See www.gov.uk/government/uploads/system/uploads/attachment_data/file/
226703/Berwick_Report.pdf.

The emphasis on developing a culture of learning and openness leading to staff being attuned to the views of people with disabilities, and their carers, would create an environment where disability hate crime would be identified earlier and victims would be heard and provided with appropriate support.

Government response

The government's response to the Mid-Staffordshire NHS Foundation Trust Public Inquiry is contained in *Hard Truths: A Journey to Putting Patients First*.[5] In addition to responding to the recommendations in the Francis Report, it also addresses the recommendations in the Berwick Report and other associated reports.

In the Foreword to *Hard Truths: A Journey to Putting Patients First*, the Secretary of State for Health, Jeremy Hunt MP, highlights the need for change, including:

- the need to hear the patient and see everything from their perspective

- the need to recognise the system providing care has extremes from excellent to unacceptably poor and that knowledge of how safe, or well run, organisations are should be shared with those using the services

- the need for stronger professional responsibility, the need to be open about mistakes and candid about 'near misses' should be clearly understood

- the need for proper accountability when things go wrong.

(2014, p.3)

The government's response recognises the importance of ensuring that those raising concerns about the quality of their care are heard and appropriate action is taken. Equally the professional responsibility of those providing care should lead to those

---

5   See www.gov.uk/government/uploads/system/uploads/attachment_data/file/ 270368/34658_Cm_8777_Vol_1_accessible.pdf.

witnessing failings in health and care systems being candid and raising their concerns with others.

Professional regulation

So far we have focused on the approach of systems regulatory bodies, as opposed to the regulation of professional activity. However, whilst systems regulators should be more alert to the information and intelligence they receive, the real opportunities for early intervention usually rest with professionals applying their individual judgement.

The Francis Report includes recommendations relating to professional regulation and those giving evidence to his Inquiry making reference to 'hindsight' and 'benefit of hindsight' on over 500 occasions. Drawing parallels to the Bristol Royal Infirmary Inquiry Report,[6] which stated that lessons needed to be learnt from the disaster to avoid a similar failing in care happening again, Francis goes on to differentiate between 'hindsight' and 'judgement'.

Any system of proportionate regulation is reliant on individual judgement being applied. Francis highlights the need for information to be fully considered when making decisions:

> a difference between a judgement which is hindered by understandable ignorance of particular information and a judgement clouded or hindered by a failure to accord an appropriate weight to facts which were known. (Department of Health 2013, p.24)

In looking at the opportunities to create an environment where victims of disability hate crime are identified earlier it is right to focus on the role of those professionals that interact with individuals. It is recognised that some victims of hate crime may have limited interaction with healthcare professionals but, however limited the engagement, it is incumbent on those providing care to consider if they are dealing with a victim.

The healthcare professional regulatory bodies all set out the expected standards of practice, but each places different emphasis

---

6   See http://webarchive.nationalarchives.gov.uk/20090811143745/http://www. bristol-inquiry.org.uk/index.htm.

on the need to act if it is considered that an individual is at risk of harm.

The General Medical Council sets out the principles and values on which good medical practice is founded.[7] This contains guidance on the duties of a doctor[8] which include: 'Make the care of your patient your first concern. Protect and promote the health of patients and the public'. Whereas the standards of conduct, performance and ethics for nurses and midwives produced by the Nursing and Midwifery Council (NMC)[9] go further and contain the duty to: 'Work with others to protect and promote the health and wellbeing of those in your care, their families and carers, and the wider community'. This goes on to say: 'You must make a referral to another practitioner when it is in the best interests of someone in your care.' Also one of the requirements developed from the NMC's principles is: 'You must disclose information if you believe someone may be at risk of harm, in line with the law of the country in which you are practising'.

Elsewhere in healthcare the approach is similar with the General Dental Council's standards for dental professionals requiring registrants to: 'co-operate with other members of the dental team and other healthcare colleagues in the interests of the patient'. The General Pharmaceutical Council produces standards of conduct, ethics and performance requiring registrants to: 'Take action to protect the well-being of patients and the public'. It goes on to say: 'If you need to, refer a patient to other health or social care professionals, or to other relevant organisations'.

From these few examples it can be seen that there is a different level of expectation on professionals to act if they feel that an individual is at risk of harm. It would be a significant step forward in the identification of victims of disability hate crime if healthcare professionals had an explicit duty, within their code of practice, to either act themselves or refer to others if they thought an individual had been harmed or was at risk of harm.

---

7   See www.gmc-uk.org/guidance/good_medical_practice.asp.
8   See www.gmc-uk.org/guidance/good_medical_practice/duties_of_a_doctor. asp.
9   See www.nmc-uk.org/Documents/Standards/The-code-A4-20100406.pdf.

Concerns and complaints

As highlighted earlier, in the Mid-Staffordshire Inquiry Report Francis recognises the persistence of those receiving poor care, their relatives and carers in ensuring that the failings at the hospital were acted upon.

There needs to be a cultural shift in the reaction of professionals and organisations to the receipt of complaints. The move to an environment where complaints are considered as a potential sign of system failings, or individual shortcomings, will also create opportunities for victims of disability hate crime, or those close to them, to share concerns with others.

Furthermore, enabling victims of disability hate crime, or their families and carers, to feel that they can raise concerns with others about the way someone is being treated will lead to greater openness and provide opportunities to address hate crimes at an early stage.

Role of the wider community

So far in this chapter we have focused primarily on the role of the health and social care regulator, and the regulation of healthcare professionals. This is due to the essential role that regulators could perform in changing the mindset of the regulated sector. Regulatory emphasis, be it system or professional, on the creation of requirements for individuals and organisations to be alert to the indications that an individual is a victim of disability hate crime will lead to an environment where hate crime is identified earlier.

Linked to this is the role that individuals and organisations in the wider community can play in supporting people with disabilities to raise concerns about the way they are being treated by others.

There are numerous not-for-profit organisations providing support, care and advocacy services and their staff, through their interactions, often form a close bond with vulnerable people. This creates an opportunity to identify when an individual is being subjected to abuse and to raise concerns with the relevant authorities on their behalf.

Recommendation 151 of the Mid-Staffordshire NHS Trust Inquiry Report relates to the way that MPs handle complaints from constituents and the potential opportunities to identify trends. Encouraging MPs to consider if issues raised with them relate to a disability hate crime will assist early intervention.

The Equality and Human Rights Commission (EHRC 2011) report *Hidden in Plain Sight* commented on the role of public authorities and the lack of confidence in those authorities:

> Respondents often said they did not feel they would be taken seriously if they reported an incident, and doubted that anything would be done, especially if the perpetrator couldn't be identified or the incident was a 'one-off'. (p.96)

Shifting the balance so that people with disabilities, their carers and advocates feel empowered to raise concerns and know that they will not be ignored is vital. As is the need for individuals within public bodies to be quick to refer concerns that are outside their remit to other relevant authorities.

Hindsight or foresight?

The continued reaction to an incident is to investigate what went wrong, thereby enabling 'lessons to be learnt'; in more significant cases an inquiry is held and recommendations produced. It is recognised that the process of trawling back through history to identify system or individual failings is a key element in seeking to establish what is required to prevent such an incident occurring in the future. Regulators take a retrospective view of the regulated sector and, in doing so, reinforce the message that what is important is past behaviours and actions. However, if the organisation or professional were encouraged to use foresight and consider what might occur in the future there is a greater opportunity to protect potential victims from hate crime and the misery associated with it.

If there is one lesson that needs to be learnt from past incidents it is that there should be greater emphasis on empowering individuals, carers and advocates to raise concerns. At the same time those receiving the concerns need to be more receptive to the potential consequences and apply foresight to enable early intervention by the appropriate authorities.

Outcomes for service users

The shift in regulatory approach across health and social care to focus on outcome regulation, where the regulator assesses the provider's delivery of services based on the outcomes experienced by service users, rightly shifts the burden of responsibility to providers to demonstrate compliance with standards. When the providers are delivering effective service this system has clear benefits and enables 'light touch regulation' and reduces the regulatory burden on providers.

However, unless the regulator develops effective systems to gather wider 'intelligence' about a provider, this one-size-fits-all approach to regulation has significant weaknesses. To work effectively the system is reliant on information from a range of sources being received and then appropriately assessed by the regulator, for example, concerns raised by service users or data from other regulatory authorities. It is, therefore, essential for regulators to be cognisant of all the factors that are impacting on service provision outcomes, especially the views and experiences of service users and their carers.

The CQC approach to outcome-focused regulation of safeguarding is set out in their *Essential Standards of Quality and Safety*.[10] Outcome 7 establishes the standard for 'safeguarding people who use services from abuse'. The standard is based on the requirement of Regulation 11 which states (p.92):

> The registered person must make suitable arrangements to ensure that service users are safeguarded against the risk of abuse by means of:
>
> 1. taking reasonable steps to identify the possibility of abuse and prevent it before it occurs; and
>
> 2. responding appropriately to any allegation of abuse.

The standard states that people who use services should have an experience where they 'are protected from abuse, or the risk of abuse, and their human rights are respected and upheld'. The standard

---

10 See www.cqc.org.uk/sites/default/files/media/documents/gac_-_dec_2011_update.pdf.

provides details of the outcomes required to achieve compliance with the standard. The CQC also provides a self-assessment supporting document.[11] This enables providers to assess their compliance against each aspect of Outcome 7.

For this approach to regulation to be successful in its aim of delivering improved outcomes for service users, it requires robust structures to identify those providers that are failing to respond appropriately to issues of non-compliance.

The findings of inquiries at Winterbourne View, Mid-Staffordshire NHS Foundation Trust and elsewhere have highlighted failings in the provider's quality assurance processes. It is universally recognised that failure to deliver appropriate care is unacceptable, but it is equally unacceptable for those tasked with the delivery of services not to have quality assurance systems that enable early intervention when care pathways are failing.

The new NHS structure in England aspires to deliver integrated care pathways with multi-disciplinary teams focusing on the needs of the individual. If this can be achieved it will undoubtedly make a significant difference to the provision of care, especially for the most vulnerable. However, the fundamental shift required to deliver this aspiration cannot be achieved by structural change alone. It requires a significant cultural shift, where those directly delivering care are empowered and feel valued, where service users are treated as individuals and where those unhappy with the standard of care they, or those close to them, receive know that their concerns will be acted upon.

Standards

Within health and social care provision there are a myriad of standards for both system and professional regulation; at the centre of these is the need to provide appropriate and safe care focused on the needs of the service user.

Standards undoubtedly have a key role in ensuring quality of service provision, but achieving compliance with a standard must

---

11   See www.cqc.org.uk/sites/default/files/media/documents/PCA_OUTCOME_
     7_new.doc.

not be the primary focus of the service provider. Aspiring to quality in service provision, with improved outcomes for service users is paramount. Taken at the most basic view it could be argued that the only standard that really matters is that of applying the test: 'Would I be happy if I, or someone close to me, was receiving this level of care or was treated in this way?' If everyone who delivered, commissioned, monitored and regulated services applied such a test and sought to attain the position where they could honestly say that the services exceeded their expectations we would know that the painful lessons from previous failings within the health and social care system have been learnt.

Recommendations for good practice

- The development of improved structures to co-ordinate action by healthcare professionals, regulators, safeguarding boards and police to enable early intervention and prevent disability hate crimes.

- The creation of systems where it is easier, at the point of engagement with healthcare professionals, for individuals, or their carers, to express concerns about being a victim of hate crime.

- Healthcare professionals should either act themselves or refer to others if they believe an individual has been harmed or is at risk of harm.

- The creation of an environment where complaints are considered as a potential sign of system failings, or individual shortcomings, which require a service provider or regulator to act.

- A cultural shift where everyone responsible for the delivery, commissioning, monitoring and regulation of services applies the basic standard test: 'Would I be happy if I, or someone close to me, was receiving this level of care or was treated in this way?'

References

Care Quality Commission (CQC) (2011) *Internal Management Review of the Regulation of Winterbourne View*. Available at www.cqc.org.uk/sites/default/files/documents/20120730_wv_imr_final_report.pdf, accessed on 17 October 2014.

Department of Health (DH) (2009) *Private and voluntary healthcare: Care Standards Act 2000. Regulations and national minimum standards consultation document.* Available at webarchives.nationalarchives.gov.uk/+/www.dh.gov.uk/en/Consultations/Closedconsultations/DH_083519, accessed on 28 January 2015.

DH (2012) *Transforming Care: A National Response to the Winterbourne View Hospital Review. Final Report.* London: DH.

DH (2013) *Report of the Mid-Staffordshire NHS Foundation Trust Public Inquiry Chaired by Robert Francis QC.* London: HMSO.

DH (2014) *Hard Truths: The Journey to Putting Patients First.* London: DH.

Equality and Human Rights Commission (EHRC) (2011) *Hidden in Plain Sight: Inquiry into Disability-Related Harassment.* London: EHRC. Available at www.equalityhumanrights.com/uploaded_files/disabilityfi/ehrc_hidden_in_plain_sight_3.pdf, accessed on 17 October 2014.

PART 4

HOW TO RESPOND TO DISABILITY HATE CRIME

CHAPTER 13

THE LOCAL AUTHORITY'S APPROACH TO DISABILITY HATE CRIME

MELANIE GIANNASI

Introduction

Local authorities acknowledge their responsibility to vulnerable adults and work in collaboration with other professions to safeguard individuals. They have well-established procedures for identifying and investigating allegations of abuse; their commitment to training staff and educating providers of care and the wider community is widely known. However an allegation is not often identified as hate crime. In 2011 the Equality and Human Rights Commission (EHRC) published *Hidden in Plain Sight* as described in greater detail earlier in this book (see Chapter 2). It highlights a systemic failure by public authorities to recognise the extent and impact of harassment and abuse of disabled people. This detailed study into abuse faced by disabled people found that, while some particularly serious offences attracted national attention, many go unnoticed and high numbers of people experiencing low-level criminality or harassment do not report it and see it as an inevitable consequence of living in a community. Many disabled people do not report harassment, sometimes because it's not clear who they should tell or often from a belief that they would not be treated seriously. The report stated that there is sometimes a focus on the victim, 'questioning their behaviour and "vulnerability", rather than dealing with the perpetrators' (EHRC 2011, p.111).

The government's response to this was to set out a commitment to tackle disability-related harassment, including plans to address the issues identified, in *Challenge It, Report It, Stop It* (Home Office 2012). The government's document outlined its proposals to tackle hate crime by challenging the attitudes underpinning this crime, encouraging victims to report incidents and by improving the ways that cases are managed, victims are supported and offenders are brought to account. The government's aim is to encourage the statutory and voluntary sectors to develop their own solutions to tackle the specific problems in their local areas.

Historical context: how has the local authority found itself in its current position?

There have been many disapproving voices about the standards and the quality of care provided for people in long-stay institutions. A DHSS publication in 1971 *Hospital Services for the Mentally Ill* and later a 1975 White Paper, 'Better Services for the Mentally Ill', were key reports marking a change in the way people received treatment and care. Psychiatry was also developing new medical and psychological tools for treatment which did not rely on in-patient treatment. This paved the way for the a change in how those with learning disabilities (LD) and mental health (MH) needs received services, leading to the closure of all long-stay psychiatric hospitals. The resulting closure of large psychiatric hospitals meant that many people hidden away from society were now more prominent in the community.

Care in the Community was the UK government's policy of removing people from hospitals and providing treatment and care locally rather than in large institutions away from the individual's community. Although institutional care was the target of widespread criticism during the 1960s and 1970s, it was not until 1983 that the Thatcher government implemented a report from the Audit Commission called *Making a Reality of Community Care*. The Griffiths Report highlighted the benefits of domiciliary care.

The programme of resettling people from long-stay hospitals was very slow and prompted the government to produce the White Paper 'Caring for People'. The subsequent introduction of the National Health and Community Care Act (1990) was the first of many pieces of legislation which fundamentally changed the way that the local authority assessed individuals and provided for their needs.

NHS and Community Care Act (1990) – Section 47(1)

Section 47(1) read:

> The Local Authority has a duty to carry out an assessment of need for community care services where a person appears to be someone for whom community care services could be provided, and a person's circumstances may need the provision of some community care services.

This was the trigger for a major change of policy which saw a move away from the local authority as the provider of all its own services for everyone who came to its door. There was the introduction of policies and procedures with limited access to people based on an eligibility criteria; the categorising of need into specific areas, with 'signposting' for people who were assessed as having lower levels of need, was a significant change. Where the local authority had provided a safety net for many individuals with LD and MH needs who may have had difficulty managing their lives within the community, the new legislation created a process which dictated that social work staff were less likely to have a long-term involvement with an individual. The focus for social care staff was short and highlighted by a process of assessment, care or support planning, review and importantly closure once the service had been set up.

Eligibility

Fair Access to Care Services (FACS) identifies whether a person has 'eligible needs' for funded social care services. If eligible needs are within the laws relating to the duty of social services to provide services, then they must be met. How they are met is up to the local authority to interpret; this results in an uneven response where one local authority may respond in a very different way from another, leading to an inconsistent approach.

In 2010 the Department of Health issued guidance to local authorities on eligibility criteria for adults to help local authorities decide who their 'most needy' members of the community were by setting out 'Eligibility Criteria'. The 'Eligibility Criteria' provide a scale by which we can assess an individual's care requirements: Low – Moderate – Substantial – Critical.

Many people who come within the low and moderate category do not receive any significant support but may be offered advice or be signposted to voluntary or charitable groups who may offer assistance. With increased funding cuts since 2010 some councils have raised the threshold, further restricting provision to those identified as having critical needs. With councils facing further spending cuts up to 2015 the tightening of thresholds is not surprising, but it is self-defeating as many people left without support services can quickly move into substantial or critical needs categories resulting in a much higher need which is much more costly.

> Under Fair Access to Care Services (FACS), individuals and carers seeking or referred for social care support are entitled to an assessment of their circumstances, needs and risks. This must ensure they can maintain as much control as possible of their lives, of the care and support that they receive, and of the opportunities to engage in training, employment, civil society and voluntary activities. (SCIE 2013, p.1)

The Social Care Institute for Excellence (SCIE) suggests that offering early intervention, proactive support and access to prevention and re-ablement services is a key point for practitioners.

Moving forward

The opportunities for people with MH needs and LD are greater now than they have ever been; many more people are successful in obtaining employment and accommodation in their own right, achieving success and independence. The opportunities for people in the past have been very limited and the loss of family support through death or inability to cope would have resulted in people being placed in residential care when they had very limited needs, only because there was no alternative in the community. The local authority social services, and housing providers, have made massive leaps forward in supporting people in community placements rather than a regulated care setting. This increase in opportunity for individuals has come with increased risks of isolation and vulnerability.

The desire for many people is to fit in at any cost. People can find themselves in unhealthy relationships with people who are not carers but are identified as 'friends' who are prepared to exploit these associations both for personal gain through exploitation and for the perverse satisfaction of bullying and intimidating someone. The risks associated with intolerance in the community from people who are prepared to express their hatred by abusing vulnerable people can be devastating.

Local authorities' response to vulnerable adults

Referrals for abuse of vulnerable adults will be investigated by the local team where the alleged abuse has taken place. All local authorities have policies and procedures for working in collaboration with other agencies to address complaints about abuse.

> Abuse is mistreatment by any other person or persons that violates a person's human and civil rights. The abuse can vary, from treating someone with disrespect in a way that significantly affects the person's quality of life, to causing actual physical or mental suffering. (Safeguarding Matters)

An investigation into alleged abuse focuses on the individual who is the victim and looks at ways to prevent this happening again. The solutions may be providing a more robust care package, ensuring better protection of finances, criminal investigation, better staff training and many other solutions. In many situations the outcome from an investigation can mean that the victim of abuse leaves their home or community to help them stay safe.

There are some issues around vulnerable adult investigation of abuse and mental capacity. The introduction in the Mental Capacity Act (MCA) (2005) provides a framework to empower and protect people who may lack capacity to make some decisions for themselves. The underlying philosophy of the MCA is to ensure that those who lack capacity are empowered to make as many decisions for themselves as possible and that any decision made, or action taken, on their behalf is made in their best interests.

The Office of the Public Guardian

The Office of the Public Guardian (OPG) is an executive agency sponsored by the Ministry of Justice. The OPG is to protect people in England and Wales who don't have the capacity to make decisions for themselves. This may be decisions around welfare and/or finances. The process involves the appointment of a deputy or attorney to act on behalf of the individual. The OPG also registers Lasting and Enduring Powers of Attorney, this is a legal document where the individual can choose an individual known as an attorney to make decisions for them. In Scotland the Office of Public Guardian for Scotland makes provisions through Adults with Incapacity (Scotland) Act 2000.

Where someone is identified as having capacity the social care staff may find it difficult to act; where an individual is clearly saying they do not want help or advice the worker has no power to compel the person to work with them. The mental capacity guidelines clearly state that just because someone makes unwise decisions this does not mean they do not have capacity to make that decision. Many people with low levels of need will no longer receive support and guidance from a social care team because they do not meet criteria. This can further increase the vulnerability and isolation of certain groups of people.

Case example

> Ben is a 23-year-old; he currently lives with his parents and two younger siblings, who are both at school. Ben was not assessed as having an LD but a physical disability; he has some difficulty with mobility. After leaving school Ben started a practical based training course at college but left in the first term as he didn't feel the others on the course liked him; Ben's mother felt that he found it difficult and was unable to concentrate. Even though Ben's mum had made several attempts to engage him in some day activities and employment Ben has spent most of

his time since leaving school doing nothing. Ben's mum rang the the social services team requesting support and discussed a referral for an assessment because she was concerned about his lack of activity and the group he was hanging around with.

From the initial discussions it was felt that Ben did not meet criteria for an assessment but his mum was offered advice and support and signposted to a local youth group Ben might have been interested in. Ben was not interested and refused all attempts to involve him.

Ben is a good example of someone who has low levels of needs but needs support and guidance to move his life forward. As he is seen to have capacity under the MCA (2005) he has the right to make decision about himself.

Ben spent a lot of his daytime hours with a group of 16 and 17-year-old youths. His mum was concerned that Ben's association with them was affecting his attitude and he seemed unhappy; any attempts to talk to him resulted in an outburst of shouting with Ben leaving the family home and threatening not to come back.

Ben arrived home one evening escorted by two police officers. He had been assaulted and picked up by the police but refused to tell them what had happened; the police had suspicions about the group he was hanging around with. They had approached the group previously and were concerned about how Ben had been treated by some other group members. There had been no previous criminal or anti-social behaviour and Ben's assault appeared to have been the first known incident. Ben refused to discuss his bruises and explained them by saying that he had fallen over.

A referral was made to the local safeguarding team and attempts were made to engage Ben. He was assessed and refused to discuss the incident but did agree to working with the social care worker to find him some accommodation and a job. Ben worked with the social worker for a short while but because he didn't get the results as quickly as he expected he withdrew, stating that he was sick of waiting for a job and the case was closed. Ben returned to his associates and the potential for further abuse.

The very real risks for Ben and others like him are highlighted in the distressing cases of Brent Martin and

Steven Hoskin whose abusive experiences ended with them being murdered by people who they perceived as their friends. Luckily for Ben his family continued to offer him support and guidance and more importantly the group of youths he was hanging around with just got bored of him and didn't want him around any more.

Although the local authority does not often view abuse against adults as hate crime, by definition every incident of abuse must be classed as a hate crime if it is generated by hostility.

Hate crimes and incidents are taken to mean any crime or incident where the perpetrator's hostility or prejudice against an identifiable group of people is a factor in determining who is victimised. (College of Policing 2014, p.1)

This desire to fit in and be liked is common to most people; the desire to maintain relationships that are unequal and abusive has a deep-seated psychological base. We often have vulnerable adults reports which highlight that a person is being physically or financially abused. As part of an investigation it may be evident that the person has considered the consequences of reporting the abuse and has chosen not to pursue an investigation because of fear of losing the support of the abuser. This kind of traumatic bonding results in 'strong emotional ties that develop between two persons where one person intermittently harasses, beats, threatens, abuses, or intimidates the other' (Dutton and Painter 1981, in Kust-Swanger 2013). Traumatic bonds can develop when there is an imbalance of power in a relationship and the individual refuses to acknowledge the abuse as a form of self preservation. The relationship is characterised by episodes of abuse and concern; this confuses the victim leaving them feeling powerless to change the situation. It is suggested that bonding with a person who is being abusive makes it easier for a victim to survive within a relationship but significantly undermines their self-esteem and self worth and effects their ability to understand danger or consider alternatives to the situation they are in.

The way forward

A lack of respect for vulnerable adults causes marginalisation in society:

> Some disabled people are targeted because of their perceived 'vulnerability'. But the sustained nature of many of the attacks, the insults, jibes, systematic humiliation and extreme violence, suggest that a significant number of people in society dislike and even hate disabled people. (Scope 2008, p.25)

The Scope report further states that the motivating factor for disability hate crimes stares us in the face: a hostility and contempt for disabled people based on the view that disabled people are inferior, and do not matter. This report highlights the need for a fundamental change of attitudes towards people with disabilities, commenting that disabled people have the same desires and rights as others: to live independently and participate as equals in their community and wider society. They are not innately vulnerable and should not 'expect' to be attacked because of who they are; nor should they have to change the way they live because of these expectations.

The Disability Equality Duty (2005) placed a proactive duty on agencies. The provisions were superseded by the Equality Act (2010) which replaced all existing equality legislation such as the Race Relations Act, Disability Discrimination Act and Sex Discrimination Act. It placed a duty on statutory bodies to:

- promote equality of opportunity between disabled people and other people

- eliminate discrimination that is unlawful under the Disability Discrimination Act (1995)

- eliminate harassment of disabled people that is related to their disability

- promote positive attitudes towards disabled people

- encourage participation by disabled people in public life

- take steps to take account of disabled people's disabilities, even where that involves treating a disabled person more favourably than other people.

The *Statement of Government Policy on Adult Safeguarding* (May 2011) announced the strengthening of protection for vulnerable adults by ensuring all local authorities have Safeguarding Adults Boards in place. However, following the uncovering of abuse at Winterbourne View care home, it is clear significant measures need to be implemented in order to ensure better standards of adult protection. As such, demonstrating their commitment to safeguarding the rights of vulnerable adults, the government has published the Draft Care and Support Bill (July 2012) and the 'Caring for our Future: Reforming Care and Support' White Paper (July 2012). Furthermore, these two government publications outline the need for a modern care and support system, which promotes well-being.

Key findings

- Many people with low levels of need will no longer receive support and guidance from a social care team because they do not meet criteria. This can further increase the vulnerability and isolation of certain groups of people. There needs to be a move back to social work practice which offers ongoing social care responsibilities with a move away from assessment, care planning, review and closure – some local authorities have already identified the need for consistency and continuity of workers to improve outcomes for vulnerable people in the community. Maintaining an ongoing working relationship/ association with a service user that prevents the loss of vital personal information about relationships and key life events can assist the service user in developing and maintaining independence. However, this is limited as it only operates within the limits of the eligibility criteria and does not encompass people who are on the edge of services.

- Wider development of adult fostering placements would be beneficial; these schemes are similar to fostering for children where an individual is matched with a family in their local community who offer ongoing support and guidance, sometimes a home. The benefits of these schemes are two-fold. They offer support, guidance and most importantly a sense of value and belonging to the individual. They can enrich the lives of a family who are matched with a person who is not a relative but who has additional needs, giving young people the opportunity to care about others. Education is critical here in creating a just society where we embrace and celebrate difference, and it helps to tackle the negative attitudes towards disabled people that can trigger abuse. These adult fostering schemes have been around for many years but they are patchy. Shared Lives Plus[1] is an adult placement service which has 10,000 Shared Lives carers in the UK. They share their family and community life with someone who needs some support to live independently. Shared Lives carers support disabled adults, older people with dementia, people with mental health problems, care leavers, disabled children in transition to adulthood and parents who have learning disabilities.

- Working with communities to tackle social isolation is an essential way to improve attitudes to vulnerable people and to raise awareness in the community. Assessment processes have focused upon the individual's vulnerability and needs rather than championing people's strengths and their networks. Many councils such as Thurrock Council[2] aim to change by handing power to individuals and communities, encouraging them to take more responsibility by using their – often untapped – strengths, skills and passions. Many councils employ community link or co-ordinators to work

---

1   See www.sharedlivesplus.org.uk for more information.
2   Thurrock Council has significantly changed the way it deals with people who are deemed ineligible for statutory adult social care services. Many councils identified the need to sign post individuals in this group but they lack resources to make it work effectively. Therefore, Thurrock has employed co-ordinators to make it work.

closely with vulnerable individuals and their communities to share strengths and find local solutions (Community Care 2014).

- People who are on the edge of services with a low level of need and who are isolated in the community can be frequent visitors to social care teams and community police services without any real intervention that may help them stay safe. These frequent visits need to be recorded to trigger further investigation or indication of increased need. This may prevent people searching for associations that are unhealthy and put them at risk of abuse. This could be recorded in the same way so that frequent referrals for low-level abuse would increase in priority and require the safeguarding team to act to address the abuse.

- In local authority safeguarding boards, membership is made up of lead officers from social services, the police, health, housing, the independent care sector, the Crown Prosecution Service, the Care Quality Commission and voluntary organisations. Such teams have an important role in the protection of vulnerable adults. Safeguarding encompasses six key concepts: empowerment, protection, prevention, proportionate responses, partnership and accountability. Social care organisations are responsible for ensuring that services and support are delivered in ways that are high quality and safe.

There is need to acknowledge disability hate crimes for what they are rather than just focusing on the abuse of vulnerable adults. The hostility and intent in any incident of abuse could be categorised as a hate crime but it is not. Most local authorities have statements addressing their approach to working alongside the police to tackle issues around hate crimes, with many funding organisations, usually voluntary or charitable groups, to promote the reporting of hate crimes. This seems inadequate in the circumstances and the local authority needs to be more proactive in its actions.

How do we intervene when someone has capacity?

Sometimes there will be situations for all professionals where episodes of abuse cannot be avoided even with the best interventions because, where individuals have capacity, they can act as they want. When someone does not have capacity it is much easier to act in someone's 'best interest' to protect them.

In decision making, professionals need to agree with the individual how they will support and educate them to make better decisions. We need to consider who has the responsibility to ensure that people are supported to remain free from abuse. This can be achieved by:

- providing information about how to get help, leaflets, support groups, organisational assistance

- developing training to educate people about their rights through schools, youth groups and community bodies

- effective signposting and organisation responses to requests for help

- staff development around awareness and responsibilities for all agencies and organisations.

There has to be wider commitment from all agencies to work with this group of people. Often the police will discuss a case with a social worker to see if support can be offered but frustration exists for all when this cannot be achieved with a reluctant individual or a criteria-based system which prevents involvement until situations become critical or substantial.

Escalating signs of abuse

There is a need for triggers which prompt professionals to intervene to help protect people from abuse. In many of the most severe cases of hate crimes, as well as lower-level abuse, common factors exist. If these triggers are present in an individual's life they need to be addressed and tackled. Currently the local safeguarding board has a responsibility to monitor people who are frequently reported as victims of abuse and this should include people who are victims of hate crimes and targeted abuse. Although this is not an exhaustive list, some of the stages and common situations are:

1. unhealthy friendships/associations

2. taunting and bullying leading to abuse, leading to raised awareness within statutory agencies

3. situational abuse which arises because pressures have built up and/or because of difficult or challenging behaviour

4. dehumanisation of abuse; dehumanisation is a psychological process whereby a perpetrator views a victim as less than human and thus not deserving of moral consideration

5. escalation of mistreatment, where the controlling behaviour becomes more frequent, less disguised, more demanding and more serious

6. accusation of criminal activity – such as paedophilia, where rumours are spread about the individual to prompt abuse from others or to justify the abuse from the accuser

7. severe attack

8. torture and death.

Recommendations

Hate crimes are not just a police matter; it is for everyone to take responsibility. At many of the early stages of an abusive relationship people will come to the attention of the statutory bodies and they should not be ignored or brushed off as not the organisation's responsibility. The response can no longer be about trying to move the victim to a safer place away from the risk and threat because the risk and threat will follow them around or come from somewhere else. The government's aims are set out in *Challenge It, Report It, Stop It* (Home Office 2012), which encourages agencies to develop strategies for managing this issue. This is insufficient and needs to be placed on a statutory footing so that all agencies take responsibility for identifying hate crimes and working together to tackle this issue head on. This can be achieved by having:

- agreed national training standards for adult protection safeguarding boards which include targeted abuse by redefining issues as hate crimes and not just issues for vulnerable adults (including obligations for action when triggers of escalating abuse are present)

- greater awareness for professional organisations; rather than just acting as a third party reporter of hate crimes there needs to be specific guidance for the local authority and other agencies to act and raise awareness when early stages of escalating abuse are identified

- changes in legislation to put hate crimes in line with other punishable crimes; if someone dies as a result of abuse this needs to be treated as murder rather than focusing on the vulnerability of the individual and in some way excusing the result as less important because the individual is disabled

- government-funded public advertising campaigns to raise awareness of people's rights to be present in the community and greater acceptance of difference

- challenges to, and controls on, media coverage that accepts discrimination and encourages discrimination, disharmony and disrespect within the community.

References

College of Policing (2014) *The Agreed Definition of 'Monitored Hate Crime' for England, Wales and Northern Ireland.* Available at www.reort-it.org.uk/files/hate_crime_definitions_-v3_0. pdf, accessed on 18 December 2014.

College of Policing (2011) *Hate Crime Operational Guidance.* London: College of Policing.

Community Care (2014) *How our new social care model works with communities to tackle isolation.* Available at www.communitycare.co.uk/2014/01/09/new-social-care-model- works-communities-tackle-isolation, accessed on 15 January 2015.

Equality and Human Rights Commission (EHRC) (2011) *Hidden in Plain Sight: Inquiry into Disability-Related Harassment.* London: EHRC. Available at www.equalityhumanrights.com/uploaded_files/disabilityfi/ehrc_hidden_in_plain_sight_3.pdf, accessed on 17 October 2014.

Griffith, R. (1986) *Making a Reality of Community Care.* London: HMSO.

Department of Health (2010) *Guidance on Eligibility Criteria for Adult Social Care, England.* London: Department of Health.

Dutton, D. G. and Painter, S. L. (1981) 'Traumatic bonding: The development of emotional attachments in battered women and other relationships of intermittent abuse.' In Kurst-Swanger, K. and Petrosky, J. L. (2013) *Violence in the Home – Multidisciplinary Perspectives.* Oxford: Oxford University Press.

Home Office (2012) *Challenge It, Report it, Stop It: The Government's Plan to Tackle Hate Crime.* London: HMSO.

Quarmby, K. (2008) *Getting Away With Murder: Disabled People's Experiences of Hate Crime in the UK.* London: Scope. Available at www.scope.org.uk/Scope/media/Images/Publication%20Directory/Getting-away-with-murder.pdf, accessed on 17 October 2014.

Safeguarding Matters (2011) 'Definition of Vulnerable Adult and Abuse.' Available at www.safeguardingmatters.co.uk/the-new-disclosure-and-vetting-service/in-the-news/recent-cases-relating-to-vulnerable-adults, accessed on 18 December 2014.

Social Care Institute for Excellence (SCIE) (2013) *Fair Access to Care Services (FACS): Prioritising Eligibility for Care and Support.* London: SCIE.

CHAPTER 14

DON'T BE AFRAID TO ASK: BECOME PART OF THE CIRCLE OF SUPPORT

DR MATT HOGHTON

In the movie *Meet the Fockers* (2004) the character Jack Byrne, played by Robert De Niro, introduces the concept of the Circle of Trust. Ruth Northway *et al.*'s important study (2013) recommended that effective 'Circles of Support' need to be developed to protect people with an intellectual disability against abuse and to provide support if abuse occurs. The focus of this chapter will be on the role of the general practitioner (GP) and their primary care team in helping people at risk of disability hate crime and explains why they should specifically take notice and if possible also refer to the multi-dimensional aspect of integrated care.

At present the main co-ordinated response to disability discrimination and hate crime from the UK public services has been by the police force and the criminal justice system. However, whilst this is clearly an important part of the solution, national organisations in health and social care need to take a lead in this unrecognised cause of ill health that affects a considerable proportion of our patients. The position of primary care in the community presents a real opportunity to help people with a disability, particularly those that rely on non-verbal communication or are dependent on carers for communication and advocacy. A disabled person is defined by the Equality Act (2010) as someone who has a physical or mental impairment that has a substantial and long-term adverse effect on his or her ability to carry out normal day-to-day activities. The act includes special rules that ensure that people with HIV, cancer and multiple sclerosis are deemed to be disabled people effectively from the point of diagnosis, rather than from the point when the condition has some adverse effect on their ability to carry out normal day-to-day activities. In the UK Home Office for National Statistics and Ministry of Justice (2013) report: *An overview of hate crime in England and Wales in 2013/14*, there were 1985 disability hate crimes reported in England and Wales by the police - an eight per cent year increase on 2012/13 figures (1843), which was a five per cent increase on 2011/12 (1753). This may be partly due to more disabled people having the confidence to report crimes but Mike Smith, Lead Commissioner for the inquiry into disability-related harassment by the Equality and Human Rights Commission (EHRC) in the 2011 report *Out In the Open* raises concerns that the current financial climate and media coverage may be creating conditions where disabled people may be targeted as 'scroungers' or 'benefit cheats'. Over the same period all hate crimes where the criminal offence was motivated by hostility based on a person's race, religious belief, sexual orientation or disability were reduced to 44,519 in 2011 compared to 48,127 crimes reported in 2010.

Jones *et al.* (2012) showed that children with a disability are at a substantially greater risk of violence than non-disabled children. Mencap's report *Bullying Wrecks Lives* (2007) surveyed 500 children and young people with a learning disability (LD) and demonstrated that this particular group was confirmed to experience high levels of disability hate crime with 82 per cent of children and young people with a learning disability experiencing bullying, with 60 per cent being physically hurt by bullies. Mencap's report, *Living in Fear* (2008), is a comprehensive survey into bullying experienced by adults with a learning disability across the UK. This disturbing report looked particularly at the nature and range of bullying and its effects on the lives of people with a learning disability. Nearly nine out of ten respondents had experienced bullying in the last year, 66 per cent were bullied on a regular basis and almost 33 per cent were suffering from bullying on a daily or weekly basis.

Beadle-Brown *et al.*'s (2013) report into the experiences of people with a learning disability and autism found that 80 per cent of respondents had experienced some form disability-related victimisation. The report reiterates the issues of underreporting of incidents, problems with the processes of reporting and with securing prosecutions, which is rare. The report highlighted the types of disability hate crime adults with learning disabilities experienced, of the 116 respondents 75 per cent had been subjected to verbal abuse, just under 50 per cent had been stared at or laughed at, 40 per cent had been physically hurt and 15 per cent had had private parts of their bodies touched (Beadle-Brown *et al.* 2013, p.80).

People with a learning disability face prejudice and widespread discrimination that often makes social inclusion difficult and may cause permanent loss of confidence in going out and integrating with the rest of society. This isolation may lead to mental health issues, lack of physical activities and behaviours that challenge. Unfortunately the report found that in 53 per cent the bullying continued after the matter was reported to a family member or a person in authority. The victims did not appear to have been listened to or taken seriously, or the offender/s could not be identified and located. It appears that bullying is often not taken seriously by staff or key workers. The emergence of the issue of 'mate crime', particularly for those patients with a mild learning disability, is a particular issue which needs highlighting.

Child protection has been an integral part of general practice in the UK for many years but safeguarding adults is a relatively new area that GPs and their team have been involved in. There may currently be a lack of awareness, confidence and experience in primary care staff in tackling this difficult issue. Other barriers included lack of time, perceived difficulty, complexity and stress in dealing with disability hate crime, and access to referral agencies. However experience gained from other areas such as domestic violence has improved GPs' ability to identify and manage people who are suffering abuse. The Commission for Social Care Inspection (CSCI), now part of the Care Quality Commission, report into *Safeguarding Adults* in 2008 identified GPs as among the least likely of local agencies to be involved in adult safeguarding boards, along with housing and probation services. The report highlighted that difficulties were reported in respect of GPs' and hospitals' understanding of confidentiality and information sharing protocols, particularly mental health services. In this report the top three main difficulties safeguarding boards faced were related to lack of resources, problems related to lack of legislative powers and lack of commitment by GPs. This may in part be due to GPs' lack of awareness of adult safeguarding, and safeguarding boards' lack of understanding of how GPs operate with the need to ensure backfill of clinical cover in the surgery. The Royal College of General Practitioners (RCGP) report (2012) *Patients, Doctors and the NHS in 2022: Compendium of Evidence* documents the considerable pressures in primary care with an ageing population, fragmentation of care, financial as well as time constraints and increased multi-morbidities but GP engagement in disability hate crime and safeguarding is vital if we are to have an integrated approach across public services.

Alison Faulkner and Angela Sweeney (2011) in their review of literature on prevention in adult safeguarding highlighted the following building blocks for prevention and early intervention identified by the CSCI:

- people being informed of their rights to be free from abuse and supported to exercise these rights, including access to advocacy
- a well-trained workforce operating in a culture of zero tolerance of abuse
- a sound framework for confidentiality and information sharing across agencies
- good universal services, such as community safety services
- needs and risk assessments to inform people's choices
- a range of options for support to keep safe from abuse tailored to people's individual needs
- services that prioritise both safeguarding and independence
- public awareness of the issues.

These are important themes but the focus has predominately been on social services. In 2011 the British Medical Association (BMA 2011) recognised the importance of GP involvement in adult safeguarding and published a toolkit for general practitioners. This important document has helped to define the GP's role and obligation to take action if they suspect vulnerable adults are being abused or neglected as well as to give them the confidence to speak out or report others for not fulfilling their duties properly. However, the full scale and unique elements of disability hate crimes are only really now starting to emerge. Mark Sherry (2010) has produced a collection of vivid accounts of hate crimes and analysis of statistics documenting these crimes in the US and the UK which is considerably improving our comprehension of the nature of this widespread hidden problem of disability hostility.

The UK Government Office for Disability Issues (2012a, 2012b) suggests that disability hate crime can be seen as:

- offensive language which may include name calling and insults

- abusive verbal or written comments which are intended to threaten or intimidate (they will also include the use of email, social networks, mobile phones)

- physical assault

- domestic violence

- financial exploitation

- damage to property

- sexual abuse and assault

- threats and intimidation.

In general practice and primary care teams there is improved confidence in helping the victims of domestic violence and the lessons learnt here can be applied to disability hate crime. As a starting point, general practitioners and their staff may wish to consider the five essential steps below to tackle disability hate crime.

Step 1 – Encouraging positive awareness and understanding of disability

Many healthcare professionals appear to struggle to understand disability and disability hate crime. Disability hate crime has similarities with other forms of hate crime but has some unique features. These include the victim usually being known to the perpetrator and the fact that it often affects 16–34-year-olds. The United Nations Convention on the Rights of Persons with Disabilities (2006) recognises that girls and young women with a disability are at particularly high risk. In the community there appears to be certain patterns that emerge such as a young person with mild learning disabilities who has a loose circle of support being befriended by individuals who financially and physically abuse the person. These crimes may be difficult to recognise without a clear familiarity with the person and knowledge of their usual behaviour. In general practice the receptionists are often the first to notice if someone is struggling either with loss of prescriptions, poor compliance or not visiting the surgery. Continuity of care from one GP can help with establishing a long-term relationship and improve the depth of understanding of the unique issues the person with a disability faces. The consequence of this is an improvement in the level of trust that any reporting will be taken seriously. It is useful to have a GP adult safeguarding and disability lead within the practice with an administrative staff member acting as an advocate for people with a disability. All staff need to have adult safeguarding and disability hate crime training annually with trainers that include people with a disability. At the same time the practice should encourage people with a disability to join the practice patient participation group and to make reasonable adjustments to ensure their participation in patient satisfaction questionnaires. All public sector services have a legal duty to provide 'reasonable adjustments' for people with disabilities including removing barriers to accessing services. Practices should recruit and employ people with a disability, as they are more likely to be able to understand the complex issues people with a disability face.

Step 2 – Improving the identification and care of victims of hate crime

GPs and their staff need to consider the possibility of hate crime if the disabled person's behaviour is unusual or they have low mood. It is essential to speak to the person alone, particularly if they are in institutional care. You need to make time to listen and emphasise confidentiality, though this may not be possible if the person is a child or dependent children are also at risk. Ask the question, 'Has anyone hurt you?' and show respect and sensitivity for the person who may find it very difficult to tell you what has happened. You will need to record accurate documentation and consider photographing any physical injuries, though bruises may take several days to appear. After assessing and treating any physical injuries, you need to consider the situation to check if there is an immediate risk or a need to provide a place of safety. Some people with learning disabilities find pictures and drawings helpful, particularly the *Supporting Victims* (Books Beyond Words) produced by Baroness Professor Sheila Hollins *et al.* (2007). Having identified a potential disability hate crime it is important to support the person in reporting the crime to the police and provide ongoing care and follow-up. If someone you support is a victim of hate crime, you should work with the police to enable them to give a statement if they want to, which may include advising the police on their support, communication and healthcare needs. All members of the GP practice need to be aware of what to do if they recognise signs of hate crime, aside from just reporting directly to police, for example third party reporting centres, True Vision, Stop Hate UK's learning disability hate crime helpline.[1] Leaflets in all the practice toilets may be useful to reassure people with a disability that it is all right to discuss disability hate crime with their GP or practice nurse.

Step 3 – Preventing hate crime

GPs can raise awareness with their local Clinical Commissioning Groups (CCGs) and ensure contract specifications ensure training

---

1   The helpline number is 0808 802 1155.

for all healthcare services. In learning disabilities the Community Learning Disability teams (CLDTs) can arrange training for people with a learning disability to understand hate crime and how to avoid it, deal with it, and to report it. In addition the CLDT can help build a team of champions who support their peers.

Adults with a learning disability in England have been able to get annual health checks from their GP for several years. This offers an opportunity to see the person when they are well and develop an ongoing relationship, which will help in the future. It is important to have a section of the health check when the person is seen alone and offered the opportunity to discuss any bullying or harassment. If carers are aware that GPs and practice nurses are monitoring, challenging and considering disability hate crime it is less likely to occur. Transition planning for young people with special education needs is often not happening and some of the placements expose these young adults to significant risks in the community with poor support and advocacy.

Step 4 – Increasing reporting and access to support by improving practitioners' confidence and building anti-bullying confidence

Identifying hate crime takes time and patience and cannot be rushed. If someone with a disability discloses a hate crime, time is needed to establish and address his or her concerns. The Disability Rights UK (2013) guides *Let's Stop Disability Hate Crime – A Guide for Disabled People* and *Let's Stop Disability Hate Crime – A Guide for Non Disabled People* offer practical advice on how to report crime and how to get help. We must need to constantly remember and monitor the dangers of segregated residential institutions that are remote from people's families and communities, as the Department of Health's (2012) report into events at Winterbourne View has reminded us again. As a GP or practice member of staff you need to consider the possibility of disability hate crime as a cause of any ill health in a disabled person. People with disabilities are likely to have co-morbidities and have long-term conditions that require monitoring by the practice nurse. These regular checks often have more time scheduled than the usual UK GP appointment of ten minutes and may give an opportunity for early detection of disability hate crimes.

Step 5 – Developing local partnerships and building inclusive and safe healthcare environments

No single health organisation can tackle this alone but a co-coordinated approach is required with sharing of information across primary care and community staff. The intention of inter-agency working expressed at government and policy level and the experiences of disabled young people and their families often differ considerably and need addressing through local ownership and shared leadership by members of the practice. Face-to-face communication with other members of the primary care team, particularly health visitors and district nurses, may reveal confirmation of concerns and further background to issues the disabled person may be facing. Consider setting up a Safe Place scheme. People who join the scheme carry a Safe Place identity (ID) card that they can show to the staff of participating shops and businesses. The card will carry that person's name and the contact number of someone they trust. If they need help, the person will present their ID card to the manager or staff at the safe place. This would involve making the surgery a recognised safe place, where the surgery trains together and displays signs to indicate they are a safe place for people with a disability to come if they are bullied or suffer a disability hate crime.

The NHS *Safeguarding Vulnerable People in the Reformed NHS: Accountability and Assurance Framework* was published in March 2013. This sets out the mandate for the NHS Commissioning Board (NHS CB) with a specific objective of continuing to improve the safeguarding practices in the NHS and helps to clarify NHS roles and responsibilities. It reiterates the key message that safeguarding is everyone's business. The NHS CB is identified as being responsible for co-ordinating and funding safeguarding training. In addition it recommends local commissioners employ and develop local GPs with a specific interest in safeguarding. All healthcare providers are required to have effective arrangements in place to safeguard children and adults and to assure themselves, regulators and their commissioners that they are working. Each general practice site should have a lead for safeguarding who works closely with the named GPs and the safeguarding boards.

There are future developments in health and social care, which may be beneficial to disabled people but may present new risks as well. These include personal health budgets, patient online access and the possible need for a new safeguarding power. By April 2014 up to 56,000 people on the NHS Continuing Healthcare scheme will have the right to ask for a personal health budget, which will empower them to have more choice and control. There are concerns that the Care Standards Act (2000) and the Safeguarding Vulnerable Groups Act (2006) systems may not be applicable to personal health budgets. The Department of Health (DH) in England has stated that by 2015 all general practices will be expected to make available online access to medical records. There are likely to be considerable benefits to patients with disabilities having access to their records but there is potential for carers to gain access to disabled people's records and use them to exploit them. Access to an at-risk adult with a disability to enable a proper assessment to take place is often the key issue to address before deciding whether any compulsory action is needed. If it is believed that a patient is being abused or neglected by a third party, such as someone with whom the person is living, and that third party refuses access to the person or refuses the provision of services to them, then it is important to gain access to assess them. The Mental Health Act (1983, 2007) in England and Wales allows an approved social worker to enter any premises (except a hospital) in which a person with a mental health disorder is living if he or she has reasonable cause to believe that person has not got reasonable care under Section 115. A police officer has a similar right of entry under Section 135 and can force an entry. However, the person needs to demonstrate evidence of a mental health disorder.

In Scotland, the Adult Support and Protection (Scotland) Act (2007) was introduced in which the wishes of an adult with full mental capacity could be 'over-ruled', creating a general principle on intervention in an adult's affairs and a specific duty to make inquiries where abuse is reported. This law in Scotland introduced the concept of assessment orders, established the power for removal orders, and the protection of a moved person's property, included the right to ban abusers from the family home and the duties of the police if banning orders were ignored, and established the right to interview an adult in private. In Scotland, social workers appear to appreciate that such powers must be used only as a last resort and are happy to use the powers responsibly and sensibly, and/or the mere threat of using the statutory power gives the social worker 'teeth' with which to investigate allegations of abuse. At present these powers are not available in England but the Department of Health has run a consultation in 2012 for a new safeguarding law.

General practitioners and primary care staff are in a unique position in their relationships with patients and their local communities to help safeguard people with a disability who suffer bullying, harassment or violence. We need a health service permeated by care, compassion, respect and support for everyone, whether they are disabled or not, to live a life free from abuse and harassment. It is time to retune our attitudes to disability and disability hate crime.

References

Beadle-Brown, J., Guest, C., Richardson, L., Malovic, A., Bradshaw, J. and Himmerich, J. (2013) *Living in Fear: Better Outcomes for People with Learning Disabilities and Autism.* Canterbury: Tizard Centre, University of Kent.

British Medical Journal (BMA) (2011) *Safeguarding Vulnerable Adults – A Toolkit for General Practitioners.* London: BMA.

Commission for Social Care Inspection (CSCI) (2008) *Safeguarding Adults: A Study of the Effectiveness of Arrangements to Safeguard Adults From Abuse.* London: CSCI.

Disability Rights UK (DRUK) (2012a) *Let's Stop Disability Hate Crime – A Guide for Disabled People.* London: DRUK.

DRUK (2012b) *Let's Stop Disability Hate Crime – A Guide For Non Disabled People.* London: DRUK.

Department of Health (2012) *Transforming Care: A National Response to the Winterbourne View Hospital Review. Final Report.* London: Department of Health.

Equality and Human Rights Commission (EHRC) (2012) *Out in the Open: Tackling Disability-Related Harassment – A Manifesto for Change.* London: EHRC. Available at www.equalityhumanrights.com/publication/out-open-tackling-disability-related-harassment-manifesto-change, accessed on 17 October 2014.

Faulkner, A. and Sweeney, A. (2011) *Prevention in Adult Safeguarding.* London: Social Care Institute for Excellence.

Hollins, S., Stone, K., Sinason, V. and Brighton, C. (2007) *Supporting Victims* (Books Beyond Words). Cambridge: Turpins.

Home Office, Ministry of Justice and Office for National Statistics (2013) *An overview of hate crime in England and Wales.* London: Home Office, Ministry of Justice and Office for National Statistics. Available at www.gov.uk/government/uploads/system/uploads/attachment_data/file/266358/hate-crime-2013.pdf, accessed on 16 February 2015.

Jones, L, Bellis, M., Wood, S., Hughes, K. *et al.* (2012) 'Prevalence and risk of violence against children with disabilities: a systematic review and meta-analysis of observational studies.' *The Lancet 380,* 9845, 899–907. Available at http://dx.doi.org/10.1016/S0140-6736(12)60692-8, accessed on 17 October 2014.

Mencap (2007) *Bullying Wrecks Lives: The Experience of Children and Young People with a Learning Disability.* London: Mencap.

Mencap (2008) *Living in Fear.* London: Mencap.

NHS Commissioning Board (NHS CB) (2013) *Safeguarding Vulnerable People in the Reformed NHS Accountability and Assurance Framework.* London: Department of Health.

Northway, R., Bennett, D., Melsome, M., Flood, S., Howarth, J. and Jones, R. (2013) *Keeping Safe and Providing Support: A Participatory Survey About Abuse and People with Intellectual Disabilities.* London: Journal of Policy and Practice in Intellectual Disabilities.

Royal College of General Practitioners (RCGP) (2012) *Patients, Doctors and the NHS in 2022: Compendium of Evidence.* London: RCGP.

Sherry, M. (2010) *Disability Hate Crimes: Does Anyone Really Hate Disabled People?* London: Ashgate.

CHAPTER 15

PUSHING AN OPEN DOOR
THE VALUE OF MULTI-AGENCY WORKING

SYED MOHAMMAD MUSA NAQVI

Different government departments, public institutions, agencies, and voluntary and third sector organisations, both locally and nationally, share the responsibility for the welfare of this country's disabled people. Professionals and practitioners within these organisations interact with them on a regular basis. They provide disabled people with various essential services, advice and expertise. Through these interactions, practitioners also gather a wide range of information about individual, social and other circumstances that underpin the lives of disabled people. The cases of Fiona Pilkington, Steven Hoskin and Bijan Ebrahimi tragically and powerfully illustrate the consequences that can occur when disabled people are harassed and multiple agencies, despite their numerous interactions, are unable to recognise the harm they are suffering, or respond effectively.

This chapter focuses on the contributions that healthcare agencies, practitioners and professionals can make in tackling hate crime whilst working with colleagues in the criminal justice system, social care, third sector and others. The chapter begins by first outlining in brief what disability hate crime means and what is known about it. Second, it explores the value that multi-agency working brings in helping overcome the challenges that disability hate crime presents. Finally, it concludes with a set of recommendations to empower professionals and practitioners, in particular those working within health and social care, to be able to reduce the impact that hate crime has on the lives of disabled people.

Disability and disability hate crime

In the UK there are over 11 million people registered as disabled, this includes 770,000 disabled children under the age of 16[1] and over 1.5 million people with learning difficulties. Disability hate crime is the abuse or harassment of a person just because he/she is disabled.[2] Hate crimes and incidents are taken to mean: any crime or incident where the perpetrator's prejudice against an identifiable group of people is a factor in determining who is victimised.

As discussed further in this volume (see Chapter 16), disability hate crime was first recognised in UK law by the Criminal Justice Act of 2003. Section 146 of the Act allows courts to punish offenders more severely if a crime was motivated by the victim's disability.

Research into issues affecting the disabled suggests that nine out of ten people with learning disabilities are attacked and harassed within a year (Mencap 2000), with nearly three quarters of people with mental health problems having been a victim of crime or harassment in the past two years (Mind 2007). Disabled children are twice as likely to be victims of bullying as their 'typically developing' peers (Allerton, Welch and Emerson 2011; Mencap 2007). Furthermore, those with learning disabilities and mental health problems are more likely to be socially excluded as well as physically and sexually abused (Petersilia 2001).[3] However, disability hate crime remains seriously 'overlooked and under-reported'.[4] Indeed for 2012/13, of the 43,748 hate crimes recorded by the police, just four per cent (1744) were recorded as disability hate crimes. This under-reporting is a result of a range of complex factors including (but not limited to): an incomplete awareness and understanding of disability, low self-esteem and fears among the disabled of not being taken seriously (Cooper 2007), lack of advocates for the disabled and social attitudes towards disability (HMCPSI *et al.* 2013). Some have argued that:

---

1   See www.efds.co.uk/resources/facts_and_statistics.
2   See www.nacro.org.uk/data/files/nacro-2004120261-429.pdf.
3   See www.mencap.org.uk/all-about-learning-disability/about-learning-disability/facts-about-learning-disability.
4   See www.bbc.co.uk/news/uk-21865264.

disability hate crime remains largely invisible. Its existence is frequently denied and disabled people who report it are routinely ignored and its perpetrators often go unpunished. (Quarmby 2008, p.60)

The tragic murders of Steven Hoskin and Brent Martin, and more recently of Bijan Ebrahimi and Sean Miles, show that, at the extreme of disability hate crime, people are murdered because of their disabilities. In common with many others, retrospective reviews of Mr Hoskin's murder demonstrate that a series of minor disability hate crimes may dramatically escalate if early symptoms are not recognised and risks reduced.[5] Similarly the inquests into the 2007 deaths of Fiona Pilkington and Francecca Hardwick have raised questions about the ability of government agencies to recognise harm caused by the harassment of disabled people. A number of subsequent inquiries have focused on the relationship between partners and their ability to communicate, assess risk and reduce harm, as well as vocalising a need for 'an effective and comprehensive training programme for practitioners'(EHRC 2011; Her Majesty's Crown Prosecution Service Inspecturale *et al.* 2013).

Multi-agency working: policy, value, challenges and best practice

At a policy level the government has encouraged different agencies and departments to work alongside each other in partnership. The Home Office's Action Plan (2009) and the Department of Health White Paper 'Valuing People Now' (2009) recognise the values of cross-governmental working, introducing measures such as the creation of learning disability partnership boards, and jointly produced and delivered educational materials and training. The more recent government plan to tackle hate crime (Home Office 2012) focuses on preventing hate crime through education by challenging attitudes, by promoting empowerment, through increasing reporting and building confidence, and through effectiveness in operational response to hate crime, with specific action points for different government agencies.

---

5   See www.respond.org.uk/campaigns/disability_hate_crime.html.

Professionals working in the different sectors of education, health, social care, local councils and the criminal justice system each have their different expertise. The logic of a cross-governmental approach stems from the simple idea that different departments of government and public institutions have various different roles and varied interactions with disabled people. In each of these interactions information is gathered about the personal and social circumstances of an individual, which, if shared between these agencies, could result in earlier interventions and better support for the disabled person. Multi-agency working and information sharing can help create a better picture of what might be going on in the life of a disabled people. This has the potential to be welfare enhancing by preventing failures such as those seen in the example of Fiona Pilkington.

Professionals working within health and social care such as GPs, district nurses, pharmacists, community nurses, social workers, professionals working with those in residential care and others have a great potential to champion the rights of disabled people, whilst working with colleagues within the police and the criminal justice system. These practitioners have an important role because they are likely to be those professionals who disabled people have the most regular access to and the greatest interaction with. Thus healthcare professionals may be most suitably placed for challenging attitudes towards disability, inspiring confidence within the disability community, supporting the victims following their ordeals, encouraging them to come forward and report hate crime and abuse, while also being ideally placed to make risk assessments and escalate concerns to other partners.

Although there is a clear logic and value to multi-agency working, as discussed earlier at a practical level, a number of challenges exist in helping practitioners realise the contributions they could potentially be making in helping to tackle disability hate crime. Fundamentally, frontline staff may not understand or be aware of what 'disability hate crime' is, or indeed even recognise and correctly assess if a disabled person is at risk. A lack of training may mean that the disabled individual who does have the confidence to come forward and report a crime may not be taken seriously and be left marginalised.

Second, organisational culture, policies and perceptions of what an individual professional's responsibilities are, may in fact mean that they do not take any action at all, including not sharing information with other agencies. An example of this is Department of Health (DH 2003) *Confidentiality NHS Code of Practice* which states:

> Information that can identify individual patients, must not be used or disclosed for purposes other than healthcare without the individual's explicit consent, some other legal basis, or where there is a robust public interest or legal justification to do so. (DH 2003, p.7)

This acts as a barrier in the reporting and recording of disability hate crime, especially when the disabled person lacks confidence to go directly to the police, or give consent, for fear they may not be taken seriously.

However, Part 5A of the Disability Discrimination Act (2005) and recently the Equality Act (2010) made it a duty to recognise the need to eliminate the harassment of disabled people. Furthermore, Section 115 of the Crime and Disorder Act (1998) over-rides the duty of confidentiality for the prevention and/or detection of crime. Safeguarding concerns offer a way for healthcare agencies and professionals to share information with social care and the police – all such safeguarding concerns could in theory be seen as a potential crime, unless otherwise advised by the police. Similarly, the 1998 Data Protection Act suggests that under 'vital interest' information may be shared 'where it is critical to prevent serious harm or distress or in life threatening situations'. The above legislations and policy framework certainly suggest that indeed 'the door is open' for agencies to work collectively.

In terms of good practice, we find the establishing of 'third party reporting centres' boosts the confidence of disabled people and encourages them to report hate crime. These reporting centres are locations other than police stations such as housing associations, charities, cafes, community centres, and online facilities such as 'True Vision' which victims may use to report crime. Similarly,

Community Safety Partnerships with representatives from a spectrum of professions have enabled a collaborative model of working with a shared sense of responsibility. Some areas, such as Stockport, are seeing the benefits of 'matrix working' and are moving towards the establishment of multi-agency hubs. Here, integration between different agencies is being enabled by simple factors such as co-location of services to make it easier to share information and expertise, which are both often resource consuming.

The upgrading of Safeguarding Adults Boards to a statutory footing is also helpful in raising the profile of disability hate crime within health and social care. In many areas these are already working closely with the Community Safety and the Learning Disability partnerships, harnessing the spirit of co-operation and inter-agency working. Finally, the recent introduction and election of Police and Crime Commissioners (PCCs) has added an element of democratic legitimacy and accountability to the system. PCCs cover wide geographical areas, with the potential of bringing consistency and co-ordination to the disability hate crime work across the different local authority areas. They can also play an important role in engaging with other stakeholders and in raising the profile of disability hate crime. In some areas they have already contributed to the development and progression of local hate crime strategies.

Recommendations and next steps

The formation of bodies such as Community Safety Partnerships and Multi-Agency Safeguarding Hubs has introduced the needed structural interventions to allow different professionals to come together and share information. At a day-to-day level a number of different recommendations emerge to make the recognition of and response to hate crime even more efficient.

First, based on the general consensus that disability and disability hate crime are poorly understood, there is a recommendation for the different partners to invest in a holistic training programme as part of Continued Professional Development, with formal mandatory accreditation for professionals. The content of this training should be tailored to allow professionals to understand how to identify and assess those at risk of being subject to disability hate crime, as well as providing clarity on the relevant legislation. Training should aim to build confidence of both staff and victims (Balderston and Roebuck 2010).

Second, in conjunction with training for frontline staff, an effective and simple risk assessment tool or framework should be developed which multi-agency practitioners could easily use. Simple guidelines can potentially even enable receptionists and support staff at practices, accident and emergency departments and hospitals to play an important role and to have confidence in sharing information with the relevant agencies.

Third, agencies should develop clear guidelines, referral pathways and policies for staff, with clear instructions on how to share information. These training courses, tools, pathways and policies should be confidence boosting, building a culture where the welfare of disabled people is an important priority for all.

Fourth, in recognition of the fact that different agencies may use a different professional language or have a different professional culture, as well as different methods of problem solving, agencies should promote inter-agency engagement and dialogue. This could be in the form of regular engagement events which provide an opportunity for professionals to come together to consider how agencies are currently working with one another and how this could be further improved. Professionals should be encouraged to disseminate this learning within their own organisations and feel empowered to make the necessary changes.

Fifth, agencies should proactively engage with disabled people on a regular basis, in creative ways. Engaging and interactive methods which allow disabled people to express themselves are helpful in overcoming communication barriers (Triangle 2010).

Sixth, at an organisational level, those organisations and institutions with frequent interactions with the disabled such as GP practices, housing associations, nursing homes and care homes, community clinics and accident and emergency departments all have the potential to act as third party reporting centres whilst also performing their safeguarding duties.

Finally, for multi-agency work to prove successful, it is important to have clearly defined governance arrangements. This requires clarity of expectations, responsibilities and direction, involvement of the right organisations and individuals, and a demonstration of strong leadership.

Needless to add, all recommendations, interventions and projects need an evaluation component to benchmark their effectiveness.

References

Allerton, L. A., Welch, V. and Emerson, E. (2011) 'Health inequalities experienced by children and young people with intellectual disabilities: A review of literature from the United Kingdom.' *Journal of Intellectual Disabilities 15*, 269.

Balderston, S. and Roebuck, E. (2010) *Empowering People to Tackle Hate Crime: Trans Women and Disabled People Working Together with Victim Services in North East England.* Manchester: EHRC.

Cooper, S. (2007) 'Was Westminster another Climbie?' *Children Now 21*, February, 12–13.

Department of Health (DH) (2003) *Confidentiality. NHS Code of Practice.* Available at www.gov.uk/government/uploads/system/uploads/attachment_data/file/200146/Confidentiality_-_NHS_Code_of_Practice.pdf, accessed on 5 December 2014.

DH (2009) *Valuing People Now: A New Three-Year Strategy for People with Learning Disabilities – Making it Happen for Everyone.* London: DH.

Equality and Human Rights Commission (EHRC) (2011) *Hidden in Plain Sight: Inquiry into Disability-Related Harassment.* London: EHRC. Available at www.equalityhumanrights.com/uploaded_files/disabilityfi/ehrc_hidden_in_plain_sight_3.pdf, accessed on 17 October 2014.

Her Majesty's Crown Prosecution Service Inspecturale (HMCPSI), HMIC and HMI Probation (2013) *Living in a Different World: Joint Review of Disability Hate Crime.* London: HMCPSI, HMIC and HMI Probation.

Home Office (2009) *Hate Crime – The Cross-Government Action Plan.* London: HM Government.

Home Office (2012) *Challenge It, Report it, Stop It: The Government's Plan to Tackle Hate Crime.* London: HM Government.

Mencap (2000) *Living in Fear.* Available at www.mencap.org.uk/sites/default/files/documents/2009-10/Livinginfear.pdf, accessed on 5 December 2014.

Mencap (2007) *Death By Indifference.* London: Mencap.

Mind (2007) *Another Assault. Mind's Campaign for Equal Access to Justice for People with Mental Health Problems.* Available at www.mind.org.uk/media/273466/another-assault.pdf, accessed on 5 December 2014.

Petersilia, J. (2001) 'Crime victims with developmental disabilities: a review essay.' *Criminal Justice and Behaviour 28*, 6, 655–694.

Quarmby, K. (2008) *Getting Away With Murder: Disabled People's Experiences of Hate Crime in the UK.* London: Scope. Available at www.scope.org.uk/Scope/media/Images/Publication%20Directory/Getting-away-with-murder.pdf, accessed on 17 October 2014.

Triangle (2010) 'A bit good but a bit not good too: children and young people's views about Specialist Health Services, The Care Quality Commission Review of Support for Families with Disabled Children.' London: Triangle.

CHAPTER 16

THE CRIMINAL JUSTICE SYSTEM RESPONSE TO DISABILITY HATE CRIME

PAUL GIANNASI OBE

In previous chapters, contributors have set out their views on the history and context of disability hate crime, about the problems experienced by disabled young people and the development of policy to try and reduce the harm it causes. In this chapter I will provide an outline of the legal framework that exists in England and Wales and will then comment on the progress made by the criminal justice agencies, who have a key role to play in reducing this harm. I will broadly follow chronological order and outline the motivations for change as well as reflecting on the quality of service offered to victims.

Legislation

As we write this book in 2014, I believe that the UK has amongst the most robust legislative framework for hate crime anywhere in the world. The hate crime report of the Organisation for Security and Co-operation in Europe (OSCE) (2012) demonstrates the massive disparity between legislation, policy and crime recording in its 57 participating States. Their guidance to States on establishing criminal legislation leans heavily on the UK model for good practice.

To avoid over-confusion, this chapter will consider the legislation in England and Wales, but there are similar provisions in Scotland and Northern Ireland.

Positive duty on agencies

In addition to the legislation to control criminal behaviour, the Equality Act (2010) creates a positive duty on public bodies, including the police and other criminal justice agencies. Essentially this compels agencies to consider issues such as hate crime.

Section 149 of the Equality Act (2010) requires that:

> A public authority must, in the exercise of its functions, have due regard to the need to (amongst other duties):
>
> a. eliminate discrimination, harassment, victimisation and any other conduct that is prohibited by or under this Act;
>
> b. foster good relations between persons who share a relevant protected characteristic and persons who do not share it.

The Act covers a number of 'protected characteristics', including disability. So, we ask ourselves, what does this mean in practice? In reality it is perhaps too soon to clearly understand how the courts would interpret these provisions as the case law has yet to demonstrate what they would consider to be a breach of the duties. The most comprehensive examination and interpretation of the duty came in the Equality and Human Rights Commission (EHRC) Inquiry (2011), which is described in greater detail in Chapter 2.

There are no specific offences of disability hate crime. The reality is that any offence can be considered as a hate crime where the perpetrator is motivated by hostility to disability. There is a deliberate disjoin between the criminal justice definition for recording and the court sentencing of offenders. This can be confusing at first sight but I will try to explain it simply here.

One of the core recommendations of the Stephen Lawrence Inquiry was that a crime should be recorded as a racist hate crime whenever the victim (or any other person) perceives it to be motivated by racism. It said that the police and other professionals should not challenge this perception, even where there is no admissible evidence that would prove this to be so. This principle was accepted by government and agencies and is reflected in the below definition of, in this instance, disability hate crime. That said, it would be unjust for a court to add additional punishment to a perpetrator where that perception was not supported by evidence to prove this to be so.

All criminal justice agencies share a common definition of 'Monitored Hate Crime' (College of Policing 2014). It includes the following concerning disability:

> [Generically] Hate crimes and incidents are taken to mean any crime or incident where the perpetrator's hostility or prejudice against an identifiable group of people is a factor in determining who is victimised.

A disability hate crime is taken to be:

> Any criminal offence which is perceived, by the victim or any other person, to be motivated by a hostility or prejudice based on a person's disability or perceived disability. (College of Policing 2014, p.3)

The definition refers to disability as including physical disability, learning disability and mental ill-health. This is slightly different from the Equality Act definition but is taken from the Criminal Justice Act (2003) described below. As you will see, the definition is inclusive and is designed to encourage reporting, to allow the broader considerations of hate crime to be applied.

The 'cornerstone' of the legislative framework is the enhanced sentencing provision which is provided by Section 146 of the Criminal Justice Act (2003). The section instructs the courts to enhance a sentence against an offender and to declare in court that they are doing so, when it is found that an offender demonstrated, or was motivated by, hostility based on disability (there are similar provisions for race, religion, sexual orientation and transgender).

For a court to apply the enhanced sentencing it must be satisfied that:

> at the time of committing the offence, or immediately before or after doing so, the offender demonstrated towards the victim of the offence hostility based on a disability (or presumed

disability) of the victim, or that the offence is motivated (wholly or partly) by hostility towards persons who have a disability or a particular disability. (College of Policing 2014, p.12)

Whilst the generic term 'hate crime' is recognised in many countries, it is very important that we recognise that the enhanced sentencing and hate crime recording do not require any evidence of 'hate', as we see above. The law requires evidence of 'hostility', a much less intense emotion. The Crown Prosecution Service (CPS) guidance (2010) states that:

> In the absence of a precise legal definition of hostility, consideration should be given to ordinary dictionary definitions, which include ill-will, ill-feeling, spite, contempt, prejudice, unfriendliness, antagonism, resentment and dislike. (p.12)

Comparison with other hate crime

As mentioned above, Sections 145 and 146 of the Criminal Justice Act (2003) have almost identical provisions to enhance sentencing for race and religion, in the case of Section 145, and sexual orientation, disability and transgender for Section 146. However, in 2007 prosecutors noticed an anomaly in respect of murder charges where the motivation was disability hostility. In all other instances 'Schedule 21' allowed for the 'starting point' for the calculation of the minimum tariff applied to life sentences to be raised from 15 to 30 years where the hostility is proved. However, disability was excluded from Schedule 21, meaning that the murders of Brent Martin and Steven Hoskin could not have this provision applied to the sentences of murder (although it could have applied to all other offences). It is important to stress that this does not mean that such crimes would automatically attract 30 years as the minimum tariff, but it relates only to the starting point for calculation of the tariff before consideration of other relevant factors.

The Crown Prosecution Service and latterly many groups and politicians lobbied for this 'anomaly' to be removed and in the Legal Aid, Sentencing and Punishment of Offenders Act (2012), provisions were added to provide parity in any future murders that are disability hate crimes.

The report of the EHRC Inquiry, *Hidden in Plain Sight* (2011), recommended that the government should consider certain elements of hate crime legislation. In response, the Justice Secretary, Chris Grayling MP, wrote to the Law Commission who agreed to review current hate crime provisions, to establish whether there would be a benefit to creating specific 'aggravated' offences, such as those currently available under Sections 29–32 of the Crime and Disorder Act (1998), which provided the following racially or religiously aggravated offences:

less serious assaults (Section 29)

criminal damage (Section 30)

less serious public order offences (Section 31)

harassment (Section 32).

In addition to these aggravated offences, the Law Commission examined whether there was a case to ask Parliament to consider the creation of an offence of inciting hatred against disabled (and transgender) people, to mirror existing offences relating to race, religion and sexual orientation.

The Law Commission reported its findings in May 2014 and the government is expected to respond to recommendations within a year of publication.

Moving forward from the Stephen Lawrence Inquiry

In Chapter 1, Tyson, Giannasi and Hall stressed the significance to all hate crime of the murder of Stephen Lawrence, or more accurately, the lobbying of the family for justice and the 1999 report of the public inquiry. The response to the inquiry introduced significant change, in terms of legislation, criminal justice policy and the culture within criminal justice agencies.

In 2003, Professor Gus John was asked to examine the CPS decision making, to identify possible racial bias within the prosecution process. His report, *Race for Justice* (2003), included the following recommendation:

Recommendation 8:
[The] CPS, through the good offices of the Attorney General should take the lead in establishing a holistic approach, across the Criminal Justice System to the issues highlighted by this research, not least in respect of the handling of race crimes by the police, the CPS and the Courts.

In response to the above recommendation the then Attorney General, Lord Goldsmith, established a task force under the chairmanship of The Honourable Mr Justice Fulford. The task force reported in June 2006 in their report, also called *Race for Justice*, and found that:

Our work revealed that there are varying levels of performance monitoring by Criminal Justice System agencies in respect of handling these crimes. The problems include a significant failure to record these crimes accurately and different ethnicity classification systems being used by the various agencies, which in turn speak a different statistical language. We consider it necessary that all the agencies track cases from the receipt of an allegation until the end of the court process using some core, common terminology.

The task force made a series of recommendations, covering all criminal justice agencies and including issues such as common definitions, training, monitoring and service delivery.

In response to the task force report, the government established a work programme, initially called 'Race for Justice', but latterly known as the Cross-Government Hate Crime Programme. The programme brought together relevant government departments, criminal justice agencies and the judiciary on a board which had oversight of the programme, hosted within the Office for Criminal Justice Reform and latterly the Ministry of Justice.

In addition to the board, the programme was established with a dedicated Independent Advisory Group to ensure that victims, advocates and academics have the opportunity to influence future policy and legislation.

Soon after the programme was established, in April 2007, it began work to agree a common definition of hate crime, which would provide clarity and also allow system changes to provide more accurate data on the extent of hate crime. Until this time hate crime evaluation had largely concentrated on race and there was no consistency as to which 'strands' of hate crime were included. At this time the CPS included domestic violence within their hate crime policy, but the police did not, which made comparative data almost impossible.

The programme considered the inclusion of disability, along with a large number of other potential 'strands' for inclusion. They ranged from attacks on people who worked in animal experimentation laboratories, through to racism.

What it found, when examining the current recording of disability as a strand of hate crime, was a huge inconsistency. Some police forces did include disability but many others did not. When those that did include disability examined what sort of crimes had become recorded as disability hate crime, there was again inconsistency with some forces recording, for example, theft of disabled parking badges. However, whilst there was no consistent recognition of disability hate crime, those crimes we discussed earlier in this book influenced the Board to accept the inclusion of disability as one of the five strands of 'Monitored Hate Crime'.

The shared definition of Monitored Hate Crime was agreed by the Association of Chief Police Officers (ACPO) Cabinet in November 2007 and, shortly afterwards, by all other criminal justice agencies.

In 2007, there were many individuals who argued against the expansion of the hate crime categories beyond race. A common argument was that we should not lose the focus on our efforts to eradicate racism and, until we have done so, we should not consider other motivations. This view was, however, rejected by government and criminal justice agencies. In November 2007 the then Attorney General, Baroness Scotland, who was the Superintending Minister for the programme, made a speech to the European Hate Crime Conference which was held in London. She said:

I have heard arguments that say that by broadening our attention, we dilute the effort to eradicate racism – I can not accept that argument. The same bigotry that fuels racism fuels other types of hate.

We must seek to provide the same high degree of service to all hate crime victims. This must mean that all areas achieve the same high standard; I can assure you that I would never allow this to mean that our efforts to combat racism should be diluted in any way.

Given this firm steer from the Attorney General, the programme examined its membership and brought in new members to reflect the broader objectives. This included the Department of Health being represented on the board and a number of disabled people joining the Independent Advisory Group.

The programme took Baroness Scotland's direction and established that there were four victims groups who were considered to be susceptible but where reporting of such crimes was less likely. They were: asylum and refugee communities, Gypsy and Traveller communities, disabled and transgender victims.

Once the definition was in place, the programme wanted to assess the quality of service provided to hate crime victims and it developed a 'Hate Crime Diagnostic Tool' to allow partnerships to examine the service they offer across the criminal justice system.

The criminal justice agencies, particularly the police and the CPS started to raise awareness about the nature and perceived prevalence of disability hate crime. Measures were put in place to gather data from April 2008. As part of this process, key leaders from each agency stated their determination to improve services to disabled victims and to increase the recording of such crimes. There was a general acceptance that what we had seen in the high-profile crimes of 2007 was merely the 'tip of the iceberg' and there was undoubtedly many more, less serious but nonetheless traumatic, crimes that never came to the attention of the authorities.

In October 2008, the then Director of Public Prosecutions, Sir Ken Macdonald QC (now Lord Macdonald of River Glaven), made a speech on the subject of disability hate crime. He said:

I am on record as saying that it is my sense that disability hate crime is very widespread. I have said that it is my view that at the lower end of the spectrum there is a vast amount not being picked up. I have also expressed the view that the more serious disability hate crimes are not always being prosecuted as they should be.

This is a scar on the conscience of criminal justice. And all bodies and all institutions involved in the delivery of justice, including my own, share the responsibility.

After the speech Chief Constable Steve Otter, who at the time led the Association of Chief Police Officers' Equality Business Area, agreed with this sentiment saying that much will have to be done to improve police understanding of disability hate crime and to encourage victims to come forward.

Criminal justice data

The shared definition of Monitored Hate Crime allowed criminal justice agencies to collate and publish hate crime data.

In September 2009, ACPO published its first set of national hate crime data (for the 2008 calendar year). It recorded data as shown in Table 16.1:

Table 16.1 ACPO National Hate Crime Data, 2008–2013

Year	Disability hate crimes recorded	Data includes police forces in England, Wales and Northern Ireland
2008	800	This was an estimated figure as collection commenced in April
2009	1294	
2010	1569	
2011	1937	
2012/13	1853	Data collection changed to record April/March

Source: Association of Chief Police Officers' Hate Crime Data 2008–2013, published at www.report-it.org.uk.

In line with the increased recording by the police, the number of prosecutions for disability hate crime recorded by the CPS has steadily increased since 2007/08 (although they recorded a reduction in the last available figures of 2012/13). They publish data based on the fiscal year and this was recorded as shown in Table 16.2.

Table 16.2 Crown Prosecution Service Hate Crime Prosecution Data 2007–2013

Year	Disability hate crimes referrals considered	Disability hate crime charges authorised	Successful outcomes
2007/8	279	187	77%
2008/9	444	292	76.1%
2009/10	720	506	75.7%
2010/11	690	726	79.8%
2011/12	643	621	77.3%
2012/13	579	640	77.2%

Source: Crown Prosecution Service Hate Crime Reports 2010 to 2014

Whilst the above data shows fluctuations, it clearly indicates a rising trend in the recording of disability hate crimes and the number of prosecutions identified as such.

The transparent publication of the data allows the public to see the progress made against the commitments made by executives within the criminal justice system, but it also allows managers to assess progress. An example of this was the response to the recorded reduction in the CPS 2011/12 report. In the weeks following on from the publication the Director of Public Prosecutions met with the ACPO hate crime lead and agreed a joint audit of disability hate crime prosecution to establish the effectiveness of the recording processes and to identify any areas for improvement.

Coroner's inquest into the deaths of Fiona Pilkington and Francecca Hardwick

As I mentioned in Chapter 3, the relevance of these tragic deaths to the area of disability hate crime was unclear until the circumstances of their deaths were established and concerns expressed by the Assistant Deputy Coroner, Olivia Davison, during the inquest which took place in September 2009. She was critical of the police and local authority responses and the jury concluded that Fiona had killed herself and her daughter 'due to the stress and anxiety regarding her daughter's future, and ongoing anti-social behaviour'; the jury went on to say they believed that the police and local authority had contributed to Fiona's decision, because of the failure to link or prioritise the crimes and incidents suffered by the family.

Criminal justice agencies recognised the gravity of the damage to public confidence in the police and partners that had been caused by the widespread coverage of the inquest. Chief Constable Otter declared the situation to be a 'critical incident', defined as:

> any incident where the effectiveness of the police response is likely to have significant impact on the confidence of the victim, their family and/or the community.

The declaration of a critical incident enabled ACPO to establish a Gold and Silver Group which has oversight of the police response and it also brought together key partners such as other criminal justice agencies and relevant government departments.

Each force appointed an executive lead officer who would feed into the Gold Group and disseminate activity back to their own force. The Gold and Silver groups met until 2011, when the decision was taken to create a permanent group under the leadership of Chief Constable Simon Cole who had, since the inquest, taken over as the Chief Constable of Leicestershire Police.

In order to support the work of the Gold Group, a series of conferences and workshops were held where Ministers, criminal justice executives and victims groups were able to present their views to local managers and practitioners.

Inspecting performance

In response to the inquiry of the EHRC discussed in detail in Chapter 2, Her Majesty's Inspectorates for the police, probation and CPS carried out a joint thematic inspection to review progress within the criminal justice response to disability hate crime. Their report which was published in 2013 made a series of recommendations for all agencies. The joint inspectors noted that many people felt that society's attitudes towards disabled people had not changed in parallel with other areas such as race. They found that the criminal justice system had introduced initiatives to improve performance but noted that progress had been slow with a new impetus being required. It challenged criminal justice agencies and society in general to adapt to improve the experience of disabled people. The report concluded that:

> Disability hate crime is a complex area and has a number of unique features. In many ways it is the hate crime that has been left behind.

Providing guidance to professionals

Since disability was included in hate crime policy, the police and CPS have provided guidance to local managers and practitioners from using presentations from policy leaders and executives a through to formal published guidance.

In 2007, the CPS published its policy concerning the prosecution of disability hate crime. The guidance included advice on presenting evidence to support the consideration of enhanced sentencing under the Criminal Justice Act, obtaining successful prosecutions and the provision of victim support, both in terms of providing support to enable disabled people to provide their evidence to the court and to deal with the psychological damage that a crime can cause to a victim.

Notably the guidance to prosecutors has particular mention of the application of 'special measures' and intermediaries.

'Special measures' were introduced by the Youth Justice and Criminal Evidence Act (1999) and are available in both crown and magistrates' courts. They are available to help the following witnesses:

- children under 17 years

- adults (17 and over) who may be considered vulnerable because of incapacity, such as a physical or mental disorder or learning disability

- witnesses whose evidence is likely to be affected because they are intimidated (for example, afraid or distressed about giving evidence).

Special measures include a range of possible support such as giving evidence through video, being shielded from sight of the defendant or public gallery, use of communication aids such as signal boards or the use of an intermediary.

An intermediary is a trained professional who is appointed by the court to act as an independent expert, to assist the victim or witness to give their evidence. Intermediaries would include language therapists and social workers who have a relevant expertise.

In 2014, the College of Policing published a hate crime strategy and the latest version of its Hate Crime Operational Guidance. The guidance covers all types of hate crime including a specific section on reducing the harm caused by disability hate crime.

True Vision

As I discussed in Chapter 3 and elsewhere in this book, addressing the under-reporting and subsequent under-recording of disability hate crime has been a key priority for criminal justice agencies and government. There are three key strands to the criminal justice response to this priority:

- raising victims' awareness of their rights to be protected from hostility

- providing accessible reporting options for victims, either directly to agencies or through third parties

- improving professionals' knowledge of hate crime recording mechanisms.

A key vehicle for delivering all of the above objectives is 'True Vision', which is the branding for ACPO's hate crime materials. It is built around a web facility.[1] The facility hosts a range of materials to inform victims, professionals and advocates and includes a

---

1   This is at www.report-it.org.uk.

range of victim-focused resources which can be downloaded and deployed locally.

True Vision also hosts a range of materials to assist individuals and groups to establish themselves as third party reporting mechanisms, whether that be as part of a formal partnership or informally in support of an individual or small group of people susceptible to hate crime. It provides resources and routes to report to the police without the need for extensive recording systems to be maintained. It also has an online reporting mechanism which allows victims or third parties to report crimes to the police in their local area, including doing so anonymously if they are unwilling to give personal details.

The central web facility of True Vision is supported by active social media use and a mobile phone application. These facilities have increased access to True Vision which, by 2014, was receiving 10,000 visits per month to the site, from users who visited an average of seven pages per visit.

True Vision acts as a central library for resources and the police have commissioned a range of targeted video and other products to help highlight their commitment to combating hate crime. One example of this is a video developed from a police/community partnership in West Mercia, which is aimed at British Sign Language users. Having posted the video, the police were able to use social media advertising to alert possible interested parties to its presence. The video was downloaded or viewed 688 times in the first month.

Community engagement

The police and CPS have both recognised, in their guidance, the importance of engaging with disabled people, whether that is at a local or national level. Whilst many events take place, the reality is that they are not equally spread and some professionals or partnerships place greater importance on efforts to engage with the community than others.

One excellent example of community engagement is the products developed by the CPS in the north-west of England.

They have produced a package which is designed to assist educators in raising awareness of disability hate crime, whether that be to disabled or non-disabled children. The products can be viewed and downloaded from the Education Support section of the True Vision website.

Conclusions

It is easy to argue that the criminal justice response to disability hate crime is either the best in the world or falling woefully short of expectations.

If we are being positive, compared to other states, the UK has: a strong legislative framework, stated declarations that disability hate crime is a priority for agencies, guidance for professionals and bodies, such as the Independent Police Complaints Commission, criminal justice inspectorates and the EHRC, who have all examined this response and made recommendations for its improvement. We have also seen a 150 per cent increase in recorded hate crime in the three years following its commencement in 2008.

However, what we also discussed earlier in this book are some of the deficiencies in this response. What we have to acknowledge is the inconsistency of the responses, as demonstrated by a comparison between areas in the police recorded crime data. The British Crime Survey data also exposes the huge gap between disabled people's experiences of crime and those that are recorded as such by the police. Whilst I accept that some of those crimes will have received a quality response but not have been noted as disability hate crime, the data tells us that less than 1 in 30 crimes appear in the statistics.

Whilst it is important to acknowledge the hard work that has been done by professionals, advocates and disabled people's organisations to raise awareness and to increase reporting, it is clear that there is still a very long way to go before we can claim that disabled people achieve true equality in this very important area, the right to live a life free from hostility and targeted crime.

References

Association of Chief Police Officers (ACPO) (2007) *Practice Advice on Critical Incident Management.* London: ACPO. Available at www.acpo.police.uk/documents/crime/2007/200708-cba-critical-incident-management.pdf, accessed on 9 February 2015.

Attorney General's Office (2006) *Report of the Race for Justice Taskforce.* London: Attorney General's Office.

College of Policing (2014) *Hate Crime Strategy and Operational Guidance.* London: College of Policing.

Crown Prosecution Service (CPS) (2007) *Policy for Prosecuting Cases of Disability Hate Crime.* London: CPS.

CPS (2010) *Hate Crime and Crimes Against Older People Report, 2009–2010.* London: CPS.

CPS (2012) *Hate Crime and Crimes Against Older People Report, 2011–2012.* London: CPS.

CPS (2014) *Hate Crime and Crimes Against Older People Report, 2012–2013.* London: CPS.

Equality and Human Rights Commission (EHRC) (2012) *Out in the Open: Tackling Disability-Related Harassment – A Manifesto for Change.* London: EHRC. Available at www.equalityhumanrights.com/publication/out-open-tackling-disability-related-harassment-manifesto-change, accessed on 17 October 2014.

EHRC (2011) *Hidden in Plain Sight: Inquiry into Disability-Related Harassment.* London: EHRC. Available at www.equalityhumanrights.com/uploaded_files/disabilityfi/ehrc_hidden_in_plain_sight_3.pdf, accessed on 17 October 2014.

HMCPSI, HMIC and HMI Probation (2013) *Living in a Different World: Joint Review of Disability Hate Crime.* London: HMCPSI, HMIC and HMI Probation.

John, G. (2003) *Race for Justice.* London: CPS.

Law Commission (2014) *Hate Crime: Should the Current Offences be Extended?* London: Law Commission.

Mind (2007) *Another Assault.* London: Mencap.

Organization for Security and Co-operation in Europe (OSCE) (2012) *Hate Crimes in the OSCE Region – Incidents and Responses. Annual Report for 2011.* Warsaw: OSCE.

Office for Democratic Institutions and Human Rights (2009) *Hate Crime Laws: A Practical Guide.* Warsaw: OSCE.

CHAPTER 17

INFLUENCING POLICY

LORD NIGEL CRISP KBE

I approach this subject as someone who knows relatively little about hate crimes against children and adults with disabilities, despite having worked with disabled people in a number of different capacities over the years. I am not unusual in this and, indeed, this lack of awareness is in many ways the point of this chapter.

The book as a whole is about how practitioners can develop the understanding and skills necessary to combat these problems. An important aspect of this is to understand how to influence policy makers and budget holders. In this chapter I will use my experience as a former Chief Executive of the NHS and consider how best to bring the importance of this issue to the attention of leaders in public service and in government and, ultimately, how to influence public policy for the better. In other words, 'What would have persuaded me in my role as Chief Executive – and people in similar roles – to give this issue priority and what are the policy and other tools available which could help improve the situation?'

The discussion that follows will address the Realpolitik – what really happens in politics – not what should ideally happen in an ideal world. In my six years as Chief Executive of the NHS, I was lobbied every day about different causes because everything in health and social care is a priority to someone. There is competition for attention and priority. What, therefore, is the best strategy to adopt? What are the best tactics?

First, we need to consider the nature of the issue itself. Hate crimes against disabled people, as other writers in this book have shown, take many forms and can easily be invisible in wider society. It may be about low-key bullying at school or on the internet, physical abuse, name calling or violence and it can be linked to social isolation and discrimination by the authorities in access to services. The crimes are personal, private and, often, insidious and long-term. The level of abuse and violence can escalate dramatically if early symptoms are not recognised and risks reduced. There are a few high-profile cases which have come to the attention of the media and the public but much more is secret and hidden away both by perpetrators and their victims.

There are also much wider issues about social attitudes which, as others have written, have deep and multiple roots in culture and cultures. Whilst Government can influence attitudes and behaviours, its impact on them is limited and needs to be exercised alongside others in society. This complexity must not be used as an excuse for inaction by government or other authorities; although it is often, in reality, a reason why action is not taken.

Politicians and policy makers may in all honesty see the issue as too complex and difficult, outside their remit, cutting across too many departments to be practical, not primarily a task for government or, saddest of all, as being too long-term a problem to be dealt with during this Parliament, this period of government or this particular planning period. It can all too easily be 'kicked into the long grass'.

In many cases, the Minister or official may simply not see what can be done about the problem. They may not have the knowledge, the experience or the imagination, even if they have the will to do something.

There are, however, many things that governments can do; albeit as part of a wider cross-societal effort. Public authorities can ensure that the policy makers and public servants understand the nature of the problem, that its scale is measured and known and that policies and practices address it and do not, unconsciously and inadvertently, aggravate the situation or make it easier for perpetrators to conceal their actions.

It is essential that this is seen as a cross-government issue and addressed by inter-departmental policies. It is not just a matter for the police, teachers or health and social workers, but one for them and others to be working on together. This is very difficult to do in reality. However, there is now a great deal of experience to draw on, going back many years in other areas of children's policy, as the following illustrations from my own field of health show.

Efforts by some parts of government to get children to exercise more in the 1980s, before childhood obesity was a major issue, were undermined by demands from other departments to sell off school playing fields. Thirty years later, with obesity now endemic, there are policy conflicts between departments promoting health and well-being and those promoting the rights of food processors and retailers to regulate themselves as to the amount of salt and sugar in foods and how they display this information for the public. Going from these general examples to individual cases, there are also many tragic instances where murderers and abusers have been able to commit their crimes and, even, escape justice because of lack of co-ordination or poor co-operation between agencies and individuals.

There are lessons about what to do and what not to do from all these examples and from the long history of inquiries stretching back from before Maria Colwell in 1973 to the appalling crimes of Soham and the death of Baby P. The recent inquest into the deaths of Fiona Pilkington and Francecca Hardwick – victims of disability hate crimes – questioned the ability of government agencies to recognise the harm caused by the harassment of disabled people and, once again, raised issues about the relationship between partner organisations and their ability to communicate, assess risk and reduce harm.

There is also much to learn from past improvements: the risks and reality of child abuse are now much better managed than 30 years ago; children with learning difficulties are no longer confined in hospitals; bullying in schools has now become more visible and preventing it has been given higher priority; and equalities and human rights legislation have provided a foundation for exposing and tackling problems. Public campaigning on smoking, funded by government and linked with legislation, is gradually having an effect; whilst campaigns on HIV helped stop the epidemic growing.

There are two things which all these examples have in common. First, many of the actions you would take to deal with one problem will help with others: exercise, obesity, smoking, bullying, adult supervision and education are all easily linked. Second, few if any of these problems are ever finally solved – for example, there is a resurgence in 'unsafe' sex as fears of HIV have almost disappeared in a new young generation – and campaigners need to be constantly vigilant and find ways to secure their advances for the long term.

The most important lesson for our purposes, however, is that government can do something about even the most seemingly intransigent problems. Progress is possible. There is a body of knowledge and experience which researchers are adding to all the time.

How, therefore, can you get Government to act? How, to put it in very immediate and concrete terms, do you behave when you get the long-awaited meeting with the Minister and his or her officials to press the case? How can you ensure that they won't simply see you as yet another special interest lobby group in the long line of such groups they will see that day? None of them will say your cause is not important, of course: there will be supportive words, but will there be action?

Supportive words, but will there be action?

Against this background I would suggest that securing an effective cross-government approach will be based around three things: first, awareness raising and building the will for change; second, changing the terms of the debate; and third, describing precisely what is wanted from government. Let me take them in turn.

Raising awareness successfully is a pre-requisite for building the will for change. Whilst there is an obvious need for raising awareness given the lack of visibility of much disability hate crime and the importance of tackling problems early, it is also vitally important that people are motivated to actually do something about it. The public, the media, public servants and even those with disabilities, their supporters and friends need to understand the nature and the scale of the problem and, crucially, to be clear what they can do about it. This, in turn, requires sensitivity to language and to audiences and the ability to gather and present the right data and evidence.

There are many good examples of raising awareness around children's issues, whether in the UK by campaigning organisations or globally, with the malaria insecticide treated bed net campaign being a particularly good one. Many of these rely on shocking stories and awful statistics. Many, too, seek to engage their audiences with the use of celebrities, fun events and all the techniques of affinity marketing. They are most likely to be successful in persuading policy makers when they are supported by hard data and evidence rather than just by anecdote and individual cases. Stories can win over the heart but data and evidence convince the mind. Both are needed.

The biggest problem, from my experience in being on the receiving end of many advocacy campaigns, is that it can be very difficult for advocates to demonstrate what works in practice because there is often very little evidence. The problem may be very clear but where is the evidence about what you can do about it that will have a real impact? An important aspect of this book is that it seeks to present the evidence in an area that is still relatively new to rigorous inquiry and evaluation. It will provide some answers to this question.

There is also a very important place for political analysis – with a small 'p' – and the careful working through of who are the potential allies and likely opponents and of how to build a coalition of support. This takes us back to the rather contradictory points I made earlier about, on the one hand, there being competition for attention and priority between different causes and, on the other, that there are many actions which address one cause which will also help with others. Here, as in much of life, the best competitive strategy may well be collaboration and the searching out of common cause with as many others as possible. This includes, of course, the very politicians and policy makers you are trying to influence.

It is vitally important that those in authority are held to account for their actions and their responsibilities – and I write as someone who has appeared before many Parliamentary Select Committees and other mechanisms of public accountability. At the same time, however, it can be very effective to seek to engage the policy makers themselves in the endeavour so that they become the internal advocates for the cause. Their interests can align with yours.

It is worth remembering that politicians and policy makers are human beings too. I have observed situations where advocates for a cause have approached ministers very aggressively or lectured them on their responsibilities – and seen just how counter productive it was. It all becomes a question of judgement: is the minister a potential ally or an opponent and what will be the most effective tactics to employ – attack or engagement?

In summary, when it comes to the issues of advocacy and building the will for change, the key issues are clarity of message, targeting the right audiences, engaging people in understanding what they can do to help, providing objective data and evidence, building a coalition with allies and finding as many third party advocates as possible, including internal champions, amongst those you are trying to influence.

The second key strategic area, which I described earlier as 'changing the terms of the debate', needs more explanation. I suspect that we all approach disability hate crimes with a feeling of outrage and the desire to protect the children and adults involved and to ensure that their rights are upheld. This is entirely right and good; however, I wonder if it is enough.

If we frame the issue only in these terms we may unintentionally foster the notion that disabled people are defined by their vulnerability and seen only as a burden on society and the state. Baroness Jane Campbell, a good friend, a tireless campaigner and radical thinker about disability, sees it very differently. She has pointed out to me that disabled people are amongst the best project managers and problem solvers in the world. If you can only move your arm or have difficulty speaking you have to solve problems all the time, learn how to cope and how to exercise some control over the external world. This is only one example of the many different talents and abilities people may have.

Leaders like Baroness Campbell have been engaged for years in changing perceptions of disabled people, re-framing the issue and taking on well-intentioned paternalism as well as discrimination and disadvantage. The simple point is that disabled people should not be seen as a cost and a drain on society but as people who can be enabled to fulfil their potential and contribute alongside everybody else.

Once we re-conceptualise the issues in this way we really can change the terms of the debate. It is not just about convincing the public and the policy makers to care enough to do something but we can describe the tangible benefits to us all of doing so. We can start to strip away some of the wider discrimination that disabled people face, which goes far beyond disability hate crimes and can affect all aspects of life. It means that alongside the terrible stories of cruelty, campaigners need to promote positive images of disabled people and their contribution.

It also means that when we approach government we are not just asking for justice and for help – and appealing to the Health, Social Services, Home and Justice Departments – but we are also challenging Business, Education and Treasury to help nurture the ability and potential of disabled people alongside those of every other citizen.

A cross-government strategy

The approach to government needs to be based on being very clear about what is wanted. This is important for many reasons, of course, but it is particularly so in terms of the way policy is made. Government policy making is not generally a simple linear process which progresses logically from need to evidence of what works to policy and implementation. In reality, it is one in which there is competition for attention, multiple stakeholders and considerations about timing and practicalities can determine what gets done and what doesn't. Moreover, politicians and policy makers are human beings and may well react as human beings to the way they are approached – you can make them champions or turn them into opponents.

Realpolitik is about power and a key consideration is where this issue sits in terms of wider Political – with a big 'P' – considerations. How does it relate to government and opposition policy, and where do other parties sit? The current government is attempting to re-write much of social policy, redefining the welfare state as it does so. There are helpful strands to this: such as the emphasis on independence and localism and, possibly, the idea of the Big Society. There are also, however, reductions in support for disabled people and there is no recognition in current legislation of the need to support disabled people to play a bigger part in society or of the contribution they can make. The opposition policies are still relatively unformed at this stage, which, of course, presents an opportunity for lobbyists and advocates.

This brief summary reveals the choices that people wanting to influence have in how they approach government. Looking at current government policy: is there enough overlap with your concerns to try to build common cause or does the approach need to be one of confrontation? Confrontation can work: governments sometimes back down and public campaigns and outrage can affect policy. In reality, the best approach may be a mixture of both: trying to find allies in government and enlist them in the coalition for change and confrontation on key issues. The approach with opposition and other parties will be similar but the energy and effort put into it will depend in turn on your analysis of the likelihood that the party will come to power soon or have any real influence on policy.

Two points stand out. First, you probably know more about the issue than the politicians and, possibly, the policy makers. You therefore need to make it easy for them to understand and to come to them with answers and not just problems, as well as the data and evidence I mentioned earlier. You need to know exactly what you want from government – what is the precise ask? Second, timing is key. You can't dictate when the time will be right but you can spot when it is. Openings exist when the issue or a related issue is in the news for some reason (often, sadly, because of a tragedy), when oppositions are planning for government and in the early part of the parliamentary cycle or the early days of a government or of a minister's term in office.

Going forward, how can we co-design a mandate or memorandum for a 'call for action'? I believe that such a call for action needs to have the three parts I have discussed in this chapter and to be combined with a vision of what success would look like.

First, we need to conceive of this as a campaign with the specific goal of raising awareness and, crucially, building the will for change. It is essential to find allies, engage people from all kinds of backgrounds in wanting to change the situation and develop energy and momentum. This needs to be a shared effort – a coalition for action – and not just another good cause in competition with the others. Internal and external champions, celebrity endorsement, shock tactics, shocking stories and fun events will all be part of this; but so too will be data and evidence. We need to be able to say that we know what the problem is and what can be done about it.

Second, the campaign needs to take place in the context of disabled children and adults being contributors to society and having the potential to do more. It must be about social justice and outrage – and it must be about protecting vulnerable children – but it must also be about shifting perceptions about disability and changing social attitudes and behaviours.

Third, the approach to government needs to be carefully thought through and well focused. Alongside the general cross-government aim there need to be aims for each relevant department. What government policies can this be linked with in Education, what legislation is needed in Health, what practices need to change in the Police, what policies are needed in Business?

This call for action is a rallying cry to help achieve a vision of a society where children and adults with disabilities are not bullied and victimised, where public servants are alert to the dangers and know how to deal with them quickly and effectively, and where children with disabilities can grow up in a world where disabled people are seen – just like everybody else – as having needs for nurturing and development as well as talents and skills to contribute.

CHAPTER 18

CONCLUSIONS AND RECOMMENDATIONS

DR ROBINA SHAH MBE AND PAUL GIANNASI OBE

This book has provided a precious insight through personal, academic and professional accounts of the circumstances in which disability hate crime and discrimination may persist and the impact it can have on victims. Whilst the abuse and discrimination of disabled people has been present throughout history, the concept of disability hate crime is relatively new, having only been included in national criminal justice hate crime policy since 2007. For this reason the data, analytics and empirical evidence is sparse. This makes this book very timely, as it will help organisations and government departments responsible for planning, delivering and providing services to better understand their challenges, and also identify some areas ripe for further research.

Finding a common definition that binds the chapters together has proven difficult because of the broad nature of abuse and the different settings in which disability hate crime takes place. Debates about hate crime can get 'bogged down' with definitions and it is fair to say there is no common consensus, yet the hostility and discrimination faced by disabled people is all too real and we cannot wait for academia and interested parties to find that consensus. Our moral and legal duties to reduce the harm caused by hate crime and discrimination is urgent, whatever we call it. However, for the purpose of this book the definition that is commonly referred to by most contributors and appears most applicable here is the definition provided by the College of Policing in their Operational Guidance (2014) and shared across the criminal justice system:

> Hate crimes and incidents are taken to mean any crime or incident where the perpetrator's hostility or prejudice against

an identifiable group of people is a factor in determining who is victimized… So any incident or crime, which is perceived by the victim or any other person to be motivated because of a person's disability or perceived disability will be recorded as such.

So what are the key challenges?

A lack of a joined-up framework between organisations emerges as a key message particularly in their pursuit to understand and respond to disability hate crime within the various public service sectors, including health, primary care, social care, education, regulation and the criminal justice system. The individual stories, discussed in the carers' and victims' chapters, describe the poor treatment of disabled people, the lack of adequate support given to them at the time of disclosure, lack of robust systems to report harm and the negligent attitudes and prejudice held by some staff working across the public sector.

There is clearly a call for change and a call for action but working in isolation will not provide the right solution; this can only be reached by working together and defining a common purpose to deliver sustainable change.

Why has it not been solved?

Various examples have been given in the chapters to explain why some services may still be failing disabled people. This appears to stem from a lack of knowledge amongst key staff groups that discrimination and disability hate crime co-exist and poor identification, fragmented practice and a lack of understanding about it has resulted in a poor experience for disabled people and their carers and families.

Some of the key themes discussed in the book are consistent across all service departments while others are unique because they lie within the jurisdictions of particular government agencies and public institutions. The contributions also illustrate the improvements that need to be considered in order to address the lack of engagement with these themes. The strategic summary of the *Home Office Action Plan on Tackling Hate Crime* further supports the view that a cross-governmental strategy offers the best framework to engage all practitioners working with disabled people. It provides the conversation piece essential to reduce the incidence of disability hate crime, to encourage reporting, to raise awareness and ultimately to improve the experience of victims of disability hate crime in relation to service and support in the community.

There is a fundamental connection and interplay between all of the issues identified above. For example, it is important to recognise the extent of under-reporting and poor recording of disability hate crime and the implications this can have for disabled people and for services that support them. The lack of awareness about disability hate crime in the NHS may lead to poor support, a restriction of access to services and therefore a disproportionate service received by disabled people. This failure to support could contribute to the poor reporting of hate crime because victims do not feel safe or do not get the support they need to share their experience.

Similarly, the criminal justice system needs to provide better support for victims through proactive work that may lead to a reduction in hostility in our communities and prevent future crimes from happening.

Systems, processes, data collection, identification and reporting mechanisms, education and training are just some of the drivers that can strengthen a consistent cross-government approach. However, it will be leadership and sharing a common vision that will provide the impetus needed to really make a difference. This must be supported by a strategy that is non-political, collaboratively driven and committed to delivering sustainable change.

How can we address the challenges?

The argument for change discussed in this book is compelling and inaction is no longer acceptable. Disability hate crime must be everyone's business.

The final call for action is captured in the section below, the summary of recommendations. This brings together the spirit and the emphasis for change from contributors united by their shared ambition for a collaborative partnership approach that is committed to challenging disability hate crime and disability discrimination in all its forms.

Recommendations

Society

- Society must accept that:
  - Hostility and sexual violence is a reality for many disabled people and this undermines our society as well as damaging victims.
  - Disabled people are at higher risk than others of becoming a victim.
  - Disabled people have the same rights as others and are deserving of protection and advocacy.

General for all professionals

- Effective leadership in all organisations individually and collectively is essential. Strong leadership of the issue in organisations is critical for dealing with harassment. Leaders must show a strong personal commitment and determination to deliver change.
- Definitive data must be made publicly available which spells out the scale, severity and nature of disability harassment and enables better monitoring of the performance of those responsible for dealing with it.
- Research is needed to provide a better understanding of the motivations and circumstances of perpetrators and this should inform the design of offender interventions.
- Work is needed to inform all frontline staff who may be required to recognise and respond to issues of disability-related harassment of the systems and processes of ensuring victims get the services they need.

- There should be a strengthening of arrangements for data sharing, including through third party reporting organisations and the police's True Vision website and with multi-agency partnerships including Multi-Agency Risk Assessment processes.

- Agencies need to ensure that disability hate crime is not subsumed under an often reactive safeguarding agenda. Safeguarding processes are a tool for responding to hate crime and vice versa. Inclusion in one should never exclude the resources of the other.

Criminal justice system

- Work is needed to develop proactive approaches to reporting incidents when they occur.

- The Criminal Justice System (CJS) needs to be fully accessible and responsive to victims and disabled people.

- Police and prosecutors must cease to concentrate on the perceived weakness of witnesses' credibility but focus instead on case building and the characteristics of the suspect.

- The CJS needs to provide effective support to meet the individual needs of victims rather than a single unified response.

- Work needs to continue to collaborate with the internet industry to better protect victims from exposure to ridicule or hostility on internet forums.

Social care professionals

- There should be agreed national training standards for adult protection safeguarding boards which include targeted abuse by redefining issues as hate crimes and not just issues for vulnerable adults, including obligations for action when triggers of escalating abuse are present. This approach should be aligned to healthcare and other relevant sectors.

- Greater awareness for professional organisations is needed; rather than just acting as a third party reporter of hate crimes there needs to be specific guidance for the local authority and other agencies to act and raise awareness when early stages of escalating abuse are identified.

- There should be changes in legislation to put hate crimes in line with other punishable crimes; if someone dies as a result of abuse this needs to be treated as murder rather than focusing on the vulnerability of the individual and in some way excusing the result as less important because the individual is disabled.

- It would be useful to have government-funded public advertising campaigns to raise awareness of people's right to be present in the community and greater acceptance of difference.

- There should be challenge to and controls on media coverage that accepts discrimination and encourages discrimination, disharmony and disrespect within the community.

Education

- Educators must engender a culture of acceptance of disabled people and diversity in general using resources developed by the CPS and organisations such as the Sophie Lancaster Foundation which are available on the True Vision website.

- Academic research is needed to better understand the motivations for hostility, and ways to alter general public perceptions are needed to reduce the misconceptions that underpin community apathy or hostility.

- All levels of educational institutions need to take systematic steps to make the whole academic community aware of disability hate crime and the disproportionately severe adverse effects it has.

- Bodies such as Community Safety Partnerships and Multi-Agency Safeguarding Hubs need to have better communication lines to ensure that they complement rather than compete to ensure effective services.

Health professionals

- Collaborative and collective leadership is needed to ensure the identification, monitoring and reporting of hate crime.

- Improved structures should be developed to co-ordinate action by healthcare professionals, regulators, safeguarding boards and police to enable early intervention and prevent disability hate crimes.

- Systems should be created where it is easier, at the point of engagement with healthcare professionals, for individuals, or their carers and families, to express concerns about being a victim of hate crime.

- Healthcare professionals should either act themselves or refer to others if they believe an individual has been harmed or is at risk of harm.

- An environment should be created where complaints are considered as a potential sign of system failings, or individual shortcomings, which require a service provider or regulator to act.

- A cultural shift is needed so that everyone responsible for the delivery, commissioning, monitoring and regulation of services applies the basic standard test – 'Would I be happy if I, or someone close to me, was receiving this level of care or was treated in this way?'

- The creation of a standard for adult safeguarding needs to be considered for primary care and general practice.

- Health and Well-Being Boards and Joint Strategic Needs Assessments will be an essential tool to link personal safety to wider improvements in personal health and well-being.

- There should be provision of appropriate support to staff and service users/patients at the time of disclosure; existing procedures need to be enhanced to support this change.

- We need raised staff and patient awareness, with advice on how to stay safe.

- Culture change is needed to encourage reference to the NHS Constitution as an important signpost to get the values and behaviours right.

- There should be internal sensitivity and support for staff who may be victims themselves and improvement of workplace safety.

- Disability hate crime should be embedded into all NHS and social care standards.

- There should be an integrated and co-ordinated 'care pathway' to identify early warning signs of disability hate crime.

- Healthcare workers (including those on the front lines such as receptionists) require appropriate training to build the confidence of both staff and victims.

- General practitioners and primary care staff are in a unique position in their relationships with patients and their local communities to help safeguard people with a disability who suffer bullying, harassment or violence. We need a health service permeated by care, compassion, respect and support for everyone, whether they are disabled or not, to live a life free from abuse and harassment.

It is time to retune our attitudes to disability and disability hate crime.

CONTRIBUTOR PROFILES

Mark Brookes

Mark Brookes worked at Values into Action, a charity promoting the rights and equality of individuals with learning difficulties, for 11 years. He now works as a Quality Advisor at Dimensions, a personalised support service for people with learning disabilities and people with autism. Mark has led many workshops about hate crime for people with learning disabilities and has worked collaboratively with Paul Giannasi on projects related to disability hate crime.

David Cain

David is an experienced former NHS Chief Executive who continues to operate at board level in the health, education and charity sectors. Wider interests include national engagement as a representative of NHS managers and civil servants and as a Trustee of a number of charities. Most recently David took up a role as Chair of an Implementation Group around Equality, Diversity and Inclusion.

Lord Nigel Crisp KBE

Nigel Crisp is an independent crossbench member of the House of Lords where he co-chairs the All Party Parliamentary Group on Global Health. He was previously Chief Executive of the NHS and Permanent Secretary of the Department of Health. He now works in health globally and has written extensively on health including the books *Turning the World Upside Down* and *African Health Leaders*. For more information see nigelcrisp.com.

Paul Fredericks

Paul Fredericks is Managing Director of Lolben Consultancy, a company providing advice and interim management services to charities, not-for-profit organisations and regulatory bodies. He specialises in governance, strategic development, quality assurance, risk management, regulatory compliance, fraud detection and prevention, organisational change and major programme delivery.

Before establishing Lolben Consultancy, he was a director of a major UK health charity and prior to that held senior positions in health and charity regulation.

At the Healthcare Commission he led the development of specialist statutory regimes aimed at enhancing patient safety. Prior to that he held a range of senior posts at the Charity Commission including heading the Compliance and Enforcement function. He is a Lay Trustee of the Royal College of General Practitioners. He studied at Cass Business School, City University and has an MSc in Voluntary Sector Management.

Melanie Giannasi

Melanie is a qualified social worker currently working for a large local authority where she manages a team of social workers providing assessment and care support services for children and adults with learning disabilities. As a social work practitioner and approved social worker under the Mental Health Act (now AMHP), Melanie has worked for a number of years as a project manager of a charity which provides fostering respite for children with disabilities. She was also a Trustee for a visual impairment charity. Melanie has had a significant career working with vulnerable adults and children, supporting people to achieve their goals, and develop their independence in a safe and fulfilling manner.

Paul Giannasi OBE (Co-editor)

Paul is a Police Superintendent working within the Ministry of Justice in the UK. He leads the cross-government Hate Crime Programme which brings all sectors of government together to co-ordinate efforts to improve the response to hate crime across the criminal justice system.

Paul is the UK National Point of Contact to the Office for Democratic Institutions and Human Rights on hate crime and has worked to share good practice within the OSCE region and within Africa.

Paul is also a member of the Association of Chief Police Officers (ACPO) Hate Crime Group and is the author of the 2014 ACPO Hate Crime Manual which offers guidance to all UK police officers and partners. He is the co-editor of the 2014 *Routledge International Handbook on Hate Crime*.

Paul was awarded an OBE in the 2014 New Year's Honours list for services to policing, equality and human rights.

Dr Nathan Hall

Nathan Hall is a Principal Lecturer in Criminology and Policing at the Institute of Criminal Justice Studies at the University of Portsmouth. He is a member of the Cross-Government Hate Crime Independent Advisory Group (IAG) and the Association of Chief Police Officers Hate Crime Working Group. Nathan has also acted as an independent member of the UK government hate crime delegation to the OSCE, and is a member of the Crown Prosecution Service (Wessex) Independent Strategic Scrutiny and Involvement Panel, Hampshire Constabulary's Strategic IAG, and the Metropolitan Police Service's Hate Crime Diamond Group.

Dr Matt Hoghton MBChB FRCP MRCGP

Matt is a general practitioner in Clevedon Medical Centre, North Somerset. He has been involved in the care of people with learning disabilities for over 25 years and is a lifelong member of Mencap. He has been the Royal College of General Practitioners (RCGP)'s Clinical Champion in Learning Disabilities and is currently the Medical Director of the RCGP Clinical Innovation and Research Centre. He was the lead investigator in the Department of Health's confidential inquiry into the premature deaths of people with learning disabilities and is a visiting researcher in Bristol University's Norah Fry Centre.

Professor Sheila Baroness Hollins

Professor Sheila Baroness Hollins is Professor Emeritus in Psychiatry of Disability at St George's University of London, Cross Bench Member of the House of Lords, and a member of the Pontifical Commission for the Protection of Minors. She is past-President of the Royal College of Psychiatrists and the British Medical Association, and chairs the BMA Board of Science. She founded Books Beyond Words for adults who find pictures easier to understand than words, to communicate about life events, relationships and well-being to people with learning and communication disabilities.

Sylvia Lancaster OBE

Sylvia is Chief Executive of the Sophie Lancaster Foundation, which she established following the murder of her 'goth' daughter Sophie in 2007. Sylvia is an experienced youth worker and, through the Sophie Lancaster Foundation charity, aims to create a lasting legacy to Sophie through education and campaigning for the UK hate crime legislation to include

Alternative Subcultures. The charity works in schools, colleges, prisons and with young offenders, challenging the often violent prejudice towards people from Alternative Subcultures to create safer communities which celebrate, rather than fear, difference. Sylvia works closely with police authorities throughout the UK, delivering training and presentations. She is a member of the UK Government Cross Party Hate Crime Advisory Board.

Dr Keri-Michèle Lodge

Dr Keri-Michèle Lodge is Higher Trainee in the Psychiatry of Intellectual Disability and Academic Clinical Fellow at the University of York. She also works as a parliamentary research assistant to Professor Sheila Baroness Hollins. Her publications have focused on identifying patients with a learning disability in primary care and improving medical students' understanding around communication with people with a learning disability. She is a sibling carer for her brother who has a learning disability.

Emeritus Professor Bob Munn

Bob Munn is Emeritus Professor of Chemical Physics at the University of Manchester and currently works as a consultant on quality in higher education for organisations in the UK and in several other countries. He had responsibility for the student experience as Vice-President for Teaching and Learning at the University of Manchester and before that as Dean of UMIST, the University of Manchester Institute of Science and Technology.

Syed Mohammad Musa Naqvi BA (Oxon) MSc (Manc)

Musa is a project manager in urgent care for NHS Stockport CCG with strong experience in health and social care research, strategy development and planning. He joined the NHS in 2011 through the NHS Management Training Scheme, working at Central Manchester NHS Foundation Trust and Central Manchester CCG, with a secondment at the Greater Manchester Police Force. He has conducted detailed qualitative and thematic analyses of healthcare and social care services and published reports with different think tanks. He maintains a strong academic interest in healthcare leadership and policy, disability hate crime, women's rights and domestic violence as well as international development and relief projects. In 2010 he started a free primary school for children in rural Pakistan, which caters for over 120 children. Musa is a graduate in Economics and Management from Brasenose College, University of Oxford. He also holds a Master's degree in Economics from the University of Manchester and a Master's degree in Leadership and Service Improvement from the Manchester Business School.

Dame Philippa Russell DBE

Dame Philippa Russell DBE is Chair of the Government's Standing Commission on Carers, a member of the Cross Government Programme Board for the Carers Strategy and of the Ministerial Advisory Group on Mental Health. She was formerly a Commissioner with the Disability Rights Commission and Director of the Council for Disabled Children. She is an Honorary Fellow of the Royal College of Paediatrics and Child Health and of the Royal College of Psychiatrists. In 1990 she was awarded the Rose Fitzgerald Kennedy Centenary International Award for women who have contributed to the field of learning disability. She is the parent of an adult son with a learning disability and has a grandson with an autistic spectrum disorder. She has extensive contacts with third sector and carer and user organisations.

Dr Robina Shah MBE FRCGP (Hon) DL JP (Editor)

Robina is senior academic lead for Compassionate Care, Patient and Public Involvement and Co-Director of the Doubleday Centre for the Patient Experience at Manchester Medical School, Manchester University. She is also the National Director for Carers at Frenkel Topping Ltd. Robina is a psychologist with a specialist interest in learning disability, patient safety, breaking difficult news and the carer/patient experience. Robina has an established research portfolio and has achieved national and international recognition for breaking new ground in her areas of specialist interest. Robina is the author of numerous books and training materials, she has also contributed to various national government reports.

Robina was the former National Lead for Disability Hate Crime, Department of Health, Ministry of Justice and member of the UK Government Task Force on Violence against Women and Young Girls. Currently, she is a member of the UK Cross Government Hate Crime Independent Advisory Group, Ministry of Justice.

Robina also has specialist advisory roles with the General Medical Council, Health Education England North West, and the Care Quality Commission. She is an Honorary Fellow and Lay Trustee of the Royal College of General Practitioners and a Board Member of the UK government's Standing Commission on Carers.

Mike Smith

Mike is Chief Executive of Real, a user-led organisation of disabled people based in Tower Hamlets, which provides information, advice, advocacy and other services to support local disabled people to participate equally within society, overcome discrimination and achieve their human rights.

Prior to this he worked for PricewaterhouseCoopers for 19 years, qualifying as a chartered accountant and specialising in company tax advice. After working in Risk Management his most recent role was Director of Policy.

Mike was appointed a Commissioner for the Equality and Human Rights Commission (EHRC) in December 2009 and has chaired its statutory Disability Committee since. In 2009 Mike chaired the oral evidence panel for the EHRC's formal inquiry into sex discrimination and the gender pay gap in the financial services sector. Mike also led the EHRC's recent formal inquiry into disability-related harassment. The inquiry's groundbreaking report, *Hidden in Plain Sight*, was published on 12 September 2011, with the follow-up report, *Out in the Open*, published on 22 October 2012.

Mike has been involved in equality and diversity organisations for the last ten years, starting off with his involvement in the disability movement in Tower Hamlets. He is currently a board member of Disability Rights UK, a member of the government's Independent Hate Crime Advisory Group, and a member of the Ministerial Advisory Group on equality in mental health. He also contributed to the reference group for the Commission on Funding of Care and Support (the Dilnot Review).

Mike was previously Chair of the National Centre for Independent Living (2005 to 2011) and a former member of the board of Stonewall (2006 to 2010), the lesbian, gay and bisexual charity.

Kathryn Stone OBE

Kathryn Stone OBE is a Commissioner for the Independent Police Complaints Commission. Before that she was Commissioner for Victims and Survivors in Northern Ireland and was CEO of Voice UK, a charity promoting support for vulnerable victims of crime. Kathryn is a qualified and registered social worker and a Fellow of the Institute of Directors. She is a member of the Ministerial Hate Crime Advisory Group.

Jemma Tyson

Jemma lectures at the Institute of Criminal Justice Studies, University of Portsmouth, where she teaches across a range of criminology programmes.

She is currently researching issues relating to disability hate crime for her PhD. In particular, her research examines criminal justice service provision for victims of learning disability hate crime, and builds upon the findings of her Master's thesis on a related topic. The latter research was conducted in partnership with the Cross-Government Hate Crime Programme, with whom she has been working as an intern for a number of years. Jemma has also represented the UK government at hate crime events overseas, and is the co-author of a forthcoming book chapter exploring the relationship between hatred and mental disorder.

Dr Catherine White OBE, MB ChB, FFFLM, FRCOG, MRCGP, DCH, DMJ, DFFP

Catherine White has worked in forensic medicine since 1995, specialising in the examination of women, men and children following an allegation of rape or sexual assault, and takes a local, national and international lead in SARC regulation and development. She has been the Clinical Director at St Mary's SARC since 2003.

She is currently the Deputy Chief Examiner for the Membership Exam of the Faculty for Forensic and Legal Medicine (FFLM), responsible for Sexual Offences Medicine. She is also a member of the Academic Committee and Forensic Science Committee for the FFLM. She was Vice-President of the Faculty between May 2010 and 2013.

Catherine sits on a number of national steering groups and committees that seek to improve the way in which services to rape and sexual assault victims are being delivered. These include the Association of Chief Police Officers (ACPO) Rape Working Group and the National SARC Steering Group.

She is a guest lecturer for the Judicial Studies Board, Serious Sexual Offences seminars and Family Courts and a member of the UK team delivering training to the French Judiciary.

She is currently a UN expert on sexual violence involved with developing forensic medical training for the Palestinian National Authority. She also provided training in Cambodia sponsored by UNICEF and CEOP (Child Exploitation online Protection) in 2006, 2008 and 2010 and in Moldova in 2008. She has written extensively on the subject, providing a comprehensive information and reference tool for experienced forensic physicians as well as ensuring that those just starting in the field of forensic examination are equipped with the detailed and specific knowledge required.

SUBJECT INDEX

AUTHOR INDEX

intermediaries ascribe high value to artisanal gold products inherently by virtue of their unique physical features or rarity. Such local mining economies are dependent on trust between artisans and intermediaries, both trading directly, with different conditions to contributions valued in the local commodity networks.

In these ways, the promise of rising volumes of fairtrade products seems incompatible with broader processes of decommodification rooted in the cultivation of embedded relational values. This promise is not easily realized. Decommodification has been promoted most successfully in traditional fair-trade handicraft and coffee sectors through intensive and direct interactions between producers and producers, fair-trade organizations and committed consumers. In coffee, rapidly expanding sales by mainstream corporations and an increasing reliance on product labeling have promoted universal and decontextualized prices and recommodification, and with these products like bananas, sugar, tea and cocoa which sit within mass-market retail chains, complex and value-added production systems, processes of decommodification founded on distinctive local and ethical consumption have been challenged even more to certify by industrial and commercial norms, values and modalities upholding production efficiency and price competition. While both decommodification and recommodification dynamics are evident in major fair-trade product arenas in new product areas, like sports balls and gold, Fairtrade appears to have had very limited success in destabilizing traditional commodity relations.

PRODUCTION AND EXPORTS

Fairtrade production and exports have grown dramatically in recent years across the global South. This growth has been spurred by burgeoning demand in major markets and by the widespread adoption of neoliberal policies which have increased market competition and fueled a search for new export niches. South th producers have sought out avenues for differentiating their products according to social or ecological attributes and, where possible, accessing markets shielded from global commodity price swings. Fairtrade producers have seen some expansion in fair trade organization market opportunities. Yet the majority of growth has been in the increasing range of Fairtrade certified products. Reflecting the persistent contradictions of working in and against the market, fair trade seeks to transform, or buttress relations exhibiting largely selling colonial-based patterns of primary product exports from South to North (Reynolds 2012).